Time and the Generations

KENNETH J. ARROW LECTURE SERIES

KENNETH J. ARROW LECTURE SERIES

Kenneth J. Arrow's work has so deeply shaped the course of economics for the past sixty years that, in a sense, every modern economist is his student. His ideas, style of research, and breadth of vision have been a model for generations of the boldest, most creative, and most innovative economists. His work has yielded seminal theorems in areas such as general equilibrium theory, social choice theory, and endogenous growth theory, proving that simple ideas have profound effects. The Kenneth J. Arrow Lecture Series highlights economists, from Nobel laureates to groundbreaking younger scholars, whose work builds on Arrow's scholarship as well as his innovative spirit. The books in the series are an expansion of the lectures that are held in Arrow's honor at Columbia University.

The lectures have been supported by Columbia University's Committee on Global Thought, Program for Economic Research, Center on Global Economic Governance, and Initiative for Policy Dialogue.

TIME AND THE GENERATIONS

*Population Ethics for a
Diminishing Planet*

Partha Dasgupta

With Robert Solow, Scott Barrett, Eric Maskin,
Joseph Stiglitz, and Aisha Dasgupta
With reflections from Kenneth J. Arrow

Columbia University Press
New York

COLUMBIA
UNIVERSITY
PRESS

Columbia University Press gratefully acknowledges the generous support for this book provided by a member of our Publisher's Circle.

Columbia University Press
Publishers Since 1893
New York   Chichester, West Sussex
cup.columbia.edu
Copyright © 2019 Columbia University Press
All rights reserved

Library of Congress Cataloging-in-Publication Data
Names: Dasgupta, Partha, author.
Title: Time and the generations : population ethics for a diminishing planet /
Partha Dasgupta ; with [five others].
Description: New York : Columbia University Press, 2019. |
Series: The Kenneth J. Arrow lecture series |
Includes bibliographical references and index.
Identifiers: LCCN 2018048438 (print) | LCCN 2018050795 (e-book) |
ISBN 9780231550031 (e-book) | ISBN 9780231160124
(cloth : alk. paper)
Subjects: LCSH: Population policy—Moral and ethical aspects. |
Nonrenewable natural resources.
Classification: LCC HB883.5 (e-book) | LCC HB883.5 .D37 2019 (print) |
DDC 174/.93639—dc23
LC record available at https://lccn.loc.gov/2018048438

Columbia University Press books are printed on permanent
and durable acid-free paper.

Printed in the United States of America

Cover design: Noah Arlow
Cover image: Vincent van Gogh, *The Sower (after Millet)*, 1888,
Van Gogh Museum, Amsterdam

To Carol's and my children, and to their children

Like the generations of leaves, the lives of mortal men. Now the wind scatters the old leaves from the earth, now the living timber bursts with new buds and spring comes round again. And so with men: as one generation comes to life, another dies away.

THE *ILIAD*, TRANS. ROBERT FAGELS, BOOK 6, LNS. 171–75
(PENGUIN BOOKS, 1998)

Contents

Part I Foundations

Part II Applications

In Memoriam

Kenneth Joseph Arrow (1921–2017)[1]

IF YOU type "Kenneth Arrow" into an internet search engine, you will find many, many tributes to him, not just from economists, nor only from people who knew him. You will read that he made momentous discoveries that spanned economics, political science, sociology, and moral and political philosophy. If you continue to look, you will discover that he made significant contributions to operations research, in particular the stability of certain dynamical systems. And if you look some more, you will read that his first publication, based on work done during the World War II as a weather forecaster in the U.S. Air Force, was on a problem in aeronautics (the path that should be taken by an airplane flying from A to B that, so as to conserve fuel, corrected for wind velocities). Arrow created an entire branch of thinking (i.e., the possibilities of designing ethical voting rules—he showed there can be no voting rule that satisfies a set of minimal normative requirements),

---

1. Kenneth Arrow was a Founding Member of the Pontifical Academy of Social Sciences (PASS), established in 1994 by Pope John Paul II. As with the Pontifical Academy of Sciences, which was established in 1936 by Pope Pius XI, the remit of PASS is to prepare studies on matters of particular interest to the Holy See. The Academies' activities, which are undertaken jointly when a chosen theme requires expertise from both, are meant to complement one another. They have a common Secretariat, housed in Casina Pio IV, Vatican City. Members of the Academies are appointed by the Pope. This is a mildly edited version of a tribute that was prepared at the request of our Chancellor, Bishop Marcelo Sanchez Sorondo, and read by me at the 2017 Plenary Session of PASS on Saturday, 29 April 2017.

and in joint work with Gerard Debreu, he helped close a long-standing attempt to conceptualize an ideal price-guided economy (i.e., the existence and efficiency of general competitive equilibria). Arrow opened new areas on which to think: the economics of financial assets (Arrow securities); identifying unique features in doctor–patient relationships that make unassisted markets unsuitable for supplying medical care; understanding the forces that drive the practice of racial discrimination; deriving the meaning of option values for environmental goods; uncovering the meaning of sustainable development; exploring the characteristics of knowledge that make it very different from marketable commodities; using the Aristotelian Principle (i.e., learning by doing) to show how practice is an engine of economic growth[2]; and so on). Even in his more discursive papers, Arrow offered insights that have repeatedly been used by others to build their own work. You will find in your internet search that he was not only admired universally for his brilliance and creativity, but, more importantly, that he was much loved. In an international ballot among economists some twenty years ago, he was voted the greatest economist of the twentieth century. Arrow was not unaware of his natural gifts, and because he did it unconsciously, he was not reticent about displaying them; however, for a reason I discovered many years ago, none of that ever grated on others (I will come to that later in this tribute). His presence may have caused others to balk before speaking, but he was never intimidating.

Those intellectual gifts included not only an exceptionally creative mind, but also the ability to read at speed, distilling from what he read their essential elements and recalling them when he had need to do so.

---

2. Appealing to what was then a sparse empirical literature within industrial economics, Arrow assumed that a firm's productivity is a function of its cumulative output to date. Borrowing from John Dewey's writings on education policy, Arrow gave his paper the title "The Economic Implications of Learning by Doing" (*Review of Economic Studies*, 1962, 29(3), 155–173). Dewey in turn had borrowed it from Aristotle: "Anything that we have to learn to do, we learn by the actual doing of it: people become builders by building and instrumentalists by playing instruments" (Aristotle, *The Nicomachean Ethics*, trans. J. A. K. Thomson; Harmondsworth: Penguin Books, 1976; p. 63). John Rawls in his *Theory of Justice* (Oxford: Oxford University Press, 1972) christened "learning by doing" the Aristotelian Principle.

And he was a voracious reader of whatever lay close to hand—books, journals, newspapers, magazines. There is a story, that at the time of his move from Stanford to Harvard in 1968, the younger members of Harvard's Economics Department devised a plan to open a discussion on a subject of which they were confident Arrow would be innocent. (I imagine they connived in this way so as to retain some form of respect for their own abilities.) In anticipation of a dinner in Arrow's honor, the group read all of what they thought was then available on how gray whales find the same breeding ground every year. The topic was duly introduced at the dinner, casually of course, and the protagonists talked at length on the subject. Arrow, as the story goes, remained quiet, but before the conversation moved on to other things, he murmured, "But I thought Turner's theory was discredited by Spencer, who showed the supposed homing mechanism couldn't possibly work." The story isn't apocryphal—I once asked Arrow if it was true . . . he didn't say "no."

We at the Pontifical Academy of Social Sciences (PASS) remember him as a dedicated Member, duly attending meetings and being fully engaged in our discussions (even while taking his renowned naps during sessions). He was proud of being Member of PASS and loved staying in Domus Santae Marthae. On every occasion we were both at a PASS meeting, he would pick me up from my room upon arrival at the Domus so that we could visit his favorite coffee shop, near the Pantheon, and catch up on our thinking.

Kenneth Arrow was born in New York City on 23 August 1921 to Lillian Greenberg and Harry Arrow, both Romanian immigrants of the Jewish faith. A younger sister, Anita (Summers)—Emeritus Professor at the Wharton School, University of Pennsylvania—survives him. The family income dropped precipitously during the Depression, so the Arrow family was poor for a number of years. Ken once said to me in passing that he walked several miles each day to school. As I understand it, his exceptional intellectual gifts were recognized early. He attended City College New York for his undergraduate studies, graduating in mathematics in 1940, and moved to Columbia University for graduate studies, obtaining his Master's degree in mathematics and statistics in 1941. There he came under the influence of the great economist/statistician Harold Hotelling, who helped him to obtain a scholarship to study for a PhD, but in the Economics Department. As Arrow told the story, Hotelling said he had no influence over the Mathematics Department, so could not be of help obtaining funds there.

During 1942–1946, Arrow's studies were interrupted while he served as a weather forecaster in the U.S. Air Force. He returned to academia in 1946, partly as a graduate student at Columbia University and partly as a Research Associate at the Cowles Commission for Research in Economics at the University of Chicago, under the Directorship of Tjalling Koopmans. In all the years I knew Ken, the two scholars to whom he showed reverence (and I mean this literally) were Harold Hotelling and Tjalling Koopmans. They had both served as his mentors during a period when he needed reassurance that the life of an academic economist was what he should aim for.

In 1947, Arrow married a fellow research associate, Selma Schweitzer, herself an economist of distinction. Together they moved to Stanford University in 1951, where Ken assumed an Assistant Professorship in the Economics Department. The couple remained there until 1968, when they moved to Harvard University. But it was not for long, because the Arrows (with their two boys, David and Andrew) returned to Stanford in 1979, where Ken was appointed Joan Kenney Professor of Economics and Professor of Operations Research. He retired from his Professorships in 1991 but continued to work in the Department of Economics in the afternoons, right to the end. Selma, who had subsequently trained as a psychotherapist, practiced well into her 80s. She died in 2015.

I got to know Ken in the spring of 1973, when he was visiting Cambridge in the United Kingdom. He had taken an interest in a typescript I had recently prepared on John Rawls' just principle of saving. Because he felt an alternative model would better fit Rawls' intentions (we published our papers separately[3]), he made it a point of seeking me out to discuss the principle with me. It was a terrifying experience. His mind not only moved at an incredible speed, but he spoke rapidly so as to keep pace. He also had the habit of changing gear mid-sentence to improve upon what he had been intending to say, on occasion recognizing even while he was formulating a theorem that it wasn't quite right and correcting it by the end of the sentence. I found this overwhelming. It meant I had to do something if I were

---

3. K. J. Arrow (1973), "Rawls' Principle of Just Saving," *Swedish Journal of Economics*, 75(4), 323–335; P. Dasgupta (1974), "On Some Problems Arising from Professor Rawls' Conception of Distributive Justice," *Theory and Decision*, 4(2), 325–344.

to retain whatever self-confidence I then had. I took to crossing the street to avoid him if I saw him approaching. But I couldn't do that all the time. Over the weeks I realized that he felt our conversations had helped improve the paper he was writing. It was only some years later that I realized Arrow was under the impression that most others he met were equal to him in intellect. In all the years I knew him, this was the one fact about the world on which I knew him to be wrong.

Arrow was one of the architects of modern economics, including the theory of public policy. But unlike his writings on social choice, risk and uncertainty, and general equilibrium theory, his publications on the theory of public policy are discursive, both in style and focus. Some are essays, with no mathematics to aid the exposition, and are written in an informal style that guides rather than directs readers toward ways in which the questions could be most fruitfully framed. Others are mathematical, have a sharper focus, and are enlivened by theorems. Arrow's style of discourse on the theory of public policy fitted his intentions. They have shaped the way the literature has developed and continue to develop.

He took public policy to be society's reasoned response to failure of markets to allocate goods and services efficiently and equitably. Utilitarianism guided him, but by paying greater attention to individuals' expressed preferences than is welcomed by moral philosophers, he avoided the authoritarian streak that has frequently marked Utilitarian writings. A deep meditation (*The Limits of Organization*, 1974) on the constraints on motivation and actions that dispersed information imposes on people reads as a tussle between the democrat and the Utilitarian in him. Arrow's democratic instincts curbed his Utilitarian leanings; his Utilitarian convictions in turn kept him far removed from Libertarianism. Arrow did not advocate dispensing with markets; instead, his work led him to characterize well-functioning mixed economies.

Although confident about the relevance of his models when establishing theorems, he was hesitant when lifting them to speak to the world we have come to know. This was a reflection of his pluralistic values. He opened his monograph of 1974 with the words of the great first-century sage, Rabbi Hillel: "If I am not for myself, then who is for me? And if I am not for others, then who am I? And if not now, when?" That tension is present not only in the monograph, but also in his other writings on public policy.

His Utilitarianism isn't the one to be found in Henry Sidgwick's great work, *The Methods of Ethics* (1907; London: Macmillan). Arrow was an Intuitionist, at direct odds with Sidgwick, who had devoted an entire chapter criticizing Intuitionism. Arrow arrived at his Utilitarian thinking from fundamental ethical axioms. That is why his version of Intuitionism is also called Value Pluralism. In this he was influenced by Tjalling Koopmans, who had provided an axiomatic foundation for Utilitarianism in an intergenerational setting. Value Pluralism encourages one to iterate between the choice of ethical parameters and the consequences of those choices for public policy. Without such experiments, seemingly plausible expressions of ethical preferences can commend policies that are in deep conflict with other values the decision-maker may hold.

At the personal level, though, Arrow was far from being a Utilitarian. You all will have felt his uncompromising stance on what he felt to be one's duties. Although he never spoke to me about it, I can't help thinking that, on personal conduct, it was family influence at work.

But above all, what made him entirely distinctive was that he never abandoned the intellectual life of the quintessential student. For him, no problem was too trivial to explore, no topic too boring to pursue. His love of mathematical calculations never deserted him. Once he had formulated a problem and uncovered a truth, he was done. He disliked writing papers.

Ken told me that after reaching age 80 he would come to PASS meetings only when absolutely required. We at PASS know of his concerns about the global environment, and we have been much engaged in recent years in trying to understand humanity's common responsibility toward Nature. At Stanford, Arrow was for many years much engaged in seminars on global conflict and the ready availability of nuclear material. We also know of his concerns about humanity's treatment of the biosphere. I shall end this remembrance tribute with a brief account of some of his activities in the period when his visits to PASS became rare.

Arrow's involvement with what we now call "ecological economics" dates back to 1990, when he joined a monthly seminar organized by a group of ecologists and economists at Stanford University. That involvement was reinforced by his subsequent association with the Beijer Institute of Ecological Economics in Stockholm. In 1993, the Institute's Director, Karl-Goran Maler, initiated an annual workshop that was to be held in the summer at the marine field station on the island of Askö in the Trosa archipelago in Sweden. Each year the designated group, composed of equal numbers of ecologists and econ-omists (members of the Institute's Scientific Board and a few invited scholars), chooses a theme for discussion and prepares a brief report. The records show that Arrow attended all but six meetings in the years since 1993 (on one occasion only because he discovered on arrival at the airport that his passport had expired). The last meeting he attended was in September 2016. By then he was bent and weak and needed to pause after every few steps. We queued to carry his backpack and lug-gage, while Paul Ehrlich, his neighbor and friend, locked arms with his to prevent him from stumbling over the uneven grounds of the island. Despite his frail state, Arrow not only took part in the discussion, he was insistent that the policies we discuss for reducing our reliance on environmental natural resources should be built on liberal values. He also took part in socializing, joining Swedish members of the Askö group in singing drinking songs in his imperfect Swedish.

In one way or other, the Askö meetings have addressed the idea of sustainable development—its meaning and its implications for the way we should live. He was signatory to eighteen policy briefs that emerged from those meetings, and he co-authored five scientific papers that formulated the notion of sustainable development and then put the notion to work on data to explore whether nations in recent years have followed development paths that are likely to be sustainable.

Above all, it was his tireless involvement with ecological econom-ics that will be remembered by those many scholars who have met him at conferences and listened to him at the teaching and training workshops on environment and development organized by the Beijer Institute over the years in various parts of the developing world (e.g., South Asia, Latin America, sub-Saharan Africa). Networks of mainly young economists in the developing world that were established with the help of the Institute found Arrow in their midst, listening to their presentations, reading their works, and sharing comments in the mar-gins of their manuscripts.

Kenneth Arrow is renowned in the West and the Far East as a teacher and mentor, not simply as that greatest of social scientists. What may not be known elsewhere is that his death is being mourned by scholars in the developing world, many of whom not only heard him lecture, but were also helped by Arrow to formulate problems they had found on their own ground. We all have cause to mourn.

Partha Dasgupta
St John's College, Cambridge

Foreword

POPULATION NUMBERS and their changes have played a part in economics at least since Malthus, and no doubt even before him. Malthus provided a descriptive theory of population size. Given diminishing returns in agriculture and the procreative habits of mankind (though that was not quite how Malthus put it), population would be driven to the particular number that yields an income per person high (or low) enough to just hold the population in check. For any smaller number, income per person would be higher and population would increase; for any larger number, income would be smaller and population would fall. As a matter of common observation, that "equilibrium" level of income per person was fairly low, and the corresponding population size might be judged to be too large. But that judgment was not the main point. Malthus did not offer an opinion about the right size or, as we would say, the optimum size of the population. Nevertheless, a Malthusian would be more likely to worry about overpopulation than underpopulation.

It is usual to place the beginnings of a theory of optimum population with John Stuart Mill. I am not enough of a scholar to understand exactly what he means by "increasing returns." It is clear enough, however, that he sees agriculture as subject to diminishing returns and industry to (some variety of) increasing returns. If the population is very small, there will be plenty of food and raw materials to go around, but the market will be too small to allow industry to exploit increasing returns adequately; thus the general level of income will be fairly low. If the population is very large, industry will be very productive, but there will not be enough food and materials; again, the general level of income will be fairly low. Something in between will be best. It is easy for any modern economist to embody these ideas in a transparent model that will yield an optimum population in the sense that some version of output per person is as large as possible, given the known technology and the available resource base.

Mill's discussion is unsatisfactory in several ways. The sharp distinction between agriculture and "manufacture" seems inappropriate now, and it probably was then. He pays little or no attention to the importance of capital investment, whether in agriculture or in industry. Most oddly, given that Mill was writing in the 1840s, as the Industrial Revolution was transforming economic life, he takes no notice of the effect of technological progress on the relationship between total employment (or population) and output per person.

Later writers, however, took their agenda from Mill in one important respect: the focus of the theory of optimum population was, for a long time, the achievement of the largest possible income (or consumption) per person. This has an off-putting consequence. A theorist with a well-developed habit of abstraction (in other words, a theorist) will want to begin with the extreme special case of a society of identical individuals. The point is to separate the question of numbers from the issue of inequality. This is certainly off-putting because even a theorist knows that, in practice, any policy designed to increase or decrease the size of the population will do so by adding or subtracting population at specific points in the distribution of income. I will follow the common practice, as does Partha Dasgupta in his Arrow Lecture, and I will do so for the standard reason: to isolate the question of numbers, and only numbers. Dasgupta understands, as well as you do, the importance of inequality.

If each of the identical members of the society has the same utility (or well-being) function that is increasing in income or consumption, then achieving maximum feasible income for everyone is obviously the same thing as achieving the maximum feasible utility for everyone. This is not simple utilitarianism, however. Simple utilitarianism wants to add up the utilities of the relevant individuals to arrive at a kind of aggregate well-being. If all individuals are alike, that means multiplying the common value of utility by the size of the relevant population. It appears to be Henry Sidgwick who got to this formulation in 1907, and it is the starting point for Partha Dasgupta's Arrow Lecture, though only the starting point. He calls it the Sidgwick–Meade criterion, because James Meade formalized it and operated with it some fifty years later.

It is worth noticing something obvious: the population that maximizes the Sidgwick–Meade criterion is always larger than the population that maximizes consumption per person (and thus utility per person), so the common utility is lower than the maximum achievable. Society loses from that but gains from greater numbers. I will come back to this after a small digression.

I have always thought it a little strange that the utility-based discussion of optimum population seems to be incurious about the possibility that people might have preferences directly about the size or density of the population. That is to say, population size might enter the common utility function as a separate argument. Some people might, like Greta Garbo, "vant to be alone." Others might be more gregarious and prefer a larger population. Should that not count? Knut Wicksell took an explicit position. He thought that finding the optimum population size was one of the most important questions of political economy; on the whole he thought that the population (of Europe, circa 1900) was too large. One reason he mentioned was simply that occasions for the more or less solitary enjoyment of the beauties of nature were becoming scarce. Of course, he was a Swede.

On reflection, however, I can think of two reasons for theory to avoid this issue. First, it would mean abandoning all hope of general results. Any interesting general proposition could be overthrown if popular preferences about population size were sufficiently adverse to it. Further, we know nothing about those preferences, and so we can not make plausible assumptions about them. Second, a general excuse is available: maybe most people would (unlike Greta Garbo) dislike a very sparse population, and they might also dislike a very crowded population, being more or less indifferent about a wide middle range of densities. In that case, it would be safe to ignore the point that I have been discussing. So I will, like Partha Dasgupta, follow the common practice.

Now I return to the Sidgwick–Meade criterion for the optimum population size: the quantity to be maximized is the product of the number of (identical) people and the common utility of (equal) consumption per person. (Partha Dasgupta proposes several important and enlightening modifications of it, and I will come back to them.) The consumption level that yields zero utility has a utility equal to zero.

There is something peculiar about the common consumption level that yields a utility equal to zero for everyone. Suppose we start at a negative utility; increasing the population (with aggregate consumption constant) makes things worse in two ways. A larger population, multiplied by a negative number (i.e., the negative utility), reduces aggregate utility; on top of that, the common consumption bundle is reduced, so each individual is worse off. Population is already too big and should be diminished. The arithmetic tells the Sidgwick–Meade utilitarian that people are already miserable, and having more people only adds to the total of misery. (When I said earlier that the Sidgwick–Meade optimum population is always bigger than the highest-feasible common-utility population, I should have added "provided that the utility level is positive." The time was not ripe then, so I add that proviso now.)

This peculiarity had naturally occurred to Partha Dasgupta's predecessors, and to the author himself. There is an obvious fix for the Sidgwick–Meade criterion: choose a consumption standard and a corresponding level of utility that defines a "good life" (or some other roughly equivalent locution). Then, for the good-life utility consumption level, calculate the excess of common utility over the good-life level and label that difference "net utility." The modified Sidgwick–Meade criterion for population size is now the size of the population multiplied by net utility (i.e., the aggregate amount of net utility). The Arrow Lecture explores this formulation with great care and broad sympathy.

It turns out to matter a great deal where the boundary between a good life and a not-good life is fixed. So how is it to be determined? Here I am led to another digression. The text of the Arrow Lecture makes regular use of an abstract Decisionmaker, the person who would presumably make this determination. At one point in the brief email correspondence quoted in the book, Kenneth Arrow asks, rather plaintively, who this Decisionmaker might actually be. Partha Dasgupta does not really answer the question: he describes the role of the Decisionmaker, but not who he or she or it *is*. I want to suggest an answer, probably controversial and not necessarily the answer that Kenneth Arrow or Partha Dasgupta would give. To paraphrase the cartoon character Pogo: We have met the Decisionmaker and it is Us. Of course, this does not mean Us in our everyday, probably selfish, and certainly sloppy capacity, but rather Us when we have decided to be thoughtful and deliberative and dignified and judicious and all those good things, as we consider matters of principle for our society.

It is hard (at least for me) to imagine a single worldwide Committee of Us arriving at consensus about this important parameter, the boundary between a quality of life good enough that We should think it worth replicating, and a poorer quality of life that would be unfortunate to replicate. The representative from Beverly Hills and the representative from Eritrea would have very different conceptions, even if they are trying very hard to think in universal terms. The best they might do is negotiate a compromise, and the very idea of a compromise in this connection has problems of its own. The notion of an abstract, not otherwise identified, Decisionmaker may already take too much for granted. I can only recommend reading the text and thinking it over.

Even apart from this difficulty, the Sidgwick–Meade criterion is not overpoweringly convincing because it seems to give a lot of weight to sheer numbers. Why is it obviously desirable to add to the population another few persons with barely positive net utility when the trade-off is a small reduction in the common net utility of everyone else? One might say: the boundary between a good and a not-good life has to be chosen so as to justify this trade-off. But that seems rather to shift the problem rather than to settle it. Over the long history of utilitarianism and its critics, there has been a great deal of seriously sophisticated discussion of this issue. The reader of this book will be treated to a seriously sophisticated example.

Eventually the text arrives in Section 8 at a destination, what Partha Dasgupta calls "generation-centered prerogatives," the germ of which, but not this precise version, is attributed to Samuel Scheffler. It is not my job to explain this criterion, only to comment on it and encourage the reader to think about it.

Generation-centered preferences require there to be generations, and thus also the passage of time. The thing about generations is that they follow one another; it is no longer possible just to talk about "the Genesis problem" of deciding how many people should go into an initially empty Earth. The "prerogative" of a generation is to regard its own well-being as more valuable than the well-being of later generations. Remembering that all members of the current and future generations share the same utility function, the simplest way to proceed is to take it that each generation, when it is current, accepts the natural utility (as a function of consumption per identical head) for itself but multiplies that function by a fraction µ for every member of a future generation. That is what the text does. (In the simplest overlapping-generations model, two successive generations are alive in each time period.) There is a sort of, but not quite, generational discount factor.

This story brings complications of a kind well-known to economists. The current generation makes its current decisions as the start of a plan for the future. But when the next generation takes over, given whatever its parents have left it, it will make its own decisions as the start of its own plan for the future. This plan will not generally coincide with what the parents had in mind when they were doing the deciding. One has to suppose that the parents realize this and take it into account in their own planning. The logic leads to a kind of inter-generational Nash equilibrium: the current generation does the best it can in its own interest, subject to the constraint that no future generation should have reason—in its interest—to deviate from that plan.

The reader should resist the temptation to dismiss all of this as the sort of hyper-rationality that sometimes infects economics. Partha Dasgupta is no babe in the woods. This is not intended as a description of the way fertility and saving decisions are made by ordinary humans: it is intended as a benchmark against which to evaluate those decisions, and perhaps to make recommendations. I can leave the argument for generation-centered optimality to the author. I only want to comment on what may or may not be an oddity.

When Partha Dasgupta comes to try out his story on a simple numerical example, to see what kind of answer it gives to the basic normative question, the author has to choose a value for µ, the fractional weight each current generation gives to the well-being of all its successors. In those examples, the values he explores are 0.01, 0.05, and 0.10. These are presumably chosen to be intuitively natural and to give reasonable results in the whole exercise. They do the latter, but, on the intuitive side, they seem shockingly low to me. I value my children's and my grandchildren's well-being as approximately equivalent to my own; sometimes I seem implicitly to act as if µ is actually larger than 1. (I surely would not extend that liberality to more distant generations, however.) So are those numbers near zero really way off base? In the artificial two-period overlapping-generations model, the implicit time-period is long, longer than twenty-five or thirty years, but I am not sure how that should affect the plausible value of µ, which deals in genealogical time, not calendar time. Nor do I see why adopting the deliberative mode rather than the personal mode should make such a drastic difference; the deliberators will take universal feelings into account. This is something to think about: where to place a new parameter is always difficult.

In the very brief Part Two of the Arrow Lecture and in the added essay by Aisha and Partha Dasgupta—what value of μ applies there?—the emphasis shifts a little. Earlier on, the main consideration has been the standard stuff of utilitarianism, with a little diminishing marginal product of labor entering in the numerical examples. Now more attention is paid to the carrying capacity of the "biosphere" and the damage that a large population can do to the environment that ultimately supports it. This shift in emphasis, even when it just takes the form of illustrative numerical examples, brings us closer to nitty-gritty issues. All I want to do in this Foreword is to mention a couple of my own reactions.

I have no trouble in sympathizing with the theorist's need to focus on the artificial case of a society of identical individuals. The closer one comes to numbers and explicit or implicit recommendations, however, the more important it becomes to give up that simplification, at least informally. Any actual change in the population of the world will be a change (or a series of changes) in the population of some geographical area, and at some point in the distribution of wealth or well-being. (There are migration flows, of course, but they are neither costless nor frictionless.) Population policy, if we are to have such a thing, will have to be combined with policy about the distribution of income and wealth. I can hear the Dasguptas saying, "Thanks, but this is hard enough work without making it more complicated." And I will agree: I am musing, not complaining.

Which leads to my second reaction. There is almost nothing, probably there is nothing at all, in the way of standard intuition about magnitudes that figure centrally in this book: for example, there is no general idea of the income level that separates a good life, one worth replicating, from a not-good life, nor about the "ecological footprint" of the current population, about which there has been some research but needs to be much more, so that estimates can be compared and discussed and improved. The likely reason for this gap, as Partha Dasgupta says, is that so little attention has been paid to the question of optimum population, especially by the sort of people who generate numbers and evolve intuitions. Maybe this book will mark a beginning.

When I promised to write a Foreword to this book, it was a reflection of admiration and affection for Partha and Aisha. That feeling has only been strengthened by reading the book and thinking about it. It took commitment and courage to tackle so broad and fundamental a problem with bare hands. The book is a fitting tribute to Kenneth Arrow, who was always willing to take a shot at any tough intellectual problem.

Robert M. Solow
Massachusetts Institute of Technology

Preface

THE ESSAY *Birth and Death: Arrow Lecture*—henceforth, Arrow Lecture—is a much revised and expanded version of some ideas I explored in my Kenneth Arrow Lectures at Columbia University (2011) and the Hebrew University of Jerusalem (2012), in my Munich Lectures in Economics (2011) and the Humanitas Lectures at the University of Oxford (2012), and in a paper with the title "Birth and Death" that I prepared for circulation in April 2016. Valuing potential lives and the related notions of optimum population and optimum saving have intrigued me ever since I was a graduate student, and I am grateful to James Meade for arousing my interest in them, and to Amiya Dasgupta and James Mirrlees for encouraging me to continue pursuing them.[1]

In one of the chapters of my doctoral dissertation (1968), I followed the Utilitarianism of Henry Sidgwick and took the good ("the ground of binding reason") to be the mathematical expectation of the sum of utilities of all who are ever born (Sidgwick, 1907).[2] I then applied the Utilitarian calculus to a series of economic models of increasing complexity and derived both the optimum size of each generation and

---

1. I had originally intended the essay "Birth and Death" (April 2016) to serve as the final set of chapters for a wider-ranging book on welfare economics I was then preparing, with the title *Time and the Generations*. It was only some months after Professor Arrow's death that I realized it would be exactly right to drop the idea of a book on welfare economics, expand the essay, and offer it to Columbia University Press as my contribution to the Kenneth J. Arrow Lecture Series.
2. References to publications cited here appear in the list of references following the Arrow Lecture.

the rate at which each generation should invest for future generations. That exercise also yielded the optimum living standard of each generation.[3] The models served as mathematical laboratories. My idea was to experiment with alternative worlds so as to try Classical Utilitarianism on for size. (I am following Rawls, 1972, in calling Sidgwick's version of Utilitarian thought "Classical Utilitarianism.") The exercises uncovered the interplay of the possible and the desirable in Sidgwick's theory. In a canonical class of models, optimum population was found to be large; the living standard supporting optimum population was shown to be proportionately not much higher than the standard of living at which life is neither good nor not-good.

I left the matter there because I didn't have the expertise to explore the borderline living standard, which Meade (1955) had called "welfare subsistence." But the notion of "hedonistic zero," or the quality of life at welfare subsistence, is central to population ethics. We confirm here that a great deal of importance rests on the quality of life at welfare subsistence. Sidgwick had discussed it when developing Utilitarianism, but his treatment of the subject was not without problems.

Mine was an exercise in applied theory. I put Classical Utilitarianism to work in worlds facing explicit resource constraints. The research strategy in my dissertation differed sharply from the one that has been pursued subsequently by Derek Parfit and those following him in their explorations in population axiology. Parfit saw ethical paradoxes in Sidgwick's Utilitarianism, which is why characterizing those paradoxes and looking for escape routes have come to dominate the writings of Parfit and thinkers following him. But even though the way Classical Utilitarianism accommodates welfare subsistence is central to those paradoxes, Parfit and those following him have made little attempt to study life's experiences at that borderline space. The authors have insisted that life there is neither worth living nor not worth living, but they haven't offered us an account of the notion that can be used for applied work.[4] As a working economist it has also been a puzzle to

---

3. Dasgupta (1969) is the published version of that chapter.
4. See Parfit (1976, 1982, 1984, 2016) on the Repugnant Conclusion, the Mere Addition Paradox, and other closely related puzzles. I discuss the central Parfitian puzzle, the Repugnant Conclusion, in the Arrow Lecture. Arrhenius, Ryberg, and Tännsjö (2017) offers an account, of the utmost clarity, of Parfitian concerns.

me that they haven't found a place for the socio-ecological constraints under which population axiology should be tested. The paradoxes were built entirely on hypothetical worlds, with no recognition of the bio-geochemical processes that shape our world. It seems to me, though, that no system of ethics should be expected to yield unquestionable directives in all conceivable circumstances, even to the same person. If we are to arrive at satisfactory policies, a suitable accommodation has to be found for the anthropologist's findings, the demographer's projections, the economist's constructions, the environmental scientist's warnings, and the philosopher's sensibilities. So it has struck me that Parfit had studied the subject entirely within the confines of the Fellows' Common Room. That is why readers will find sharp criticisms of Parfitian concerns in the Arrow Lecture.

Soon after my student days I came to have reservations about Classical Utilitarianism as applied to population ethics (Dasgupta, 1974a). The problems I found in the theory were different from the ones that had moved Parfit and those following him. In giving expression to my worries about Sidgwick's ethics and to find ways to overcome its deficiencies, it seemed to me that the right place to start is with the considerations my wife and I had entertained in our discussions about when to have children and how many to have. As unrestrained emotions can come into play in the home, I sensed it is good discipline to dampen them when developing population ethics. So I thought the right thing to do is to start at home and move toward the Common Room in careful stages.

Not having been trained in philosophy, I have found the subject difficult; so difficult, in fact, that over the years I have fumbled about to find ways to express what it is I found wanting in Sidgwick's theory and why I was also unmoved by Parfitian concerns. And I am all too conscious that readers may find me fumbling even now. The Arrow Lecture builds on a series of work (Dasgupta, 1969, 1974a, 1989, 1994, 2005a), essentially a decadal engagement with population ethics. The construction I was led to years ago (Dasgupta, 1974a) can be called Generation-Relative Utilitarianism, which is the name I gave to it. I have persisted with it even though I had not, until recently, constructed an example of a situation concerning birth and death that points directly to the theory. It has taken me all this time also to realize that the conception I was trying to advance in those attempts was built on considerations that led the philosopher Samuel Scheffler to advance agent-centered prerogatives (Scheffler, 1982).

Kenneth Arrow had also made use of agent-centered prerogatives (Arrow, 1981), but because he had done it in an attempt to construct a positive theory of income distribution, he hadn't offered an ethical justification for them (see also Arrow, 1999). Previously Phelps and Pollak (1968) had made use of the same construct to develop an account of intergenerational saving. As theirs was a descriptive theory, they hadn't probed the ethical status of agent-relative social preferences. The considerations I now advance, based on a modified version of the problem posed by Sleeping Beauty, have been so re-drawn as to make agent-centered prerogatives central to population axiology. The version of those prerogatives I need is only an attenuated form of the ones uncovered by Scheffler. Generation-Relative Utilitarianism curbs births—it doesn't discriminate against people.

It is natural to be drawn to population ethics. I know of no other human activity that is at once so private in motivation and public in its consequences as procreation. And yet welfare economists shy away from the subject. We are all faced at some point in our lives with choices that are not unrelated to the possibilities of creating persons. A couple considering parenthood look into their own desires and needs as well as the socio-economic constraints they face. They consider the effect of an addition on all existing family members, and they consider the kind of life that would be on offer to the potential child. Anthropologists and demographers study problems arising from the first pair of considerations, whereas population axiologists focus on the third.

But there is a fourth class of considerations that couples will want to think through. They will want to consider the potential effects of their newborn child on others outside their family, including people who will appear in the future. I have in mind here in particular the environmental consequences of new births. In the world we know, those consequences are not mediated by the price system nor by social norms of behavior. But this tells us that procreation should not be seen as an entirely private matter. It isn't a private matter also because parental motivations are shaped by the social milieu. We look at others' behavior when choosing what to do, and we know that others look at the choices we make when they choose what to do. No doubt we each are negligible on the societal stage, but the effects we each impose on others when summed across all of us is not negligible.

Readers will recognize that I am talking here of "externalities," which are the unaccounted-for consequences of our actions for others, including future people. The presence of externalities explains why and how it can be that a people are settled on a pattern of reproductive behavior they all would prefer to alter but cannot because no couple has the necessary motivation to change their behavior unilaterally.

Anthropologists, demographers, and development economists in recent years have, however, focused on yet another problem, also of vital importance. They have pointed to the inequalities in power between the genders, most especially perhaps in the poor world. So the inner workings of households in poor countries have come under scrutiny in studies of population and development. The United Nations' declaration of 1994 (UNFPA, 1995) on the primacy of women's reproductive rights was in part built on that recognition but in part also in response to coercive measures in place in a few regions.

The environmental externalities I am alluding to are of an adverse kind. Their presence tells us that there is a clash of rights between households and those who are affected by households' reproductive decisions. Moreover, the line joining women's reproductive rights, their expressed desire for children, and their need for family planning assistance is not simple at all. Translation of women's reproductive rights into family planning programs is full of pitfalls, if for no other reason than deducing needs from expressed desires is wholly unreliable. In the accompanying essay, reprinted from *Population and Development Review* (Dasgupta and Dasgupta, 2017), Aisha Dasgupta and I explore the clash of rights to which reproductive intentions give rise. We also argue that contemporary methods of eliciting women's reproductive needs underestimate their actual need for family planning. Talk of family planning and population policies, and we tend to hear alarm bells ringing "coercion" and "restrictions on family size." But more than 60 years of research on externalities has uncovered a wide range of policies that can reduce the externalities even while avoiding command and control.

In a previous work (Dasgupta, 1993) I studied the processes that shape fertility behavior, household poverty, and the local environmental resource base in the world's poorest societies. Work by anthropologists and demographers had pointed to population overshoot in rural parts of South Asia and sub-Saharan Africa, and I wanted to understand why that had occurred. Economic analysis suggested to me that the presence of open-access resources (e.g., sources of water, forest products) encourages fertility as households rush to convert those resources into private goods, which include household size. In poor communities, the causal chain can lead to the existence of poverty traps, where poverty, high fertility, and degradation of the local environmental resource base reinforce one another. Once caught in them, escape is difficult, and many households spend their lives in them.[5]

Adverse externalities also plague the global economy. Vital parts of the biosphere remain free to all to do what we want with them. They are the global commons. Freedom in the commons encourages fertility and so gives rise to positive feedback, other things equal.[6] Over time, the feedback would be expected to stretch the biosphere's ability to supply its products on a sustainable basis. The deduction isn't inconsistent with experience. Environmental scientists have uncovered a large body of evidence that says humanity's demand for the biosphere's products and services in recent years has exceeded its ability to supply them on a sustainable basis. Habitat destruction accompanying our use of land and water and the contamination of the atmosphere and the oceans reflect the imbalance between demand and supply. Global climate change is the most widely discussed of environmental problems, but contamination of the oceans and biological extinctions are also ominous events. Environmental problems are accentuated in those cases where insults to the biosphere are not easily repaired. In cases such as biological extinctions, they are irreversible. Degradation of the biosphere would now appear to be the central weakness in our relationship with our descendants.

Suppose then that by some miracle human society is able to eliminate the adverse externalities accompanying our activities. Suppose too that economic inequalities are ironed out. Given current and prospective technological possibilities, can we say anything about the maximum level of economic activity the biosphere is able to support over the long run? If we can, what does the answer say about optimum population numbers? The latter parts of the pair of essays in this monograph study those questions in two different ways and arrive at tentative answers. My treatment is minimalist. I work with the simplest models possible for addressing the questions at hand, and I cut corners so as to find the quickest ways to reach answers.

---

5. A brief, non-technical account of those pathways is in Dasgupta (1995).
6. This is proved via a simple model in Appendix 2.

The numerical estimates are based on data that are cruder than the data even we economists are used to using. The data are crude in part because very few research groups have tried to estimate our global demand from the biosphere and the biosphere's ability to meet that demand on a sustainable basis (ecology continues to be an underfunded discipline). They are crude in part also because the questions are immensely hard to answer. But the supply of data responds to the demand we make for them. It is not so much the numbers we reach in this monograph that matter as their implied suggestion that the biosphere's workings ought now to be taken seriously by macroeconomists studying the long run and moral philosophers exploring population ethics.

The two essays here approach the question of globally optimum population numbers along parallel routes. In both the Arrow Lecture and the paper with Aisha Dasgupta, economic possibilities are assumed to be circumscribed by the biosphere. In turn, the biosphere is modeled as a gigantic renewable natural resource. In the Arrow Lecture I solve for Generation-Relative Utilitarianism in that world. Depending on the parameters chosen to reflect the biosphere, human technologies, and our values, the numerical solution yields not only the size of the optimum global population, but also the (corresponding) optimum standard of living. In the paper with Aisha Dasgupta, we took the approach of choosing a standard of living deemed comfortable and then estimating the global population that the biosphere would be able to support at that standard on a sustainable basis. The estimates also vary with values of parameters that reflect human technologies and the workings of the biosphere. In the Arrow Lecture, I study the sensitivity of both optimum population and optimum living standard to alternative values of welfare subsistence and the generation-relative weight awarded to potential people; in the paper with Aisha Dasgupta, the sensitivity of sustainable population is studied by choosing alternative living standards deemed comfortable. In a central range of parametric specifications in both studies, optimum population size is found to be considerably less than the current 7.6 billion people. The numerical studies in the latter parts of the two essays are meant to help construct a population ethics that accommodates contemporary sensibilities regarding birth, life, and death, and to then put it to work on quantitative data about humanity's reliance on the biosphere. The idea is to develop methods of analysis and get a sense of the numbers involved; nothing more.

Possibilities of technological advances that influence our dependence on the biosphere are discussed in both essays. As with all discussions on the shape of future technologies and institutions, we are in the realm of speculation. It is easy enough to construct theoretical models in which innovators introduce new technologies that continually raise the living standard of a growing population even while making demands on the biosphere that don't exceed its ability to supply goods and services at a sustainable rate; but there is no evidence from the past that it will prove feasible, and much evidence since at least the middle of the last century that it will not (see Sections 10–12). So I avoid speculating on the shape of future technologies and point to those institutional failures that provide incentives to entrepreneurs to design technological innovations that are rapacious in their use of the biosphere. In the Arrow Lecture, I also offer a brief review of studies that have looked to historical, and even archaeological, evidence for understanding the successes and failures of past societies to meet environmental stresses.

Population axiology is rooted in Utilitarianism, albeit that of a broad form. In contrast, political philosophers and welfare and development economists have introduced a number of non-Utilitarian modes of reasoning. This gives population axiology a quaint flavor, all the more because the subject remains detached from the others. It is an unsatisfactory state of affairs. So, in Section 3 I study one prominent non-Utilitarian theory of distributive justice and argue that it is an expression of Utilitarianism itself. A theorem that relates human well-being to an inclusive measure of wealth also informs that differences between Utilitarian and Resourcist theories are a lot less striking than some scholars maintain. Formal arguments including proofs are presented in Appendices 5 and 6.

Transmission of assets from one generation to the next is what binds the generations together. A recurring question in welfare and development economics and in political philosophy is that of the rate at which a generation should save for its successor, given its state of development. Population ethics addresses the problem of optimum saving, but it has been customary to study the saving problem for a world where projections of future population size are given. Frank Ramsey, who in his famous 1928 paper, "A Mathematical Theory of Saving," initiated the study of the problem of optimum saving, pursued the question using Classical Utilitarianism as his guide for a world in which population is a given constant. Rawls (1972) has also studied the problem of saving, but he applied a different reasoning so as to arrive at a just saving principle. In Appendix 3, I take a detour to interpret the principle and relate it to Utilitarian saving rules.

Although the two essays in this book are closely related, they speak to different audiences. I had prepared the essay "Birth and Death" in April 2016 with philosophers also in mind, while Aisha Dasgupta and I developed our paper for demographers and development economists. The latter essay is self-contained. To make the Arrow Lecture also self-contained, I have borrowed material from the joint paper. There is in any case an overlap between the two essays, as they both study population ethics.

The first drafts of these two essays were prepared between 2014 and 2016. A grant from the Leverhulme Trust in 2013–2015 had brought me in contact with Christopher Cowie, who read drafts of "Birth and Death" and explained Parfitian puzzles to me. Simon Beard, who joined me at the Centre for the Study of Existential Risk at Cambridge in the spring of 2016 on a grant from the Templeton World Charity Foundation, read, commented on, and corrected previous drafts of the Arrow Lecture. Their guidance has been invaluable. At the Faculty of Economics, Gustavo Paez asked me to explain what is to economists an unfamiliar field of inquiry, and then he offered to help me prepare the figures that accompany the text.

Over the years I have learned much about population ethics from discussions and correspondence with Kenneth Arrow, Scott Barrett, Simon Blackburn, Caroline Bledsoe, Christopher Bliss, John Bongaarts, John Cleland, Susan Cochrane, Joshua Cohen, Gretchen Daily, Aisha Dasgupta, Carol Dasgupta, Zubeida Dasgupta-Clark, Mary Douglas, Anantha Duraiappah, Paul Ehrlich, Robert Goodin, Jack Goody, Lawrence Goulder, Jan Graaff, Frank Hahn, Richard Hare, Geoffrey Heal, Ann Kinzig, Simon Levin, Robert Lucas, Georgina Mace, Karl-Göran Mäler, Eric Maskin, David Mitchell, Christopher Morris, Pranab Mukhopadhyay, Subhrendu Pattanayak, Charles Perrings, Edmund Phelps, Peter Raven, John Rawls, Martin Rees, Jeffrey Sachs, Paul Seabright, Amartya Sen, V. Kerry Smith, Robert Solow, Joseph Stiglitz, Robert Sugden, Sylvana Tomaselli, Alistair Ulph, David Ulph, Jeffrey Vincent, Menahem Yaari, and Stefano Zamagni. I have also been stimulated by the criticisms of my previous writings on population ethics by John Broome (Broome, 1996, 1999, 2004). In preparing "Birth and Death," I benefited from the insights of Kenneth Arrow,

Shamik Dasgupta, Paul Kelleher, Thomas Korner, Kian Mintz-Woo, Tapan Mitra, Ingmar Schumacher, Itai Sher, Robert Solow, Gerhard Sorger, and Larry Temkin. The final version of the Arrow Lecture also reflects the impact of comments I received from Ken-Ichi Akao, Simon Blackburn, Krister Bykvist, Timothy Campbell, and Shamik Dasgupta. I have been moved to prepare additional material in response to the probing questions that Hester van Hensbergen put to me on the modern intellectual history of environmental and growth economics. I am grateful as well to Robert Solow for graciously preparing a Foreword to this book, and to Scott Barrett, Eric Maskin, and Joseph Stiglitz for their most thoughtful comments on the material here. I have not responded to them in the Arrow Lecture; I have instead prepared a consolidated set of responses that follows their comments.

My editors at Columbia University Press, Bridget Flannery-McCoy and Christian Winting, have been most encouraging during the publication process, and I am especially grateful to them for enabling me to produce a monograph in which the honoree's presence is felt throughout. And as always, I am grateful to Jake Dyer, Ryan Hilton, Craig Peacock, and Sharon Swann at the Faculty of Economics of my university for their help with the logistics of preparing a text on disk. Sections 1 and 10 of the Arrow Lecture are a reworking of Sections 6–8 of Dasgupta and Dasgupta (2017), and I am most grateful to Aisha Dasgupta for the many discussions we have had while preparing our paper on the place of reproductive rights in population ethics. The influence of Amiya Dasgupta, Kenneth Arrow, and Robert Solow on the way I conceive economics has become increasingly evident to me.

I included a number of remarks on population axiology in my Arrow Lecture in Jerusalem because Arrow had shown interest in my previous work on the subject.[7] He was present on both occasions. In an afternoon-long session in the summer of 2013, in his office at Stanford University, Arrow raised several further problems with Classical Utilitarianism. It had become a custom of mine to send him drafts of papers I had just completed. Accordingly I sent him "Birth and

---

7. The Arrow Lecture at Columbia University was directed more on the concept of intergenerational well-being and the rates at which we should discount marginal changes to future consumption. Both of these issues enter the essay on birth and death.

Death" in April 2016. The paper had incorporated the points he had made three years previously. He was nearly 95 years old, but he found the energy to send me three e-mails, in rapid succession, on June 6.

Arrow visited Cambridge in late June on his way to attend the annual Jerusalem Summer School in Economic Theory. He had previously written to say he wanted to discuss population ethics with me and would like to spend a couple of hours in my office to do just that. We met on June 21.

Because I had hoped philosophers would find "Birth and Death" useful in their thinking, I had simplified the mathematical reasoning when developing Generation-Relative Utilitarianism. To display its differences from Classical Utilitarianism, I had assumed that the biosphere supplies a pure consumption good, like manna from Heaven. There was no production in the model, so no labor was needed to produce the consumption good. Arrow didn't like that. In his third e-mail he complained that I had overlooked modeling labor as an input in production. He wrote that humans are born with both mouth and hands ("and a brain," he added). He told me at our meeting in Cambridge that he didn't approve of compromises in exposition when something significant is missing (in this case, labor, in an essay on population ethics). If scholars found a problem interesting, he said, they should work through it and not demand simplified versions to ease their reading. My 1969 paper had contained a complete capital model, in which output is produced by labor in conjunction with produced capital and land. When I reminded him of that paper (it had evidently slipped his mind), he said that as I had already introduced production possibilities into population ethics in my early work, it was all the more reason to include labor in my new essay. In preparing the Arrow Lecture, I have cast population ethics in a model in which human labor, in conjunction with the goods and services supplied by the biosphere, produces consumption goods.

That still leaves out produced capital (roads, buildings, machines). The economic model that was used to study Classical Utilitarianism in Section 3 of Dasgupta (1969) contains labor, a constant flow of the biosphere's goods and services, and a produced capital that can be accumulated for future people so as to enable them to enjoy more prosperous lives. Unlike the analysis presented in this monograph, attention was not restricted to stationary states. The analysis there was fully dynamic, and the Classical Utilitarian optimum was shown to converge to a stationary state. That finding justifies the attention I give in the Arrow Lecture to stationary states. I have also extended the previous model to include renewable natural resources. The analysis is presented in Appendix 4.

Because I am anxious to engage with population ethicists, I have labored over the exposition in the Arrow Lecture, particularly in Part I, where Generation-Relative Utilitarianism is constructed. I have also inserted an unusually large number of footnotes to explain technical details and to show how the analysis can be extended to richer models. The account is developed in steps. I first apply Classical Utilitarianism to a timeless model of production and consumption; then I study Generation-Relative Utilitarianism in the same model, but in a setting where decisions are made in two stages. Existing people choose the number of people to be created, knowing in advance that they will share economic activities on an equal basis with the next generation. This involves backward induction, an essential ingredient in population ethics. I make use of the analysis in the timeless world to extend Generation-Relative Utilitarianism to a world that is moving through time in a stationary mode. Such laborious exposition isn't the sort I am used to; I have nevertheless undertaken it here because it may help readers who want to see how population axiology can be applied to data, but who don't engage in optimization exercises as a matter of course.

Arrow's three e-mails of June 6, 2016, are reprinted here. To me they remain affectionate letters from a revered teacher to an errant pupil. He begins his third e-mail by complaining that he doesn't understand who the Decision-Maker could be in the exercise I had conducted on Classical Utilitarianism. In my meeting with him on June 21, I reminded him that for many decades I had been delegating that particular exercise to the Decision-Maker at Genesis. He also does not like the high welfare-subsistence rate I had assumed in a numerical exercise and chides me for not following through with the suggestion, which I had made in the draft, that our well-being depends not only on our own standard of living but also on that of others.[8] I am now puzzled about why I was timid on the matter, because socially

---

8. Robert Solow independently urged me to do derive the implications of socially embedded preferences for population ethics.

embedded preferences are central to the analysis of reproductive rights in the essay I had already prepared with Aisha Dasgupta, and I had co-authored a paper with Arrow in which we analyzed the problem of optimum saving in a world where people are conscious of their status and express it through conspicuous consumption (Arrow and Dasgupta, 2009). A formal analysis of socially embedded preferences is now included in the Arrow Lecture (Section 5.6 and Appendix 1).

In the third e-mail, Arrow performs mathematical operations to better expose the workings of Classical Utilitarianism. For me, working through his calculations was a familiar exercise, for he had produced a simplified version of the model in Section 3 of Dasgupta (1969). The e-mail ends with a study of Classical Utilitarianism in a world where the productivity of labor is independent of population numbers (an out-and-out extreme case) and where output per head supports a positive quality of life. He notes that Sidgwick's Utilitarianism commends a population policy that is discontinuous at that extreme value and remarks that there is something wrong with the theory. At our meeting in Cambridge, I said it shouldn't come as a surprise when a moral theory displays unexpected features in complex environments, nor should unexpected features per se be a reason for doubting a theory. I also said a theory that has no surprises in store should be regarded as shallow. I reminded him that Frank Ramsey, in his famous paper on the optimum rate of saving in a Utilitarian world, had found that the very meaning of what constitutes an answer to the problem takes a sharp turn when the utilities of present and future people are awarded the same weight (Ramsey, 1928). Arrow was tired from his journey from Stanford, so I sensed he didn't have the strength to carry on with the discussion. I don't know whether he agreed with me.

Partha Dasgupta
St John's College, Cambridge

Random Thoughts on "Birth and Death"

KENNETH J. ARROW

Subject: "Birth and Death"
From: Kenneth J. Arrow
Date: 06/06/2016, 06:28
To: Partha Dasgupta

Hi Partha,

I'm still working my way through your chapter. It is entirely too stimulating (there are some other papers I should be completing); I stop and try to calculate a model stemming from your work. I attach a few scattered thoughts; I will have more to say when we meet.

As ever,

Ken

Subject: "Birth and Death"
From: Kenneth J. Arrow
Date: 06/06/2016, 06:56
To: Partha Dasgupta

Hi Partha,

The "thoughts" (about a day's work) seem to have disappeared. I am a bit upset. I have a new operating system in old computer; that may be the problem.

I can reconstruct the arguments all right, but I have some more urgent things to do until next weekend.

Hasta la vista.

Ken

Subject: Random Thoughts on "Birth and Death"
From: Kenneth J. Arrow
Date: 06/06/2016, 09:04

To: Partha Dasgupta

SOME RANDOM THOUGHTS ON "BIRTH AND DEATH"

I. In discussing a preference structure, I always want to find a set of decisions that have to be made. I have always found difficulty in thinking about population because I couldn't identify clearly the decision. If the choice is between existence and non-existence, one alternative refers to a person but the other refers to—what? In the standard evaluations of health, we use as a real-life measure the choices between jobs with differing fatal accident rates and correspondingly different wages. A single individual is being compared in two different circumstances.

II. James Joyce refers to, "the God-possibilized individuals whom we nightly impossibilize." Here there does seem to be a choice—by the potential parents. Your "generation-relative utilitarianism" may point in this direction. But, of course, in that case, it is not (at least, not entirely) the utility of the potential person that is relevant; there is a direct (instrumental) utility to the parents.

III. Sophocles on C^S: Glancing at your chapter raised vague memories of a chorus from one of Sophocles' plays about Oedipus and his children. It occurs in, "Oedipus at Colonus," about two-thirds of the way through. This is Gilbert Murray's translation

Not to be born, by all acclaim,
Were best; but once that gate be passed,
To hasten thither whence he came
Is man's next prize—and fast, Oh fast!
For, once he has unloosed his hand
From Youth and Youth's light vanities,
What blow can from his path be banned?
What griefs will not be surely his?
Strife, envy, falseness, blood and hate,
Till, last, the curse of curses, lone,
Despised, weak, friendless, desolate,
Old age hath claimed his own.

This sets a high (literally, infinite) value for C^S, though it is connected with the decay due to age, and so may point to a value depending on both age and the technical ability to mitigate consequences.

Paul Baran, who was a colleague of mine in the Stanford Economics Department for 14 years after I joined in in 1949, had a semantically and logically complex variation on this thought. "Best of all never to have been born! But who has such luck? Not one in twenty"

IV. C^S in previous periods: If we go back even a few thousand years and certainly if we go to a pre-agricultural era or even parts of the world today, we observe consumption levels vastly lower than even current average world levels. Either we have to say that most of mankind for most of its existence should not have lived or we have to make utility a relative concept, an idea you briefly raise and shrink from (or at least say that other ethicists would disapprove of).

V. A major issue to me is the specification of the production conditions. As I say, I have not completed my reading of your chapter by a long shot, but you have used the Sidgwick–Meade model of a fixed amount of goods available for consumption. As an old saying has it, "Man is born with a mouth—and two hands." (I may add, "and a brain.") Even in a hunter-gather society, you can collect more fruit or hunt more animals with a larger population. If N is population (assumed equal to labor force) and C is per capita consumption, then the constraint is,

$$NC = F(N, K),$$

where F is concave and homogeneous of degree 1. If we maximize $NU(C)$ with this constraint, we get,

$$[EU(C)/EC]\, s_K = 1, \text{ where } s_K = F_K K/F,$$

the share of rents in total output. [Note: EU/EC is the elasticity of U with respect to C. Meade and Sidgwick assume N plays no role in production, so that for them, $s_K = 1$. It not hard to see that, if technological progress is land-augmenting, then, at the optimum, N increases in proportion to land productivity while C remains constant (generalizing a conclusion that you had already come to).

The conclusions are not very institutive and may cast doubt on the utilitarian criterion.

This doubt is, to my mind, increased by one final observation. Let us specialize the production assumption by assuming that F is Cobb-Douglas, so s_K is a constant, say, a. It can be shown that EU/EC is a decreasing function of C in the interval beginning at c^S and ending with the C-value where $EU/EC = 1$. Hence C *decreases* as a decreases to 0, approaching c^S. This is especially odd, since a small a means that output is mostly determined by human effort and little sensitive to nature. Incidentally, there is a discontinuity at $a = 0$. At that point, per capita consumption is determined by production conditions. If this level is above the zero-utility level, then N will be infinite.

I really don't know how to interpret this last conclusion. There may be something wrong in the model, or, as I think, something wrong in the Sidgwick–Meade criterion.

Figure 0.1 Kenneth J. Arrow and Partha Dasgupta, Nässlingen Island, Sweden, September 1994

Time and the Generations

Birth and Death

Arrow Lecture

PARTHA DASGUPTA

PEOPLE HAVE children for many reasons. The mix of motivations depends on the customs and institutions we inherit, as well as on our character and circumstances. That children are valuable in themselves is emotionally so compelling that it may seem too obvious to require acknowledgement, but social anthropologists have shown that children are not just valuable to us because of the innate desire we have to bear and rear them, but also because they represent the fulfillment of tradition and religious dictates, and because they are the clearest avenue open to self-transcendence. A common refrain, that our children are priceless, is an expression of how innately valuable they are to us.[1]

---

1. One such injunction emanates from the cult of the ancestor, which takes religion to be the act of reproducing the lineage. See Fortes (1978). "Socially Embedded Preferences, Environmental Externalities, and Reproductive Rights" (Dasgupta and Dasgupta, 2017), which is reprinted later in this volume, reports anthropological findings on the motivations that guide fertility behavior.

In places where formal institutions are underdeveloped, children also substitute for other assets and are thus valuable for the many benefits they bring to their parents. This is most apparent in the poorest regions of the world. Children serve as security in old age in places that have neither pension schemes nor adequate capital and land markets. They are also a source of labor in households possessing few labor-saving devices. Children mind their siblings, tend to domestic animals, pick berries and herbs, collect firewood, draw water, and help with cooking. Children in poor countries are valued by their parents also as capital and producers of goods.[2]

1. Economic Demography

Those childhood activities are so unfamiliar today in the West that they direct us to study the motivations governing procreation by contrasting rich regions from poor regions. There are notable exceptions of course, but broadly speaking fertility rates and mortality rates are high and health status and education attainment are low in poor countries, whereas the corresponding statistics in rich countries read the other way. Table 1, which presents a snap shot (roughly, the period 2014–2015), speaks to that by displaying data published by the World Bank, where countries are classified according gross domestic product (GDP) per capita. I have labeled the two categories "rich" (the World Bank labels them "high-income countries") and "poor" (the World Bank labels them "low-income countries"). Countries have been known to make a transition from the latter category to the former category (that's what economic development is usually taken to mean), and there are regions that were prosperous once but have since declined; moreover, the bulk of the world's population and a majority of the world's poorest people live in neither rich nor poor countries, and international statistics say there are enormously rich people in poor countries. It nevertheless pays to study sharp contrasts, as in Table 1.

---

2. In South Asia, children have been observed to work in household production from age six.

TABLE I
Social Statistics from Rich and Poor Regions (Year 2014–15)

	Rich	Poor
Population (millions)	1,420	620
Gross domestic product per capita (international dollars)	41,000	1,570
Total fertility rate *	1.7	4.9
Under-5 mortality rate (per 1,000)	7	76
Life expectancy at birth (years)	80	60
Youth literacy	100	68
Civil liberties	High	Low
Political liberties	High	Low
Government corruption	Low	High

* Total fertility rate is the number of births that a woman expects to have during her reproductive years. The number 2.1 is usually taken to be the total fertility rate that, over the long run, would lead to a stable population.

Sources: World Bank (2016), UNPD (2015), Freedom House (2017)

Reproductive decisions and our use of the natural environment have consequences for others, including our descendants, that are unaccounted for under prevailing institutions and social mores (e.g., markets, government policy, communitarian engagements, religious injunctions). Economists use the term *externalities* to denote those consequences of our decisions for others that are not accounted for. The qualifier "not accounted for" means that the consequences in question follow without prior engagement with those who are, or who will be, affected. The required engagements don't have to be face-to-face. Many of our actions can be expected to have consequences for our descendants, but if the actions were taken with due care and concern (we take many actions—for example, saving for the future—with our descendants very much in our mind), they would not give rise to externalities. We begin to engage with future people when we deliberate whether current rates of carbon emissions into the atmosphere will place an unjust burden on our descendants. The presence of externalities explains why and how it can be that a people are settled on a pattern of reproductive behavior and environmental-resource use they would all prefer to alter but do not because no one has the necessary motivation to change their behavior unilaterally. Externalities raise deep ethical issues. Not only do they extend to contemporaries and can be expected to extend to future people, it is also that some people will be born in consequence of the decisions we take, while some conceptions that would have taken place had we acted otherwise will not take place.[3]

Caldwell (1981, 1982) drew on an idea that is suggested by Table 1, that the intergenerational transfer of wealth is from parents to children in rich countries but from children to parents in poor societies. The suggestion has been easier to confirm in rich countries, where the rate of investment in children's education has been found to be as high as 6–7 percent of GDP (Haveman and Wolfe, 1995). Because a vast range of activities in poor societies are undertaken outside the institution of markets, it is especially hard to identify the direction in which resources there flow across the generations. Nevertheless, the Caldwell hypothesis has been questioned for poor societies. Studies have found that, even there, the direction is from the old to the young (Lee, 2000, 2007). Further investigations may find hidden transfers from the young to the old in poor societies that confirm Caldwell's thesis, but as of now it would seem that throughout the world intergenerational resource transfers are made by the old to the young.

Differences in the social statistics in Table 1 are striking. They are traceable to kinship structures, marriage practices, and rules of inheritance. The implied line of thinking says that over the long run it is differences in institutions, beliefs, and social norms of behavior that lie behind differences in reproductive behavior among peoples.[4] Theoretical models have been built on that premise. Causality isn't traced to differences in income or wealth. It is not that fertility and mortality rates are high and health status and education attainment are low in poor regions *because* people there are poor; rather, it is that very low

---

3. The latter should be thought of as consequences to the potential parents. Decisions on consumption and production also create externalities. They are connected to reproductive externalities. Here I focus on decisions regarding reproduction. We uncover the pervasiveness of externalities in Section 5.7, Section 10, and Appendices 1 and 2.

4. We should expect institutions and the norms of behavior that support them to originate in some measure on geography: tropical regions vs. temperate regions, drylands vs. wetlands, sedentary vs. migratory societies, and so on.

incomes go hand in hand with those features of life. The variables are mutually determined over time.[5]

Table 1 is a snapshot. It says that, in comparison to people in rich countries, people in poor countries receive less basic education, have more children, die younger, enjoy fewer political and civil liberties, and suffer from greater failure in governance. There is no suggestion that poor societies will remain poor, nor that rich countries may not find their place reversed in the long run. Regional differences in fertility, education, and output per capita were slight until the start of the Early Modern era (roughly, 1500 CE). Global aggregates of earlier eras look much the same as their regional aggregates.[6] Although regional aggregates have diverged since then, global aggregates (a weighted

---

5. For theoretical models that speak to the mutual determination, see Dasgupta (1993, 2010), Brander and Taylor (1998), Harford (1997, 1998), Dasgupta and Ehrlich (2013), and Bohn and Stewart (2015). Crist et al. (2017) offers a description of the mutual determination using global figures. Sub-Saharan Africa has long been regarded as special, even among poor regions (Goody, 1976; Fortes, 1978; Bledsoe, 1994; Guyer, 1994; Bongaarts and Casterline, 2013). In an early review of fertility intentions, Cochrane and Farid (1989) noted that both the urban and rural, the educated and uneducated in sub-Saharan Africa have more, and want more, children than their counterparts in other less developed regions. Even young women there expressed a desire for an average of 2.6 more children than women in the Middle East, 2.8 more than women in North Africa, and 3.6 to 3.7 more than women in Latin America and Asia. Updated versions of these figures are available, but it is worth considering the data from the mid-1980s because the income gap between Africa and the rest of the developing world was smaller at that time than it is now.

  Evolutionary biologists distinguish reproductive strategies in the animal kingdom that correspond to the two extreme types of fertility and human capital outcomes displayed in Table 1. An r-strategy gives rise to many offspring combined with low parental investment, and each offspring has a low probability of survival. In contrast, a K-strategy gives rise to few offspring over a longer lifespan and high parental investment. The motivation driving animals is inclusive fitness. Each of the strategies is an equilibrium, depending on the underlying evolutionary game.

6. The classic on this is Maddison (2001), who provided estimates of expectancy of life at birth, population size, and output from 1 CE to 1998 in various regions of the world.

average of regional statistics) have shown a steady move toward and beyond "fertility transition," that is, transition from high fertility and mortality rates to low fertility and mortality rates.

Economists have offered a number of explanations for the historical experience.[7] What is common to them is a presumption that parental choices over fertility, consumption, and investment determine long-run outcomes. The models trace the relative urgencies of parental needs, desires, and obligations to the constraints on choices faced by parents in each generation.[8] Some authors stress economic constraints, and others pay attention to social and ecological constraints. A few (as in Dasgupta and Dasgupta, 2017, reproduced here) speak especially to the pervasiveness of reproductive and environmental externalities. Economic demographers have commonly avoided moral theories in their study of reproductive behavior.

In contrast, philosophical discourses on population have been built on normative reasoning, directed at four questions: (i) What are the nature, ground, and limits of parental responsibility for existing children? (ii) Does producing a child interfere with the rights of children the couple already have? (iii) Do individuals have a duty not to have children whose lives are likely to be bad for them (negative well-being)? Do they have a duty to have children whose lives are likely to be good for them (positive well-being)? (iv) How should one value possible populations so as to decide which would be best?

One way to contrast the two disciplinary approaches is to say that the economic demographer's task is to explain Table 1, while the aim in population ethics is to produce a normative theory that one could use to evaluate the behavior patterns that give rise to Table 1 and prescribe better ones. Question (iv), which stands in sharp contrast to those that demographers study, is at the heart of "population axiology," which attempts to uncover the ethics involved in what Parfit (1984: 356) called Different Numbers Choices. To me it remains a puzzle though that population axiologists haven't subjected their reasoning to a world facing socio-ecological constraints of the kind we have now come to know.

---

7. See the references in note 5, and Galor (2011).

8. "Parental choices" are only a contemporary way of alluding to choices that are often, perhaps even usually, influenced by the extended family, kinship, the couple's peer group, and the power relationship between the couple. On this, see Dasgupta (1993, 2010).

In Part I, population axiology is studied with an eye on resource constraints (i.e., the biosphere's ability to supply goods and services). I try to integrate demographic and environmental concerns while accommodating contemporary sensibilities surrounding birth, life, and death. In Part II, the formulation is applied to quantitative data on humanity's reliance on the biosphere. My idea there is to obtain a sense of the numbers involved, nothing more.

2. Utilitarian Ethics

In his statement of Utilitarianism, Sidgwick (1907: 415–416) wrote:

> . . . if we take Utilitarianism to prescribe, as the ultimate end of action, happiness as a whole, and not any individual's happiness, unless considered as an element of the whole, it would follow that, if the additional population enjoy on the whole positive happiness, we ought to weigh the amount of happiness gained by the extra number against the amount lost by the remainder. So that, strictly conceived, the point up to which, on Utilitarian principles, population ought to be encouraged to increase, is not that at which average happiness is the greatest possible . . . but that at which the product formed by multiplying the number of persons living into the amount of average happiness reaches its maximum.

The account is read by philosophers as saying that the basis for evaluation is not gains and losses to people, but gains and losses in total utility. An ethics grounded on the latter reflects the view that lives have an intrinsic value, and that the better the life is for the person as measured in terms of utility, the greater is the value. Sidgwick took utility to be a numerical measure of happiness. His Utilitarianism asks us to evaluate alternative states of affair in terms of the sum of personal utilities: State of affairs X is judged to be superior to state of affairs Y if total utility in X exceeds total utility in Y, period.[9]

---

9. I am grateful to Krister Bykvist for correspondence on the way Sidgwick should be interpreted. The ground of binding reason in Sidgwick's population ethics is total human happiness ("happiness as a whole"), not the algebraic sum of gains and losses to people.

Sidgwick's theory, which Rawls (1972) called Classical Utilitarianism, involves two related notions: personal happiness, whose numerical measure is individual utility; and summation as the required operation for combining individual utilities. Sidgwick (1907: 119–150) contains three chapters on empirical hedonism, where the sense in which "happiness" is used is a lot more considered than is suggested in the frequent criticism that Classical Utilitarianism views humans to be mere pleasure machines. Nevertheless, I am reluctant to give the impression that the ethical theory I am led to relies on Sidgwick's notion of the personal good, so I shall use the term "well-being." Griffin (1986) contains a measured, book-length analysis of the concept in its many guises, but he also develops his preferred interpretation. Briefly, he thinks of personal well-being as a measure of the extent to which one's *informed desires* are realized. He also discusses measurement problems.

The qualifier "informed" is meant to bear ethical weight. We are to interpret the fulfillment of informed desires as a flourishing life. To be informed is taken to include, for example, to practice reasoning when sifting evidence. While composing this essay I have kept Griffin's conception in mind, but the mathematical structure of the ethics that is constructed here is not tied to his formulation of the idea of well-being.

Personal well-being will be denoted by a numerical function U. It is assumed to be a function of the standard of living. By living standard I mean an aggregate measure of all the factors that influence personal well-being. In the formal models that I study here, those factors are represented by an all-purpose consumption good.

The presumption that the sole factor in well-being is consumption may seem otiose. It is widely held that personal and social engagements are central to how one's life gets shaped. Chance, of course, plays a role. And there are factors such as genetic endowment, which at least for now are not subject to choice by the individual. We may regard them as parameters of the U-function. Because all engagements require goods and services, we may think of engagements as production activities in which goods and services are inputs. Partaking of a meal (alone or in the company of others) is an engagement, but food items are the inputs that make the meal possible. Friendship involves an investment of time, which is a scarce resource. And so on. Goods and services come with various characteristics, and for each person there is (given the resources at his command) a best way of obtaining the commodities that are best suited for the activities that are, from his point of view, the best for him to engage in. Of course, the best way of obtaining goods and services with those characteristics involves further engagements (e.g., getting a job, making contacts); but the regress is circular, meaning that it is closed. The economist's presumption that the only things people care about are goods and services should be seen as a filtered expression of their projects and aims. Commodities have instrumental value; they don't necessarily have intrinsic worth. However, irrespective of what a person values, he will be found to value commodities. The U-function postulated here should be interpreted in that light.

Part I of this essay studies Sidgwick's theory as amended when happiness is replaced by well-being, and then offers reasons why we should still move away from it. I depart from the amended theory in two ways. First, I alter the way individual well-beings are aggregated by the decision-maker and propose an alternative that commends itself. I am drawn to the alternative because population axiology is not only about identifying desirable demographic states of affairs, but also about the reproductive choices people can justify to themselves. Answers to the latter problem do not follow from resolutions of the former exercise. Second, I am drawn for several reasons to a different reading of the idea of a neutral life, which is a central notion in population axiology. We shall call the theory I am led to Generation-Relative Utilitarianism.

Differences between Total Utilitarianism and Generation-Relative Utilitarianism are exposed in Part II. There I apply both theories to quantitative data on humanity's reliance on the biosphere.

3. Ends and Means

Humanity's future will be shaped by the portfolio of assets we inherit and choose to pass on, and by the balance we strike between the portfolio and the size of our population. Assets are durable objects. Their durability enables us to save them for our own future, offer them as gifts to others, exchange them for other goods and services, and bequeath them to our children. Durable doesn't mean everlasting. Assets depreciate (e.g., machines suffer from wear and tear, trees die), but they are not fleeting. Perhaps because financial capital has figured prominently in economists' writings, the qualifier "capital" is sometimes added to assets, as in "capital assets."

3.1. Capital Goods

Durability distinguishes assets from services, such as live performances, which vanish as soon as they are produced. It is true that a memorable performance is remembered long after, but memory of a performance differs from the performance itself. Memory confers durability to the performance by creating a substitute product. Recording serves a similar, in some ways a more faithful, purpose. But even though we can enjoy the recording, it's a recording we are enjoying, not the actual performance.

Assets acquire their value from the services they provide over their remaining life. A refrigerator preserves food products by keeping them cool. It provides that service until it breaks down beyond repair. The refrigerator's worth is a measure of the benefits it provides over its remaining life. How that measure should be constructed is something we discuss below. The important thing to remember here is that an asset's future performance is built into it today.

In common parlance, to say an object is an "asset" is to convey the idea that it has positive worth; assets are taken to be goods. But one virtue of moving from the literary to the formal is to extend the use of concepts so as to bring disparate objects under a common intellectual framework. So we note that assets not only contribute directly to our well-being, but indirectly too, as sinks for pollution (contemporary carbon emissions into the atmosphere are a prominent example). One way to conceptualize pollution is to view it as the depreciation of assets. Acid rains damage forests; carbon emissions into the atmosphere trap heat; industrial seepage and discharge reduce water quality in streams and underground reservoirs; sulfur emissions corrode structures and harm human health; and so on. The damage inflicted on each type of asset (respectively, buildings, forests, the atmosphere, fisheries, human health) should be interpreted as depreciation. For natural resources, depreciation amounts to the difference between the rate at which they are harvested and their regenerative rate (Appendix 4); the depreciation that pollutants cause on natural resources is the difference between the rate at which pollutants are discharged into the resource base and the rate at which the resource base is able to neutralize the pollutants. The task in either case is to estimate depreciation. Economists have tried to estimate the damage over time that an additional ton of carbon emitted into the atmosphere today is likely to inflict on agricultural production, submerged coastal habitats, human health, and so on. In 2016 the U.S. Environmental Protection Agency proposed a range of values for the social cost of carbon, based on alternative assumptions. The range was 11 to 56 U.S. dollars. Resources are "goods," while pollutants (the degrader of resources) are "bads." Pollutants are the reverse of resources, and polluting is the reverse of conserving.[10]

In common parlance assets are often called "capital goods." But economists in the past confined the use of that term to assets that are material (tangible), durable, and alienable (i.e., whose ownership is transferable)—a piece of furniture, an orchard, a lathe, and so on. One reason for the latter restriction is the desire to work with assets that can be measured and compared with one another. It's not enough to say that houses can be measured in physical units (floor space, say); they need to be compared with other capital goods, such as automobiles. We need a common unit. Valuing assets is a way to do that. Goods that are both material and alienable can be exchanged in markets. As a possibly crude, first approximation, market prices offer a measure of their value to us.

In recent decades, economists have introduced Nature into economics by viewing it as a capital good. In Part II, we build on that way of looking at things and apply it to the biosphere as a whole. Of the myriad assets that make up Nature, land is perhaps the most familiar. The market price of a hectare of agricultural land at the outer edges of a farm includes the ecological services it provides the rest of the farm, but it excludes the services that the neighboring farm may enjoy (the latter would be a positive externality). So the market price of the hectare is likely to be an underestimate of its worth to the economy as a whole. Valuing a watershed is harder, but again it is manageable. Among the services it offers is purifying water. One way to value that service is to estimate the cost of purifying that same flow of water by other means, such as a water-purification plant. In a well-known study of a degraded watershed (i.e., the Catskills in upper New York State), Chichilnisky and Heal (1998) found that constructing a water-purification plant so as to provide New York City with clean water would have had cost far more than restoring the watershed (fortunately,

---

10. A formal demonstration of the equivalence is in Dasgupta (1982).

the latter is what had been decided by the authorities). Of course, a watershed provides many other services whose value is often not measurable. So we would have an underestimate of the value. Then there are objects of Nature that communities would rightly refuse to value (sacred groves). That measurability is perforce incomplete is no argument for not trying measurement. Economists call the assets that comprise Nature "natural capital."

What about a person's knowledge, skills, reputation, and state of health? They are non-alienable (knowledge, skills, and reputation are also intangible). Nevertheless, contemporary economists include them on the list of capital goods by calling them "human capital." We economists use market wages and salaries to estimate the value of human capital to the individual possessing it. The term "human capital" reminds us that assets can be ends, they can be means to ends, or they can be both. Reading is a pleasurable activity, but it is also necessary in a job that requires literacy. Similarly, a person's health is both a desired end for him and a means to employment. These examples suggest that valuing human capital on the basis of their market prices is to underestimate their worth. Working with biased estimates can nevertheless be revealing. Recent work on human capital using market prices has shown that, as a share of national wealth, it is larger than other capital goods by at least two orders of magnitude (Arrow et al., 2012).

Once you include knowledge, skills, reputation, and health in the category of capital goods, it's hard to know where to stop. Should you not include institutions, such as the State or the market system? After all, they too are assets. There is then the temptation to go for broke and speak of institutional capital, knowledge capital (e.g., science and technology), and cultural capital. Today some people even refer to religious capital. You could then take an extreme position by calling *all* assets capital goods. I first discuss the advantages in doing that. I then show that there are severe disadvantages.[11]

In a ground-breaking work, Putnam (1993) studied the role social networks play in facilitating civic engagement. The underlying thesis was that network activities help create trust among members by,

---

11. There is a huge literature in which cross-country data are used to show that various types of capital goods are factors in economic performance, usually growth in GDP. See for example Jones and Romer (2010), who find that the quality of institutions matters for economic performance.

among other ways, enabling members to learn who are trustworthy, which in turn helps people engage in civic activities. Using Italy as his laboratory, Putnam uncovered contemporary data on memberships of choral societies and football clubs in each of the twenty states in the country. Calling the trust that is created in such networks "social capital," he found that the networks not only discipline the nation's state governments in their role as suppliers of public services, but that they also have a long temporal reach. Regions where civic engagement was greater hundreds of years ago enjoy greater levels of civic engagement and better governance today. Putnam identified civil society as the seat of social capital. His finding says that, while civic engagement contributes directly to one's well-being, they are also of instrumental value: accumulation of one type of asset (social capital) improves the quality of another type (state government).[12]

As these examples show, there are many ways of classifying assets. However, only one has proved useful in empirical work. It is one thing to recognize that a durable object has worth, and it is another thing to measure that worth. Try, for example, to compare the value to a nation of good governance with the real estate value of its capital city. The requirement that a durable good be measurable if it is to be called a "capital good" was at the basis of the complaints Arrow (2000) and Solow (2000) made of attempts to regard social capital on par with buildings, roads, labor, and land. We take heed of their caution in our study by creating a three-way partition of capital goods: *produced capital* (e.g., buildings, roads, ports, machines, instruments), *human capital* (e.g., population size, health, education, reputation, knowledge, skills), and *natural capital* (e.g., ecosystems, sub-soil resources). The remaining set of assets (e.g., institutions and practices—more generally, social capital—and publicly available knowledge) we will call

---

12. Networks can have negative social value, for example criminal gangs. Dasgupta (2000) studied the formal economics of social capital by introducing it in models of economic growth and development. Dasgupta and Serageldin (2000) and Grootaert and von Bastelaer (2002) contain empirical papers on the measurement of social capital. Ghate, Jodha, and Mukhopadhyay (2008) contains applied studies on the strengths and weaknesses of social capital as a lubricant of human interchanges. The authors do that by studying the management of local common property resources in South Asia.

enabling assets because they confer value to the three classes of capital goods by facilitating their use.

Enabling assets have to be produced, they do not appear out of nothing. Knowledge in the sciences, technologies, and the arts and humanities, for example, are created and acquired, and they are created and acquired by people (human capital) in combination with produced capital (books, laboratories, and equipment) and natural capital (raw materials). We study the real economy here. Financial capital facilitates exchange (among people and across time), and so in our reckoning it too is an enabling asset. In our classification, there are three categories of capital goods and a wide range of enabling assets.[13]

3.2. Inclusive Wealth and Social Well-Being

At this point we do not specify the economy under study. The economy could be a person, a household, village, town, district, nation, the whole world. In Part II, we will apply the account of population ethics we develop in Part I to the world as a whole. Here we seek a way to aggregate the three classes of capital goods in the economy, for without aggregation we would be left with a catalogue of capital goods and no idea how they relate to one another in people's activities and engagements.

To aggregate disparate objects, we need a common currency. The currency we use in this essay is well-being, and by the value of a capital good we mean its social worth as perceived by the concerned individual (e.g., a citizen) when assessing the normative properties of the economy in question. When developing formal models to illustrate the choices that population ethics points to, I shall call the concerned citizen the *decision-maker* (DM). In the body of the Arrow Lecture, we

---

13. Here I am following the classification in Dasgupta and Mäler (2000). Of the three categories of capital goods, produced capital has the oldest pedigree, being the substance of Classical Political Economy of the 18th and 19th centuries. (Land of various qualities served as an additional, indestructible factor of production.) The paper that placed human capital in the category of capital goods and created the modern literature on human capital is Schultz (1961). A huge contemporary literature in ecology and environmental economics has introduced natural capital in economic reasoning.

appeal to Generation-Relative Utilitarianism to define the social worth of all goods and services, not only capital goods. But the propositions I discuss here have a far wider reach. They apply to any conception of social well-being which recognizes that we are dependent on assets (be they capital goods or enabling assets) for anything we do and any kind of person we strive to be.

It transpires that the right way to aggregate the social worth of our three classes of capital goods is to add them. That's the social worth of the totality of capital goods to which the economy has access at any given date. By social worth we mean not only the worth to people who are alive at that date, but also to future people. We call the social worth of the three classes of capital goods *inclusive wealth*. The qualifier signals that the notion of wealth adopted here differs from the one in common use in two ways: the social worth of capital goods—they are called *accounting prices*—are not necessarily market prices; and, in addition to produced capital, wealth includes human capital and natural capital. The inclusion of human capital says, among other things, that personal characteristics of the individual with access to a piece of capital good matter. A piano in the possession of someone who can play the piano has a higher accounting price than it would have were it in the possession of someone innocent of music, other things equal of course.

A person's well-being is shaped by the extent to which her projects and purposes are realized. They in turn are rooted in her engagements, both with her own self and with others (we develop the idea further in Section 4), which means accounting prices of goods and services are person-specific. It also means that the degree of fairness in the distribution of well-being influences accounting prices. So as to avoid repetition, we will sometimes drop the qualifier "inclusive" from inclusive wealth.

An economy's institutions and practices endow capital goods with their social worth, which is why we are calling them enabling assets. The same portfolio of capital goods would have greater worth to people if the society in question were to bring about changes to its institutions and practices that, for example, created greater trust among people. Those changes would express themselves through an altered set of accounting prices. A writing desk has a higher accounting price in someone's study than in a war zone. An economy can become wealthier simply by improving the quality of its enabling assets.

A more familiar means of wealth creation is to ensure that (net) investment, aggregated across the three classes of capital, is positive. These claims are proved formally in Appendices 4 and 5.

Why should we be interested in inclusive wealth? The reason is this:

Call the numerical measure of well-being across the generations *social well-being* (Sects. 8–9). The accounting price of a capital good is the extent to which social well-being would increase if the economy were provided with an additional unit of it. The idea of accounting prices generalizes quite naturally to all goods and services. We have now nearly reached the point to which we have been heading. If assets in their totality are the basis of social well-being, and if accounting prices of capital goods measure their contribution at the margin to social well-being, there must be an intimate connection between inclusive wealth and social well-being. That is indeed so. It can be shown that social well-being increases over time if the corresponding measure of inclusive wealth increases over time, and social well-being declines over time if inclusive wealth declines over time.

The equivalence of inclusive wealth and social well-being holds also in policy evaluation. At any given date, a change in policy that increases (decreases) social well-being also raises (lowers) inclusive wealth. Of particular interest are investment projects (e.g., road construction). The point to note here is that to undertake an investment project is to reallocate some capital goods from their use under the status quo to their use in the project. We may then interpret an acceptance of the project as a change in policy—marginally, of course, if the project happens to be small relative to the size of the economy. Because the project is to be evaluated using accounting prices for goods and services, its profitability can be read as "social profitability." We confirm below that the project would contribute positively to social well-being if it was socially profitable, but contribute negatively to social well-being if it was socially unprofitable.

Inclusive wealth and social well-being are thus two sides of the same coin whether we ask if society has progressed over a period of time (the question of interest in sustainability analysis) or whether we evaluate alternative policies at a moment in time (that's where social cost-benefit analysis applies). We will call this the *Wealth/Well-Being Equivalence Theorem*. The theorem is stated formally and proved in Appendix 5. The theorem implies that inclusive wealth is the right measure of social well-being, not GDP nor any of the other measures that have been suggested in recent years, such as the United Nations' Human Development Index.[14]

The wealth/well-being equivalence theorem directs us to expand our common-sense notion of investment. To invest in a capital good is to increase it beyond what it would be if there were no investment in it. We are talking of *net* investment here, that is, investment net of depreciation. And because we are interested in inclusive wealth, we

---

14. The UN's Human Development Index (UNDP, 1990) is a linear aggregate of GDP per capita, life expectancy at birth (human capital), and literacy (human capital). The equivalence of movements in social well-being and movements in inclusive wealth in a general setting was proved by Dasgupta and Mäler (2000) and Arrow, Dasgupta, and Mäler (2003a, 2003b). Dasgupta (2004) is a book-length treatment of the idea of sustainable development and the role that the wealth/well-being equivalence theorem plays in it. Agliardi (2011) extends the theorem by introducing a stationary stochastic process that drives consumption. To facilitate empirical work, the authors of these works identified circumstances in which average well-being across the generations moves in the same manner as per-capita inclusive wealth. Dasgupta (2014) and Irwin, Gopalakrishnan, and Randall (2016) are non-technical accounts of the wealth/well-being equivalence theorem and its extensions. Arrow et al. (2004) studied the connections between sustainable development and optimum development. In an interesting and important paper, Yamaguchi (2018) unearths the differences between conceptualizing social well-being in its total and its population-average forms. Arrow et al. (2012, 2013) applied the theorem by estimating movements in wealth in five countries (Brazil, China, India, the United States, and Venezuela) over the period 1995–2000. The theorem was the basis of a report commissioned in 2011 by the Prime Minister of India, Manmohan Singh, to recommend a methodology that would introduce natural capital in the country's national accounts. I served as the commission's chairman (see Dasgupta et al., 2013). Yamaguchi, Sato, and Ueta (2016) applied the theorem to a region in Japan. UNU-IHDP/UNEP (2012, 2014) and Managi and Kumar (2018) contain pioneering estimates of the wealth of more than 120 countries, akin to estimates the World Bank provides annually of the GDP of nations. Tomlinson (2018) has applied the theorem to the recent economic history of Nigeria. The theorem has also been used to motivate the development of methods for estimating of accounting prices (Fenichel and Abbott, 2014; Fenichel, Abbott, and Yun, 2018; Appendix 5).

may call net investment "inclusive investment" (Hamilton and Clemens, 1999, called it "genuine saving"). Our common-sense notion of investment, however, carries with it a sense of robust activism. When the government invests in a building project, the picture drawn is of bulldozers levelling the ground and tarmac being laid by men in hard hats. But the notion of capital goods we are using here extends beyond produced capital to include human capital and natural capital. That training people to be teachers is investing in human capital is simple enough. To leave a forest unmolested may not suggest much like investment, but it is an investment because it enables the forest to grow. To allow a fishery to re-stock under natural conditions is to invest in the fishery; and so on.

This could suggest that inclusive investment amounts to deferred consumption, but the matter is subtler. Providing additional food to undernourished people via, say, food-guarantee schemes not only increases their current well-being, but it also enables them to be more productive in the future and to live longer. Because their human capital increases, the additional food intake should count also as investment. Note, though, that food intake by the well-nourished doesn't alter their nutritional status, which means the intake is consumption, not investment. Our equivalence theorem suggests that by "net investment" in an asset we should mean the value of the change in its stock.

We are talking of ends and means here. Despite the equivalence theorem, ends (i.e, enhancing social well-being) are the right starting place for population axiology, as is the case in Sidgwick's Utilitarianism. Ends (i.e, human flourishing) are also the starting point of Rawls' contractual theory of justice. His theory is emphatic in regarding persons to be inviolable in certain respects of their personhood and insists that persons are to be treated equally (Appendix 3). Ends are the right starting point because they are antecedent to means. One can articulate ends even without asking whether they can be realized, but it makes no sense to talk of means if the ends they are meant to advance aren't articulated first. The wealth/well-being equivalence theorem doesn't deny the antecedence of ends; the theorem says that, if the means to a set of ends have been identified, it doesn't in principle make any difference whether we examine the extent to which the ends have been (or are likely to be) furthered by a change to an economy or whether we estimate the degree to which the means to those ends have been (or are likely to be) bolstered by that change: the two point in the same direction. The wealth/well-being equivalence theorem draws attention to the fact that no matter what conception of ends citizens may adopt, the source of the means to those ends lies in a society's capital goods. Their accounting prices serve to tie them to the ends. The theorem says the weapons and human capital deployed by the state to abduct awkward citizens from their homes in the middle of the night are to be awarded very large, possibly unboundedly large, negative accounting prices. Likewise, steel put to use in making ploughs differs from steel used to manufacture guns. Accounting prices of capital goods depend on their location and the use to which they are put. The equivalence theorem is utterly wide in its reach.

The equivalence between inclusive wealth and social well-being holds as tightly in a society where the ends are far from being met due to the misallocation of the means or unjustified usurpation of the means by the powerful, as it would in a society where they are met as far as is possible under the prevailing scarcities of the means. The equivalence of ends and means will be confirmed repeatedly in this essay.

That inclusive wealth is equivalent to social well-being is not an empirical law; rather, it is an analytical proposition. Being an equivalence relationship, it does not say whether a society is doing well or badly, whether it is well governed or badly governed. But both theory and experience say that it is commonly easier to measure the means to the ends than it is to measure the ends themselves, which is why in empirical work we are drawn to the means. Consider, for example, a proposal to build a social housing project on an unused piece of wetland. The project's feasibility report contains estimates, expressed in dollars perhaps, of the investment involved (e.g., draining the land, constructing the buildings and ancillary structures). The report estimates that construction requires so many labor hours in each year of the investment phase, so many types and quantities of machines and equipment and intermediate goods, and so on. The report also estimates the expenditure incurred by various parties and the transfer of resources that the project envisages among them during the project's life (e.g., government, tax payers, people who will occupy the homes). If the public are environmentally minded, they will insist the report also itemizes the services the wetland currently provides to the local community (e.g., filtering water) and a description of the animal and bird populations that make it their habitat. Their disappearance will be seen as a loss. All that information, and it is usually very detailed, are in the form of flows of goods and services. The problem is to evaluate the project.

It won't do to simply ask whether the project will enhance social well-being, for that would be to re-ask whether the project should be accepted or rejected. The idea is to put the project data to use by applying accounting prices to the items. Decades ago, welfare economists proved that the project can be evaluated by estimating the present value of the flow of social profits (net social benefits) that arise from it. By "present value" we mean a weighted sum of the flow of the project's benefits and costs over time. The weights are called "social discount factors," which transport benefits and costs in the future to the present (Sects. 9.1 and 9.2; Appendices 4 and 5). It can be shown that the project should be accepted if its present value is estimated to be positive (unless, that is, a close variant of the project with an even higher present value is identified) or rejected if it is found to be negative. That's known as the "social present value criterion." The word "social" is crucial here, for it means that accounting prices are to be used to value goods and services, not market prices. The criterion also tells us that the accounting price of a capital good is the present value of the flow of social benefits that would be enjoyed if the economy were to be provided with an additional unit of the good.[15]

The present value of a project's flow of social profits (dollars per year) has the dimensions of stock (dollars, period). You will have by now guessed (rightly!) that a project's "present value" is none other than the change to inclusive wealth brought about by the redeployment of capital goods from elsewhere to the project. It thus transpires that the criterion for project evaluation that was developed by welfare economists decades ago is implied by the wealth/well-being equivalence theorem. Notice, though, that the social present value criterion for investment choice is a far cry from the demand commonly made by economists and political commentators that economic policies should be chosen so as to enhance GDP. A macroeconomics that sees growth

---

15. Prest and Turvey (1965) is an early survey of the then-existing literature on social cost-benefit analysis. Little and Mirrlees (1968, 1974), Arrow and Kurz (1970), and Dasgupta, Marglin, and Sen (1972) are book-length treatments of the theory and of ways to make use of the social present-value criterion in project evaluation. Accounting prices of environmental resources are especially hard to estimate, but there is now a sophisticated literature establishing techniques for estimating them. See Freeman (2002) and Haque, Murty, and Shyamsundar (2011).

and distribution of GDP as the aim of public policy is inconsistent with basic welfare economics. I have no explanation for how and why that incongruity has been allowed to fester in economics.

There is a subtler reason for evaluating policies and assessing the progress or regress of economies in terms of the means to our ends. It is a mistake to suppose we come armed with our ends. For the most part, they are inchoate in our minds. Studying means clarifies the trade-offs involved in promoting our ends. The interplay of the "is" and the "ought," to use that well-worn distinction, helps us better understand our ends. In Part II, we conduct sensitivity analysis so as to take advantage of that interplay.

3.3. Placing a Value on Opportunity Sets

The wealth/well-being equivalence theorem also puts into perspective controversies over the objects of interest in distributive justice, such as whether they should be personal well-beings or resources or Rawlsian primary goods or opportunities or human capabilities.[16] The equivalence theorem says that the choice is a matter of convenience and context. We are talking of convenience in practical work, not the relative status of the two notions. Well-being is a measure of human flourishing. It serves as the primary notion in the ethical reasoning we pursue here.[17]

In contrast, consider "human capabilities," which have been defined as the alternative combinations of functionings that are feasible for a person to achieve (Sen, 1985, 1992, 1999, 2009). Functionings— earlier we called them "engagements"—are in turn the various doings and beings a person rationally values, and they are frequently interpreted by Capabilitarians as different kinds of life. A person's capability represents the effective freedom she enjoys in selecting from different functionings, meaning that capabilities are *sets* of functionings. Despite the theory's acknowledgement that functionings are objects that people rationally value, the distinguishing feature of Capabilitarianism is its view that the value of a capability to someone is not derived from

16. Rawls (1972), Dworkin (1981a, 1981b), Sen (1985, 1992, 1999, 2009), Cohen (1989), and Barry (1990), among many others.

17. In Section 13, we study the place of the value of Nature, qua Nature, in our sensibilities.

the worth to her of the functionings that are included in the (capability) set (otherwise Capabilitarianism could be read simply as a version of Utilitarianism; see Arrow, 1995); instead, the set is valued directly. (Sen, 1999, contains a clear statement of that line of reasoning.) There would seem to be a reason behind the move. The theory has been proposed as a rival to Utilitarianism and to the reasoning Rawls (1972) deployed for identifying citizens' choices behind the veil of ignorance.

Capabilities are examples of what economists call "opportunity sets."[18] Imagine that a person is able to place a value, measured in terms of her well-being, on every element in an opportunity set presented to her. The value she ascribes to the opportunity set would then be the worth to her of the element in it she values most highly. It follows that if the person were offered a choice between alternative opportunity sets, she would be able to rank them and identify the one most valuable to her.

Capabilitarianism doesn't subscribe to that way of reasoning. It values capabilities directly, which is why the theory faces an insuperable problem: it admits no machinery for comparing capabilities if none is a subset of any of the others. There is then much talk among Capabilitarians of the virtue of normative theories that yield partial orderings of the objects of choice, not complete orderings.[19] The theory is certainly able to say that slavery is bad, that health is a basic need, that in the modern world education is necessary for a flourishing life, and that freedom of speech is a cherished goal; but it is unable to say much more. And those particular value judgments are reached by all moral theories Capabilitarianism has been designed to contend with.

Why should someone wish to value opportunity sets if she knows the value of their elements to begin with? Why doesn't she simply choose the best element from the opportunity sets available to her? The reason is that the person typically has insufficient knowledge

---

18. In economics, a familiar example of an opportunity set is the set of commodity bundles an individual can afford to purchase in a market economy.

19. Let R be a binary relation of elements of a set X. We say R is a *complete ordering*, or simply an *ordering*, if it is reflexive (for all x in X, xRx), transitive (for all x, y, z in X, xRy and yRz implies xRz), and complete (for all x, y in X, either xRy or yRx). The binary relation R is said to be a *partial ordering* is it is reflexive and transitive, but not complete.

about herself and the world she lives in but knows she will learn more about both with the passage of time. This is why she is aware she would be able to make more satisfactory choices if she waited rather than tie her hands by choosing an ill-informed best element from an opportunity set now. No doubt waiting has a cost, but if the cost is smaller than the gain from keeping her options open for a while, she would rationally choose to keep her options open. That's why there is a case for selecting an opportunity set now and waiting to choose an element from it when she can better identify the element she rationally desires most. This involves backward induction, a style of reasoning I deploy when developing population ethics.

Consider that the acquisition of skills (an aspect of "human capital") involves the use of resources, which means there are tradeoffs among them. But not all skills are of equal value to all, nor even to the same person. Numeracy and literacy are basic skills in the modern world, and they prove vital to people no matter what they wish to be and do and no matter what circumstances they face. Investing in education in the early years of one's life (the decision is, of course, made on the child's behalf) is a way of keeping her options open on the choice of further education and the profession she pursues when she has become an adult. The child's future options are the elements of the opportunity set her parents are investing in on her behalf today.

A theory that values the capacity to form life plans but doesn't relate that value to the realization of those plans and the experiential states that go with them as and when they are carried out throws away material of ethical substance. Capabilitarianism does that in abundance and does it as a matter of principle. The theory says, for example, that the reason headaches are bad is that they limit our ability to function; it appears to be is uninterested in the fact that headaches are painful. Capabilitarians could no doubt retort that people have good reasons to abhor headaches, but Capabilitarianism does not admit information on a person's ranking of states of affairs she wants rationally to avoid. How is the Capabilitarian to know, for example, how headaches are to be compared to toothaches? Patrick Suppes' exploration of the normative force of freedom (Suppes, 1987) showed that freedom to choose can't carry ethical weight unless there is an independent machinery for valuing the objects of choice.

The line separating an instrumental value from an intrinsic value can be wafer-thin when the instrument advances a value that is deeply held. What is taken to be an intrinsic value could well be an instrument for advancing a more deeply held value. Nevertheless, we should suppose, as many do, that freedom has an intrinsic value, and that the very sense of a flourishing life includes freedom. An engagement that is freely chosen would then contribute more to a person's well-being than that same engagement would were it to be thrust on her. The characteristics of the engagement under the two circumstances would thus differ. Moreover, the value of an engagement to someone would depend on what other engagements were available to her. These additional considerations can be readily embedded in the account of capabilities we have reviewed here (see Sher, 2018).

Arrow (1995) appealed to the instrumental value of freedom to show that Capabilitarianism is an expression of Utilitarian reasoning. I have focused on that line of reasoning here because to add an intrinsic value to freedom would not change the character of the argument. To choose a functioning before the world reveals itself any further is to lock oneself into a situation from which there is no recourse if the choice proves to be incongruent with one's more informed values. To choose instead a capability (it's a set of functionings, remember) is to keep one's options open until things become clearer. But in order to know which capability is the best against an uncertain world, it is necessary to value, howsoever imperfectly, the consequences to the person of her choices in alternative, uncertain states of affairs. Functionings themselves have to be valued. The abiding attraction of Utilitarianism is that it offers a way to do that. The theory does that by using the person's well-being as currency.

It was Arrow's point to demonstrate that choosing capabilities is akin to purchasing options in the market for securities. Such choices reflect a desire for flexibility against future uncertainty. The argument is formalized in Appendix 6.[20] In Appendix 3, this line of reasoning is extended to show that Rawls (1972) was entirely right to base his theory of justice on "primary goods." In Rawls' account, primary goods are the objects that citizens, behind a veil of ignorance, know they will need no matter what they will subsequently discover about themselves,

---

20. Arrow and Fisher (1974) and Henry (1974) applied the idea of option values to provide a new argument in support of conservation science. Arrow (personal communication) attributed the idea to Weisbrod (1964).

including their own good, and their social world. More particularly, he saw primary goods as necessary for self-respect, by which he of course meant *informed* self-respect. That Rawls' focus in his great work was on primary goods should not detract from the fact that human flourishing is at the heart of his theory of justice. I also argue in Appendix 3 that Rawlsian primary goods are the ingredients of inclusive wealth.[21]

4. Synopsis

"Classical Well-Beingism" reads distinctly odd, so we will call the theory that evaluates states of affairs in terms of the sum of individual well-beings Total Utilitarianism. In part I, we study the foundations of population ethics. Sections 5–6 explore how far Total Utilitarianism is able to guide population ethics before running into trouble. In doing that, I respond to several strands of criticisms that have been leveled against the theory. To uncover what Total Utilitarianism is able to deliver, I put it through its paces in a timeless world endowed with a stock of natural capital. In the formal models we work with below, I shall be thinking of the world as a whole. Natural capital is therefore to be interpreted as the biosphere.

4.1. The Genesis Problem and Actual Problems

Total Utilitarianism would be least open to problems of interpretation if it were applied to a world devoid of people. In Section 7 I argue why. Nevertheless, in Section 5 I assume there is a Decision-Maker (DM). DM knows that if humans work on the biosphere, they can produce the consumption goods. DM also knows that the larger the number of people created, the greater would be the output, albeit at a rate that diminishes with increasing numbers. The model is presented in Sections 5.1–5.2. We should think of the model as responding to the Genesis Problem.

---

21. Rawls (1972: 424–433) observed that a way to identify one's good is to acknowledge the Aristotelian Principle: " . . . [O]ther things equal, human beings enjoy the exercise of their realized capacities (their innate or trained abilities), and the enjoyment increases the more the capacity is realized, or the greater its complexity."

Choices studied in population ethics differ from those in (standard) decision theory. A central idea in population ethics is that of a life which goes neither well nor not-well (Sect. 5.1). Life at that border is the point of reference against which DM deliberates additional births. Sidgwick (1907: 124) spoke of "neutral feeling" (he also called it the "hedonistic zero") as the point from which positive, or for that matter negative, happiness is measured. The notion can be extended to a person's life, and Sidgwick did that. We may then speak of a "neutral life" as a life in which happiness algebraically aggregates from birth to death to hedonistic zero. The interpretation of a neutral life I am drawn to, however, differs from the one Sidgwick offered (Sects. 5.4 and 6).

Decision theory studies choices that don't affect population numbers. Numbers being the same no matter which policy is chosen, comparisons of personal well-beings are the only things that have mattered to decision theorists. Decision theory does not recognize the idea of a neutral life because it is not needed. In population ethics, it is an essential ingredient.[22]

The notion of a neutral life can be transferred to lives evaluated in terms of consumption activities. Meade (1955) called the living standard in a neutral life "welfare subsistence." It is natural to refer to it here as "well-being subsistence." I assume DM knows that a person's well-being is a function of her consumption level, and that marginal well-being is a declining function of consumption.

DM is a Total Utilitarian and knows in advance that humans will be identical to one another in every respect (i.e., their productivity, their ability to convert consumption into well-being, and so on). The optimum distribution of consumption is therefore an equal distribution of total output. The problem before DM is to determine the optimum tradeoff between population size and the representative person's consumption level. Its solution is Total Utilitarianism's answer to the Genesis Problem, the subject of Section 5.

In the model I deploy to test Total Utilitarianism, DM commends a large population. The optimum living standard is shown to be

---

22. Formally, decision theory requires only that personal well-beings are uniquely measurable up to positive affine transformations. Luce and Raiffa (1957) and Raiffa (1968) are classic expositions. In contrast, we will need to demand that personal well-beings are uniquely measurable up to positive linear transformations (Sect. 5.3).

proportionately not much higher than well-being subsistence. For a central class of parameter values, the ratio is shown to be less than *e* (the natural base of logarithms). We study the sensitivity of optimum population numbers to alternative values of the parameters defining personal well-being functions and production possibilities (Sect. 5.5). In a series of publications, Parfit (1976, 1982, 1984, 2016) and others following him have faulted Total Utilitarianism for the tradeoff it commends between population size and average well-being. The authors have also suggested modifications to the theory so as to avoid what they see are paradoxes arising in the theory. Parfitian modifications are studied in Sections 5.6 and 5.8.

I have found no suggestion in Sidgwick (1907) that the idea of a neutral life is independent of a person's social environment. In contemporary writings on population axiology, the question of whether it is or it is not is ignored. But if the neutral life is independent of the social environment, so is well-being subsistence. That assumption, in wide use among economists, is hard to square with a commonplace human experience. Whether a person sees his life as going well depends in part on his expectations and aspirations; those in turn are (again, in part) dependent on what others in his society aspire to and are able to achieve. I take a minimalist approach to this range of issues and sketch a world in Section 5.7 and Appendix 1 where personal well-being is socially embedded. Well-being subsistence in the model increases with the average living standard in society. I study ways in which population ethics is affected by that feature of the human experience.[23]

In Section 6 we find that Sidgwick (1907) erred in his reading of a "neutral life." The error can mislead one into thinking that, when someone says Total Utilitarianism advocates large populations (as I have just done), they must also mean that the theory can commend states of affair where people have lives that are barely worth living. To make that inference is wrong.

In Section 7, a modified version of the plight of Sleeping Beauty is used to show that Total Utilitarianism's weaknesses don't lie where contemporary population axiologists claim they do, but elsewhere. The problem with the theory is that it speaks to Genesis, not to actual choices made in an inhabited world. One may even say that potential

---

23. Williams (1976) and Nagel (1976) have shown that whether a life is exemplary depends on what life throws at us. I abstract from this in the text.

parents face a far more difficult set of choices than DM. DM can afford the luxury of conflating the good with what one should do, whereas potential parents don't enjoy that privilege. I explore a way to amend Total Utilitarianism for what should be called Actual Problems, as opposed to the Genesis Problem. The amendment I work with involves in an otherwise Utilitarian reasoning the adoption of an attenuated form of agent-centered prerogatives over choices open to people. The influence of Thomas Nagel and Bernard Williams will be transparent, although both authors have shown in their writings a far more critical attitude toward Utilitarian-Consequentialism than I do here. But the modern philosophical source that comes closest to what I am after is Scheffler (1982, 1985). Potential parents evaluate states of affairs on the basis of a weighted sum of personal well-beings, where the weight they place on potential well-beings of children they could have is less than the weight they place on their own well-being and on the well-being of children they already have, knowing in advance that they will want to share resources with the children they produce on an equal basis with themselves. The amended theory is Generation-Relative Utilitarianism. The backward induction involved in this reasoning is essential to the theory. The gap between ex ante and ex post reasoning distinguishes Generation-Relative Utilitarianism from Total Utilitarianism because the latter admits no gap.

Generation-Relative Utilitarianism invokes a weak form of agent-centered prerogatives. It curbs births, and it doesn't sanction applying a lower weight on others' well-being even on grounds of prerogatives. But depending on the relative weights deployed by decision-makers, the gap between ex ante and ex post reasoning can have huge implications for optimum population size.

In Section 8, Generation-Relative Utilitarianism is put to work in a timeless world where present people deliberate how many further people to create. As in the model studied in Section 5, the world in Section 8 is endowed with a capital asset, the biosphere, that can be used to produce a consumption good. Generation-Relative Utilitarianism is shown to recommend a smaller population and a higher living standard than Total Utilitarianism. Using stylized values of ethical parameters, we find that Generation-Relative Utilitarianism can recommend high living standards and correspondingly small populations.

Parfit (1976) and following him Broome (2004: 157–162) have argued that Generation-Relative ethics is incoherent because it doesn't yield a binary relation among states of affair. In Section 8.3, it is shown that the theory only appears to be incoherent, and that it does so because Parfit insisted that decision-makers view states of affair from nowhere. That's a natural requirement to make of DM, but not of we mortals. Generation-Relative Utilitarianism evaluates states of affairs from inside the states of affairs themselves.

It may seem odd that a model that reflects a timeless economy could be of use in applying population ethics to an economy that moves through time. In fact, a timeless economy is nearly identical to an economy that moves through time over an indefinite future but in which economic variables (e.g., population and consumption) are constant. The latter is known as a "stationary economy." The connection is demonstrated in Section 8. When we come to study the stationary economy, the asset people are assumed to work with is taken to be an aggregate of all capital goods, including the biosphere.

Discounting for time and the generations in ethical deliberations over saving and fertility is not the same as exercising agent-centered prerogatives. In Section 9.1, I show why. I also argue there that a world where investment, when chosen wisely, has a positive return directs us on grounds of fairness to discount the well-beings of future generations.[24]

So as not to contaminate agent-centered prerogatives with time discounting, I eschew the latter in Section 9.3 and thereafter. It's a modeling strategy designed to develop Generation-Relative Utilitarianism in a minimalist setting. As in the timeless economy of Section 8, I assume that personal well-being is a function of personal consumption: people are egoists. In each period, adults apply labor to capital goods to produce and then share with their children the all-purpose consumption good. We find that the recommendations of Generation-Relative Utilitarianism can be carried out only if there is an implicit understanding among the generations that each generation will choose the size of the next generation and act as a trustee of the biosphere it has inherited. Being trustees, the generations protect the biosphere from excessive use; not to mention, from unacceptable damage.

---

24. Most writings on the ethical basis of intergenerational saving have been built on Utilitarian thinking. However, in his contractual theory of justice, John Rawls also sketched a principle of saving (Rawls, 1972: ch. 5, sects. 44–45). We study the principle of just saving in *A Theory of Justice* in Appendix 3.

4.2. *The Biosphere as a Commodity*

Part II moves away from that scenario. Section 10 summarizes studies that have recorded substantial declines in the biosphere's productivity over the past decades. Those declines can be traced to the environmental and reproductive externalities people inflict on one another. Today, growth in atmospheric carbon concentration is the canonical expression of adverse externalities, but humanity faces wider and deeper threats to our future from the biological extinctions now taking place (see, e.g., Cardinale et al., 2012), which are also morally more reprehensible. Proximate causes of extinctions include global climate change, but they also include the destruction and fragmentation of natural habitats and over-exploitation of biological communities residing there. We are converting land into farms and plantations, destroying forests for timber and minerals, applying pesticides and fertilizers so as to intensify agriculture, introducing foreign species into native habitats, and using the biosphere as a sink for our waste. And these things are taking place at scales that are orders of magnitude greater than they were even 250 years ago.

Adverse externalities arising from our use of the biosphere in great measure arise because Nature is mobile: birds and insects fly, water flows, the wind blows, and the oceans circulate. That makes it hard to establish property rights to key components of the biosphere. By property rights I don't only mean private rights; I include communitarian and public rights. This is why much of the biosphere is an "open-access resource," meaning that it is free to all to do as we like with it. Hardin (1968) famously spoke of the fate of unmanaged common property resources as "the tragedy of the commons." But while Hardin's analysis was entirely appropriate for global commons (e.g., the atmosphere, the oceans), it was less than applicable to geographically confined resources such as woodlands, ponds, grazing fields, coastal fisheries, wetlands, and mangroves. Because local commons are geographically confined, their use can be monitored by community members. There were exceptions, of course, but in times past those resources were managed by communities; they were not open-access resources. Reviewing an extensive literature, Feeny et al. (1990) observed that community management systems enabled societies to avoid experiencing the tragedy of the commons. Social norms of behavior, including the use of fines and social sanctions for misbehavior, have guided the use of local common property resources.[25]

In poor countries, the commons continue to supply household needs to rural people (e.g., water, fuelwood, medicinal herbs, fruits and berries, manure, and fibers and timber for building material). Some products are also marketed (e.g., fish, fuelwood, dung, wood and fiber products). But as in so many other spheres of social life, communitarian practices have, over the years, strengthened in some instances (e.g., community forestry in Nepal) and weakened in others. They weakened, for example, when communal rights were overturned by central fiat. To establish political authority after independence (and also to earn rents from timber exports), a number of states in sub-Saharan Africa and Asia imposed rules that destroyed community practices in forestry. Villages ceased to have the authority to enforce sanctions on those who broke norms of behavior. But knowledge of local ecology is held by those who work on the commons, not by state officials, who in addition can be corrupt. Thomson et al. (1986), Somanathan (1991), and Baland and Platteau (1996), among others, have identified ways in which state authority damaged local institutions and turned local commons into seemingly open-access resources. Then there are subtle ways in which even well-intentioned state policy can cause communitarian practices to weaken (Balasubramanian, 2008; Mukhopadhyay, 2008).[26]

4.3. Common-Property Resources and Fertility Intentions

Even when a common is managed by the community and outsiders are kept at bay, we should ask whether access to it is based on household

---

25. The literature on this is extensive. See Ostrom (1990), Marothia (2002), Ostrom et al. (2002), and Ostrom and Ahn (2003).

26. In recent years, democratic movements among stakeholders and pressure from international organizations have encouraged a return to community-based systems of management of the local commons. Shyamsundar (2008) is a synthesis of the findings in nearly 200 articles on the efficacy of a devolution of management responsibilities—from the state to local communities—over the local natural-resource base. Her article focuses on wildlife, forestry, and irrigation. The balance of evidence appears to be that devolution leads to better resource management, other things equal. Shyamsundar offers a discussion of what those other things are.

size or whether each household has a fixed share of its output. In Appendix 2, it is shown that, when larger households are entitled to a greater share of the commons' goods and services, households have an incentive to convert natural resources excessively into private assets, which includes household size. In sub-Saharan Africa, larger households are (or until recently, *were*) awarded a greater quantity of land by the kinship group. That practice encourages fertility. What is true in the case of local commons to which households have access regardless of their size holds true in the case of global commons, to which we all have access regardless of our household size. Even humane systems of property rights can give rise to adverse externalities.

How important are local commons in household income? Despite the importance of the question, there is little in the form of quantitative evidence. Casual empiricism suggests they are less significant in advanced industrial countries than in poor rural societies. In the former, local resources are either owned privately or under the jurisdiction of local authorities or, as in the case of places of especial aesthetic value, national parks. That is not so in rural areas in poor countries. In a pioneering study, Jodha (1986) reported evidence from semi-arid rural districts in Central India that, among poor families, the proportion of income based directly on local commons was 15–25 percent. Cavendish (2000) arrived at even higher estimates from a study of villages in Zimbabwe: the proportion of income based directly on local common property resources was found to be 35 percent, the figure for the poorest quintile being 40 percent. Jodha (2001) is a collection of his studies on the place of the local commons in the lives of the rural poor. To not recognize the significance of the local natural resource base in poor countries is to not understand how the poor live.[27]

4.4. Our Impact on the Biosphere

Being a measure of the social worth of an economy's capital goods, inclusive wealth is a stock. In contrast, GDP, which the market value of the final goods and services an economy produces, is a flow variable.

---

27. I have previously tried to build an account of the lives of the rural poor in poor countries in a treatise (Dasgupta, 1993) and more recently in a brief introduction to economics (Dasgupta, 2007a).

The rogue word in GDP (gross domestic product) is "gross," because the index doesn't include the depreciation of capital. This is why it is possible for GDP to grow for a period while inclusive wealth declines. Even if produced capital and human capital were to grow in magnitude, inclusive wealth would decline if natural capital were to decline in quality, or quantity, at a high enough rate. But if wealth were to continue to decline, GDP would eventually have to decline. You cannot degrade the biosphere indefinitely and expect living standards to rise continually.

Section 10 contains evidence that humanity's enormous economic success in raising GDP and the many benefits that have come with it in recent decades have involved an unsustainable conversion of natural capital (the biosphere) into produced capital and human capital. Population ethics directs us to look not only at the state of the world as it is today, at what has been achieved, but it also requires of us to peer into what lies ahead. There are intellectuals who insist we are living in the best of times (Pinker, 2018), but in Part II we find evidence that we may well be living simultaneously in the worst of times.

Ehrlich and Holdren (1971) introduced the metaphor, I = PAT, to draw attention to the significance of the biosphere's carrying capacity for population ethics. The authors traced the *i*mpact of human activities on the Earth system to *p*opulation, *a*ffluence (read, the standard of living), and the character of *t*echnology in use (including knowledge, institutions, social capital). We can imagine that our impact on the biosphere is proportional to the demands we make of it. The demands we make of it in turn increase with rising economic activity, as measured by global output of goods and services. That even today's poorest societies can be expected in time to make fertility transitions to population replacement levels (perhaps even to below replacement levels for a while) is no reason to think that humanity's demands for the biosphere's goods and services will cease to exceed its ability to supply them. That is why it is a mistake to ignore the Ehrlich–Holdren observation that the biosphere responds to the demands we make of it, not to changes in the demands we make of it (e.g., those that accompany declines in fertility rates) nor to changes in the rate of change in the demands we make of it (e.g., those that accompany declines in the rate of growth of the global population). A long-run global population of 11.2 billion (the United Nations' projection of global population by 2100; see Fig. 2 in "Socially Embedded Preferences,

Environmental Externalities, and Reproductive Rights" later in this volume) is likely to make a vastly greater demand on the biosphere than a population of, say, 2.5 billion (the global population in 1950). The Ehrlich–Holdren study also tells us that by population number we should mean "weighted population number," in which each person is given a weight according to the impact he has on the biosphere.

To give precision to the idea of the biosphere's human carrying capacity, I identify it as the maximum population that can sustain itself at a standard of living equal to well-being subsistence (Sect. 5). That move will be rejected by commentators who question whether it is meaningful even to talk of human carrying capacity, let alone to estimate it. They say the constraints imposed by a finite biosphere can be overcome if humanity were to accumulate other forms of capital assets at sufficiently high rates. Dasgupta (1969: Sect. 3) applied Total Utilitarianism to a model of consumption and accumulation in an economy endowed with a fixed factor of production (land) to find that indefinite accumulation of produced capital, even if feasible, would not be desirable. It was shown that, no matter what levels of capital stocks the economy may have inherited from the past, Total Utilitarianism would recommend a population and savings policy that, over time, takes the economy to a stationary state. The argument extends to a world guided by Generation-Relative Utilitarianism. That finding informs our exercises here.

The notion of the biosphere's human carrying capacity is developed in Section 10, where I use statistics on the state of the global environment to put flesh into population ethics. In Section 11, Generation-Relative Utilitarianism is applied to data on the global demand for the biosphere's services. I use that data to estimate the maximum demand we can make of today's biosphere on a sustainable basis. I then arrive at quantitative estimates of optimum population and the optimum living standard in a world constrained by *today's* state of the biosphere. This is an unsatisfactory research strategy, but I know of no study that seeks to determine sustainable supplies of ecological services were the biosphere allowed to improve in quality from what it is now. So I am obliged to take the current state as the basis of the computations.

Because we study global estimates here, I am able to lay bare differences between Total Utilitarianism and Generation-Relative Utilitarianism. I also test to see how sensitive Generation-Relative Utilitarianism is to the choice of well-being subsistence and the weight placed on generation-centered prerogatives. In a central case, we find that optimum population size is lower and the optimum standard of living is higher than they are (respectively) in the contemporary world. In view of the pervasiveness of the externalities that we inflict on one another, there is a strong case for consumption policies, twinned with public expenditure to help households plan their families in an informed way. Successful programs in today's poor countries have involved not only the government, but also charities and non-government organizations. Community engagement in family planning is an essential ingredient in any such program.[28]

It is today commonly thought that accumulation of produced capital and advances in technology will see us through, that they are the means of avoiding further dependence on the biosphere even as global living standards rise. This suggestion is the subject of Section 12. There I review historical and archaeological studies where scholars have identified successes and failures of past societies to meet local environmental problems. We are concerned in this essay with our global impact on the biosphere, and that should make one circumspect. The evidence collated in Sections 10–11 suggests that the international economy is so interconnected and extensive that whatever progress we may enjoy in economizing on one resource base can be expected to lead to greater pressure on some other resource base. Globally, reductions in consumption and reproductive externalities cannot occur without international engagement. A pre-condition of any agreement the global community is able to reach is a common acceptance that every generation is a trustee of the biosphere it has inherited.

Like Total Utilitarianism, Generation-Relative Utilitarianism offers a way to get a measure of the loss that is suffered when someone dies. And like Total Utilitarianism, the theory can be used to get a measure of the loss that would be entailed if the human race were to become extinct. Loss in the latter case would be forward looking, reflecting the value of lives that would be foregone on account of extinction, as viewed from a generation-relative perspective. In a remarkable work, the writer Jonathan Schell (1982) drew our attention away from

---

28. This is one of the conclusions in "Socially Embedded Preferences, Environmental Externalities, and Reproductive Rights" (Dasgupta and Dasgupta, 2017).

that line of reasoning and spoke of the loss each of us would suffer if we were to learn that no one will follow us. In Section 13, I review Schell's argument and modify it by enlarging the scope of that loss.[29] By extending the sphere of human motivations, we avoid a free-rider problem to which Schell's ethics could be vulnerable. I then use the deep human need to live through time rather than in time to arrive at a view of stewardship of Earth. Acknowledgement of stewardship points also to an implicit understanding among the generations to protect and promote the biosphere's ability to support life. But it arrives at it from a different direction from the one we are led to by Generation-Relative Utilitarianism. The amended account of a person's well-being is not meant to be a substitute for Generation-Relative Utilitarianism; rather, it is a complement to it. Nor is the implicit understanding among generations contrary to Generation-Relative Utilitarianism's idea of agent-based prerogatives. The viewpoints may speak different dialects, but they speak the same language. Or so I will argue.

Part I

Foundations

5. Genesis Under Total Utilitarianism

Total Utilitarianism was applied to a timeless economy by Meade (1955) and extended by Dasgupta (1969) to a world facing an indefinite future. In the latter publication, it was shown that the theory encourages large populations. I first reproduce that finding by working with a stripped-down version of the model in Section 3 of Dasgupta (1969).

5.1. Production and Consumption Possibilities

We imagine a timeless world, endowed with a finite stock of assets, of size K. We may think of K as an aggregate measure of produced capital and the biosphere, but often, to stress the salience of the biosphere in

---

29. The passages there are taken from Dasgupta (2005a). In a penetrating essay, Scheffler (2013) has further developed that line of thought.

population axiology, I shall refer to K as the biosphere. In the latter case we may think of K as being measured in units of biomass (tons, say). People are both producers and consumers. For convenience I keep knowledge and institutions separate from K (see below).

The Decision-Maker (DM) knows that humans will be identical to one another in every respect (e.g., their productivity, their ability to convert consumption into well-being, and so on). DM also knows that when it is applied to the stocks of assets, human labor can produce an all-purpose consumption good. Each person supplies a fixed amount of labor. As the world is timeless, stocks (e.g., the biosphere) and flows (e.g., ecological services) are the same. We will distinguish stocks from flows when we come to model the world economy moving through time (Sect. 9; Appendix 4).

Let Q be output of the consumption good. If population size is N, we follow Dasgupta (1969: Sect. 3) and Arrow's letter #3 and assume that

$$Q = AF(K, N), \quad A > 0 \qquad (1)$$

In equation (1), F is assumed to be homogeneous of degree 1, increases with K, N at diminishing rates, and $F(0, N) = F(K, 0) = 0$.

A is a parameter in the model, not a variable. It is called "total factor productivity" in the economics literature, and it can be interpreted as an aggregate measure of the society's knowledge base and its institutions. Because the model is timeless, I take K to be a parameter as well. That rules out accumulation or decumulation of all assets in the economy, a move that requires justification. Justification for working with a timeless economy can be found in Dasgupta (1969: Sect. 3), which studied an economy where production possibilities at any moment in time have the same structure as that in equation (1), but which moves through time, so that produced capital can be accumulated if it is so desired. The biosphere was taken to be a fixed factor of production, rather as the "indestructible land" that was imagined by Classical Political Economists of the late 18th century. In Dasgupta (1969: Sect. 3), it was shown that Classical Utilitarianism recommends that the economy be steered toward a stationary state in the long run. The stationary state in question depends on production possibilities and ethical parameters. In a stationary state, nothing changes over time, so it is rather like the timeless economy we are studying here. I want to focus on population size, N. I want to do this so that we can

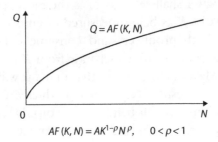

$$AF(K, N) = AK^{1-\rho}N^{\rho}, \quad 0 < \rho < 1$$

Figure 1 Population Size and Total Output

uncover in a simple way how the various other features of an economy affect N's optimum value.

We assume that either K or A (or both) is "large," which implies that the optimum value of N is large, which in turn means that it is a good approximation to regard N as a continuous variable. N is the sole variable in the model. Figure 1 depicts Q as a function of N.[30] We write marginal output $(dAF(K, N)/dN)$ as AF_N. It follows from the properties of the F-function that output per person $(AF(K, N)/N)$ exceeds output of the marginal person (AF_N) and that both are declining functions of N. Figure 2 depicts average output and marginal output as functions of N.

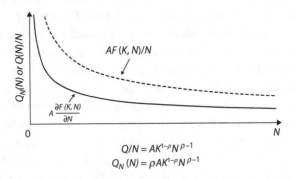

$$Q/N = AK^{1-\rho}N^{\rho-1}$$
$$Q_N(N) = \rho AK^{1-\rho}N^{\rho-1}$$

Figure 2 Population Size and Average and Marginal Outputs

---

30. All functions are assumed to be twice continuously differentiable. That enables us to use the calculus for solving for optimum population size. To assume otherwise would lead us into matters that are inessential to population axiology.

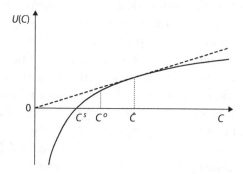

Figure 3 Personal Well-Being and the Standard of Living

If C is someone's consumption level, her personal well-being is $U(C)$. The U-function is assumed to increase with C but at a diminishing rate. We write marginal well-being $(\mathrm{d}U(C)/\mathrm{d}C)$ as U_C, and the consumption derivative of marginal well-being, $\mathrm{d}^2 U/\mathrm{d}C^2$ as U_{CC}. Thus $U_C > 0$ and $U_{CC} < 0$.[31]

Positive well-being records life as good for the person, and negative well-being records life as not good. U is positive at large values of C but negative at small values of C. It follows that there is a unique value of C at which U is zero. We interpret C to be the living standard, and we write the standard of living at which $U = 0$ as C^S. Thus $U(C^S) = 0$. Meade (1955) referred to C^S as "welfare subsistence." It would be more accurate to call C^S "well-being subsistence," which is what I do here. Figure 3 depicts a U-function with those features.

Because the economy is timeless, there is no scope for investing or disinvesting. All that is produced is consumed.

5.2. Social Well-Being and the Sidgwick–Meade Rule

In applying Total Utilitarianism's reasoning to population ethics, it is cleanest to apply it to Genesis. I argue below that Genesis is also the

---

31. Edgeworth (1881) routinized the assumption of diminishing marginal well-being.

scene where Total Utilitarianism doesn't run into any meaningful trouble. Therefore, we imagine Earth to be devoid of people.[32]

Let N be the number of people to be created. From equation (1), we know that total output $Q = AF(K, N)$. Because people are identical and marginal well-being declines as the living standard increases, an equal distribution of Q among all who are created is the ideal. If N people were created, each would receive Q/N units of the consumption good. Thus $C = Q/N = AF(K, N)/N$.

Social well-being is an aggregate of personal well-beings. If we denote social well-being as V, Total Utilitarianism says

$$V = NU(C) = NU(AF(K, N)/N) \tag{2}$$

We are in search of the value of N at which V is at its maximum. Differentiating V in equation (2) with respect to N and setting the differential coefficient equal to zero tells us that optimum N satisfies the condition:

$$U(C) = ((AF(K, N)/N) - AF_N)U_C = (C - AF_N)U_C > 0 \tag{3}$$

Equation (3) is fundamental to Total Utilitarianism. We will call it the Sidgwick–Meade Rule. The intuition behind it is this:

At the optimum, neither a small hypothetical increase in population nor a small hypothetical decrease would alter social well-being. Suppose now a marginal increase in numbers is contemplated by DM (the argument associated with a marginal decrease is analogous). The additional person would share Q equally with the population that was originally contemplated. The increase in additional well-being that would obtain if that person were created would be her well-being, which is $U(C) = U(Q/N)$. But there would also be a decrease in well-being because all others would have slightly less consumption, amounting to the difference between average consumption and the contribution the

---

32. In his letter #3 of June 6, 2016, Arrow complained that he could not tell who the decision-maker is in the model. In my conversation with him in Cambridge later that month, I reminded him that I had for many years interpreted the model as being pertinent to a Total-Utilitarian Decision-Maker at Genesis.

additional person would make to total output. That potential loss in well-being in symbols is $((AF(K, N)/N) - AF_N)U_C$. At the Genesis Optimum, the potential gain and the potential loss in social well-being must be equal. The Sidgwick–Meade Rule asserts this.

Denote the solution of equation (3) by C^O and the corresponding population size by N^O. So $AF(K, N^O)/N^O = C^O$ where N^O is the optimum population size and C^O is the optimum living standard. Let $\hat{C}$ be the consumption level at which average well-being equals marginal well-being. The Sidgwick–Meade Rule says $C^O < \hat{C}$. That is shown in Figure 3.

5.3. Measurability, Comparability, and the Aggregation of Personal Well-Beings

There is no absolute scale for measuring personal well-being. Standard decision theory, for example, yields a measure that is unique up to positive affine transformations. That says if U_i is a measure of individual i's well-being and if α is a positive number and β is a number of either sign, then $\alpha U_i + \beta$ is an equally valid measure of i's well-being. The ordering of states of affair represented by U_i is the same as the ordering represented by $\alpha U_i + \beta$. In the latter scale α represents the unit and β the level. We say U_i in that case is a "cardinal" measure. Concerned as it is with well-being differences among alternative states of affair, the theory does not require the notion of zero well-being.[33]

Population ethics, in contrast, requires that lives that go well be distinguished from those that don't go well. A life that goes neither well nor not-well is calibrated to be zero (in Sidgwick's system of ethics it is the hedonistic zero). Personal well-being is "strongly cardinal" if its measure is unique up to positive linear transformations (i.e., proportional transformations). That says if U_i is a measure of i's well-being and if α is a positive number, then αU_i is an equally valid measure of i's well-being. A population ethic that is derived from Total Utilitarianism requires individual well-beings to be strongly cardinal.

When applying Total Utilitarianism to the Genesis Problem, we made an implicit assumption that well-beings are fully comparable

---

33. For fixed populations, Harsanyi (1955) built Utilitarianism on the basis of the theory of choice under uncertainty.

across individuals. There was no need to mention it because people were assumed to be identical in all respects. In a heterogeneous population, the assumption should be made explicit. Without full comparability of personal well-beings, it would not be possible to construct an ethics with which to derive population policies.[34]

The idea of full comparability we need here is familiar from weights and measures. The weights of objects (measured, say, in a vacuum-sealed flask at ground level in a given latitude) are fully comparable. Suppose we find x to be a heavier object than y. If that is to be a meaningful finding, the units in which they are measured must be the same; it's no good measuring x in ounces and y in grams. Reference to grams and ounces tells us that we can say a lot more than merely that x is heavier than y: we can say how much heavier x is proportionately than y. The reason we can is that, if x is found to be twice as heavy as y using one system of units (ounces), it will be found to be twice as heavy as y using any other system of units (grams). And that's because an ounce is proportional to a gram. We can move from one system of units to another with impunity so long as the corresponding transformations (grams to ounces) are applied consistently.

We can say even more. Because physical theories tell us that addition and subtraction are legitimate (even required) operations on weights, each scale in the set of admissible scales is proportional to any other scale in the set, and all scales that are proportional to a scale in the admissible set are also in the admissible set. Non-linear scales don't belong.

Personal well-beings are taken to be fully comparable here if multiplying each individual's well-being by a constant positive number α is ethically of no significance. Other things equal, the Total Utilitarian would rank the pair of personal well-beings {4,11} above the pair {5,9}, because 15 is bigger than 14. Full comparability says that if we multiply each individual's well-being by a positive number α, the ranking of the resulting pairs remains the same. They remain the same

---

34. Sen (1970) is the classic text on the measurability and interpersonal comparability of individual well-beings in fixed populations. By extending his analysis to population ethics, it is easy to show that dropping full comparability would yield only a partial ordering of population policies. Partial orderings may be the best that the ethicist can hope for in practice, but no theory of social ethics should start with partial orderings.

because $4\alpha + 11\alpha$ (= 15α) is bigger than $5\alpha + 9\alpha$ (= 14α) for all positive α. The Total Utilitarian can choose any value of α he likes without compromising his ethics.

Measurability and comparability of personal well-beings are closely related to possibilities of aggregating them into a measure of what we have been calling social well-being. There would be few restrictions on the social well-being function if personal well-being were measurable in an absolute scale. Because there *is* no absolute scale, DM has to be circumspect before identifying an ethically defensible social well-being function. Social well-being functions cannot be chosen willy-nilly.[35]

Total Utilitarianism aggregates personal well-beings by summing them. The theory requires personal well-beings to be strongly cardinal and interpersonally fully comparable. The reasoning confirms that the Sidgwick–Meade Rule is invariant with respect to α.[36] Well-being subsistence, C^S, remains the same under all proportional transformations of the U-function. That's because $\alpha U(C^S) = 0$ for all positive α. In the model we have used here to study the Genesis Problem, α was set equal to 1 so as not to add another symbol.

5.4. Zero Well-Being

Sidgwick (1907: 124–125) spoke of "neutral feeling" when suggesting ways to identify C^S:

> If pleasure . . . can be arranged in a scale, as greater or less in some finite degree, we are led to the assumption of a hedonistic zero, or perfectly neutral feeling, as a point from which the positive quantity of pleasures may be measured . . . for pain must be reckoned as the negative quantity of pleasure, to be balanced against and subtracted from the positive in estimating happiness on the whole; we must therefore conceive, as at least ideally possible, a point of transition in consciousness at which we pass from the positive to the negative.

---

35. Koopmans (1972), Hammond (1976), d'Aspremont and Gevers (1977), Maskin (1978), and Blackorby and Donaldson (1982) are studies on the connections between measurability, comparability, and aggregation of personal well-beings.

36. If $U(C)$ is replaced by $\alpha U(C)$ in equation (3) and U_C by αU_C, α cancels from the two sides.

It is not absolutely necessary to assume that this strictly indifferent or neutral feeling ever occurs. Still experience seems to show that a state at any rate very nearly approximating to it is even common: and we certainly experience continual transitions from pleasure to pain and *vice versa*, and thus (unless we conceive all such transitions to be abrupt) we must exist at least momentarily in this neutral state.

Zero well-being is a defining notion in population ethics. Sidgwick's reference to neutral feeling invites us to assess life from the inside. But the idea of neutral feeling and the corresponding idea of a neutral life also point, even if several steps removed, to a comparison of life with non-existence. That latter exercise requires calibrating well-being in terms of something outside our experience, which is why the exercise is regarded as questionable by some philosophers. Yet, when in deep despair, people have been known to say they would rather not have been born, an utterance that doesn't sound incomprehensible. Comparison of life with non-existence is an unavoidable exercise in population ethics because reproduction is never a certainty. Suppose a couple understands that there is a 90 percent chance of producing a happy child and a 10 percent chance they will be unable to conceive. Neutral feeling in Sidgwick's sense cannot cover the latter event in the couple's reasoning because the intended child doesn't exist there.[37]

Nagel (1979: 2) famously suggested that death is not an unimaginable condition of the living person: ". . . the value of life and its contents does not attach to mere organic survival: almost everyone would be indifferent (other things equal) between immediate death and immediate coma followed by death twenty years later without reawakening."[38] He also suggested that death is a mere blank, and that it can have no value whatever, positive or negative. I am unable to tell whether Nagel meant the blank can't be used as a benchmark against which other states of affair are compared; but he went on to suggest that one can imagine non-existence by imagining being in a coma for the rest of

---

37. There are philosophers who advocate evaluating states of affair in terms of an impersonal good (Griffin, 1986, offers an account of that viewpoint). As the example in the text suggests, even for them comparison of life with non-existence would seem to be a required move.

38. The point is developed in Section 7, but I apply it to a different purpose from Nagel's.

one's life. For Nagel, non-existence is the real blank, and being totally unconscious for the rest of one's life is a simulation of that blank.

We are thinking of someone's life as a whole, not her life at a moment in time. There are thinkers who believe the whole is the sum of its momentary parts; there are others who believe the whole to be a non-linear function of those parts. We don't need to adopt a position on that because, except for the model we analyze in Sections 9 and 11, there will be no occasion to slice someone's life into parts. The U-function here is calibrated by using Nagel's "blank" as a point of reference. Without loss of generality I am attaching the number 0 to that point. Zero well-being is therefore the measure of a person's life that, taken as a whole, goes neither well nor not-well for her. In view of the additive structure in Total Utilitarianism's conception of aggregate utility, $U = 0$ is also the level of well-being at which, in DM's judgement, an additional life adds no further value to the world that contains it.

I have heard it said that $U = 0$ is the point of indifference between dying and continuing to live, or the point of indifference between life and death. In Section 6, we uncover the reason that such an interpretation is misconceived. The reason also steers us away from the thought that in the contemporary world C^S is an absolute poverty line, in the sense in which the notion has been articulated in such figures as the World Bank's "1.90 dollars a day." As DM would see it, every life of poverty represents a bad state of affairs for that individual, and so it makes the state of the world less good than it would otherwise be. In the contemporary world, C^S would be higher than the World Bank's poverty line. C^S is the living standard at which life is neither good nor not-good. Determining C^S in a society will always prove contentious, but the move can't be bypassed in population ethics. It involves a deep and difficult value judgment. I discuss C^S further in Section 5.7 in the context of socially embedded well-being functions.

5.5. Optimum Population Size

Total Utilitarianism says social well-being is the product of population size (N) and average well-being (U). Loci of $\{N, U\}$ pairs for which NU is constant are called isoquants of NU. The isoquants of NU, being rectangular hyperbolae, asymptote to $U = 0$ as N tends to infinity (Fig. 4). As Rawls (1972: 162–163) noted, that means tradeoffs between N and U in the product NU are such that no matter how small is U, so long

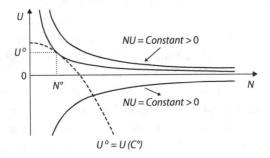

Figure 4 Isoquants of Total Utility

as it is positive a sufficiently large N can compensate for a reduction in U (as long as it remains positive, of course). Parfit (1984: 425–441) found that feature of Total Utilitarianism repugnant, so he called it the Repugnant Conclusion. There is a reverse form of the Repugnant Conclusion, aptly known as the Reverse Repugnant Conclusion. It too is a feature of Total Utilitarianism, and it says that for any world where a given number of people have lives of extreme distress, there is a worse world where a large number of people have lives just below $U = 0$ (see Mulgan, 2002). But it is the Repugnant Conclusion that has given rise to an enormous literature, so we study it in detail.[39]

The question arises whether Total Utilitarianism commends large populations when it is tested in a world facing resource constraints. Dasgupta (1969) had previously shown it does; the theory advocates population numbers at which the standard of living (C^O) is proportionately not much above well-being subsistence (C^S). I review the argument here and conduct a sensitivity analysis of the optimum with respect to various parameters of the model.

The simplest expressions of $AF(K, N)$ and $U(C)$ are power functions:

$$AF(K,N) = AK^{(1-\rho)}N^\rho, \quad A > 0, 0 \leq \rho < 1 \tag{4}$$

---

39. See, among others, McMahan (1981), Sikora (1981), Hurka (1983), Sterba (1987), Temkin (1987), Cowen (1989), Arrhenius (2000), Räikkä (2002), Tännsjö (2002), Broome (2004), Huemer (2008), and Parfit (2016). Arrhenius, Ryberg, and Tännsjö (2017) contains an outstandingly clear account of the Repugnant Conclusion and its ramifications for population axiology. I am grateful to Christopher Cowie for discussions on both the Repugnant Conclusion and the Reverse Repugnant Conclusion.

$$U(C) = B - C^{-\sigma}, \quad B > 0, \sigma > 0 \tag{5}$$

Equation (4) is widely used by economists to reflect production possibilities. The parameter ρ reflects the productivity of labor. Output is an unbounded function of population numbers, but Nature imposes a restraint on the rate at which output can expand with population. The latter is reflected in the condition $\rho < 1$. ($(1 - \rho)$ is the productivity of K.) It will be confirmed below that optimum population size is a continuous function of ρ so long as it is less than 1. Arrow ("Some Random Thoughts on Birth and Death," letter #3) observes that optimum population is discontinuous at $\rho = 1$ and remarks that there is something wrong with Total Utilitarianism. I have excluded the case from equation (4) purely on empirical grounds, but I suggest below that we should not even otherwise be bothered by the discontinuity.

The other limiting case ($\rho = 0$) corresponds to a world where the biosphere offers a pure consumption good. That too is an unrealistic assumption, but if kept within the classroom for illustrative purposes it is not an absurd assumption.

Ideal national income accounting would interpret ρ to be the share of total output attributable to labor. There is an enormous empirical literature offering estimates of ρ. They tend to lie in the range of 0.6–0.7. Because I am including the biosphere in the accounts, ρ should be taken to be smaller. In numerical exercises I will assume, solely for computational ease, that $\rho = 0.5$.

$U(C)$ in equation (5) is defined by two parameters, B and σ, both positive numbers (Fig. 5). U is bounded above, the least upper bound being B. Ramsey (1928) spoke of B as Bliss. $1 + \sigma$ is the absolute value of the percentage rate at which marginal well-being changes with each percentage rate of increase in consumption (i.e., $1 + \sigma = -\mathrm{dlog}(U_C)/\mathrm{dlog}C$),

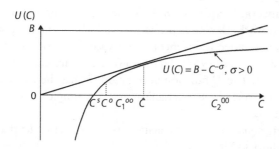

Figure 5 Personal Well-Being and the Standard of Living: An Iso-Elastic Form

which is why $1 + \sigma$ is called the "elasticity of marginal well-being with respective to consumption." The elasticity exceeds 1 in the U-function of equation (5). Note also that $C^S = B^{-1/\sigma}$.[40]

Let e be the base of natural logarithms. We know from elementary number theory that it approximately equals 2.72. On using equations (4) and (5), the Sidgwick–Meade Rule reduces to

$$C^O/C^S = [1 + (1 - \rho)\sigma]^{1/\sigma} < e^{(1-\rho)} < e \approx 2.72 \qquad (6)$$

Equation (6) is the Sidgwick–Meade Rule in a convenient form; it relates the optimum living standard directly to well-being subsistence.[41]

For ecologists it proves more natural to recast equation (6) in terms of population numbers. Let N^S be the maximum human population the biosphere can support if everyone consumes at the level C^S. We call it the biosphere's *human carrying capacity*. It follows that N^S can be determined from the relationship

$$C^S = AK^{(1-\rho)}[N^S]^\rho/N^S = AK^{(1-\rho)}[N^S]^{\rho-1} = A(K/N^S)^{1-\rho} \qquad (7)$$

The bigger K is (or for that matter, A), the larger N^S is. Using equation (7) in equation (6) yields

$$(N^S/N^O)^{(1-\rho)} = [1 + (1 - \rho)\sigma]^{1/\sigma} < e^{(1-\rho)} < e \approx 2.72 \qquad (8)$$

It will prove useful to combine equations (7) and (8) and write them jointly as

$$C^O/C^S = (N^S/N^O)^{(1-\rho)} = [1 + (1 - \rho)\sigma]^{1/\sigma} < e^{(1-\rho)} < e \approx 2.72 \qquad (9)$$

---

40. The U-function in equation (5) is bounded above but unbounded below. In applied work, the latter property should be an unacceptable feature because unboundedness is inconsistent with the axioms of choice under uncertainty (Arrow, 1965). Here, however, we are engaged in theoretical reasoning. The U-function in equation (5) has the virtue of revealing the structure of Total Utilitarianism in a very simple manner. I return to this presently.
41. To confirm equation (6), use equations (4)–(5) and the fact that $[C^S]^{-\sigma} = B$ in the Sidgwick–Meade Rule.

Neither the size of the biosphere (K) nor A plays a role in determining C^O/C^S, nor for that matter N^S/N^O.[42] If K (or A) were to be bigger, Total Utilitarianism would respond entirely by adjusting the optimum population size N^O. This could be seen as an expression of pro-natalism, but pointing in the opposite direction gives a different impression. Suppose, for example, K were to be smaller. The same feature of equation (9) now says that the adjustment to the optimum would be made entirely through a reduction in population size; the standard of living would be fully protected. When applying the theory to global economic statistics in Section 11, I return to this feature of the calculus of Total Utilitarianism.

SENSITIVITY OF C^O/C^S AND N^S/N^O TO σ Equation (9) says Total Utilitarianism favors large populations. The optimum living standard is less than $e^{(1-\rho)}$ times the well-being subsistence, no matter what value of σ DM settles on. The equation also says that carrying capacity is less than e times the optimum population size. To illustrate, suppose $\sigma = 1$ and $\rho = 0.5$. Then $C^O/C^S = (N^S/N^O)^{(1-\rho)} = 1.5$, which means the optimum living standard (C^O) is only 1.5 times well-being subsistence and carrying capacity is only 2.25 times the optimum population size (N^O). If the biosphere's carrying capacity is reckoned to be 12 billion people, the optimum global population size would be about 5.3 billion.

No doubt the idea of the biosphere's carrying capacity points to a range, not to an exact figure. Technological advances and improved efficiency in the way resources are used in production raise carrying capacity (Sect. 12). The notion, moreover, is not independent of ethical values (eq. (7)). The point remains though that Earth's life support system is bounded. N^S reflects that fact. Whether Total Utilitarianism should be seen to be advocating overly large populations ("pronatalist", as some would say) depends entirely on the standard of living (C^S) at which $U = 0$. Identifying C^S involves a value judgement. Once it has been identified by DM, the factors determining C^O are the ethical parameter σ and labor productivity ρ.

Utilitarian value pluralists have interpreted $1 + \sigma$ also as a measure of the aversion to inequality in the distribution of living standards.[43]

---

42. I owe this observation to Kenneth Arrow in a previous correspondence.

43. Pioneering contributions to the modern literature on measures of income inequality are Kolm (1969) and Atkinson (1970).

Moreover, Utilitarian decision theorists say that when a person's well-being is measured on the basis of her attitude to risk in her living standard, $1 + \sigma$ is also a measure of her risk aversion.[44] To obtain a feel for the way $1 + \sigma$ influences the optimum living standard (and, simultaneously, the optimum population size), we subject the Sidgwick–Meade Rule to a full sensitivity test. To do that we compute C^O/C^S in equation (9) using alternative values of σ. Notice that to vary σ is to vary well-being subsistence (eq. (5)), but that's another acknowledgement that identifying well-being subsistence involves a value judgment.

How does C^O vary in relation to C^S as σ assumes different values? Equation (9) says that C^O/C^S (which is the same as $(N^S/N^O)^{(1-\rho)}$) is a declining function of σ. That is intuitive. The larger σ is, the greater is the curvature of the U-function, which means the lesser is the normative significance of average consumption relative to population numbers in social well-being $NU(C)$.

Equation (9) also says that the larger σ is, the closer C^O/C^S (i.e., $(N^S/N^O)^{(1-\rho)}$) is to 1.[45] If the biosphere's carrying capacity is 12 billion people and σ is taken to be large, the optimum population is close to 12 billion. Strong social aversion to consumption inequality (alternatively, strong risk aversion) goes with large optimum populations. I have known this result since my student days, but I still find it puzzling that inequality aversion (alternatively, risk aversion) should play so influential a role in population ethics. Admittedly, the theory we are invoking here says that all who are born are to be treated equally; even so, it isn't *a priori* obvious why an attitude toward consumption inequality (alternatively, consumption risk) should so influence the ideal size of population. Ex post it is obvious of course.

In equation (5), σ has been assumed to be positive. The limiting case, $\sigma = 0$, corresponds to the logarithmic U-function. The elasticity

---

44. The classics are Pratt (1964) and Arrow (1965). Dasgupta (2008) offered reasons why the plausible range of values for σ is $(0,2]$. Empirical studies of choice under uncertainty have usually revealed σ to lie in the range $(0,1]$.

45. That's because $[1 + (1 - \rho)\sigma]^{1/\sigma} \to 1$ as $\sigma \to \infty$.

of U_C equals 1 in this case. To study that limiting case, let us without loss of generality choose the units of consumption so that

$$U(C) = \log_e C \tag{10}$$

That means $C^S = 1$. Notice that $\log_e C$ is unbounded both below and above. Using equations (4) and (10) in the Sidgwick–Meade Rule yields $C^O = e^{(1-\rho)}$. Note also that $e^{(1-\rho)}$ is the upper limit of $[1 + (1 - \rho)\sigma]^{1/\sigma}$ (eq. (9)). We have therefore confirmed that $\log_e C$ corresponds to the U-function in equation (5) for the case $\sigma = 0$.

There remains the case where the elasticity of U_C with respect to C is less than 1. The U-function is

$$U(C) = C^\varphi - D, \; 0 < \varphi < 1, \; D > 0 \tag{11}$$

The elasticity of U_C in equation (11) is $1 - \varphi$, and $C^S = D^{1/\varphi}$. Notice that the U-function in this case has exactly the opposite asymptotic properties as those of the U-function in equation (5). In the previous case, U was bounded above but unbounded below. In the present case, the U-function is unbounded above but bounded below. That makes a difference to the character of optimum population.

Application of equations (4) and (11) in the Sidgwick–Meade Rule yields

$$C^O/C^S = (N^S/N^O)^{(1-\rho)}) = [[1 - (1 - \rho)\varphi]^{-1/\varphi} \tag{12}$$

It is simple to check from equation (12) that C^O/C^S, when it is expressed as a function of φ, is not bounded above. But then, C^S is not bounded above either. Correspondingly, N^S is small when φ is small, and so is N^O small. In what follows, we shall confine our numerical calculations to the case where U-function satisfies equation (5).

Equations (5), (10), and (11) exhaust the class of U-functions for which the elasticity of U_C is independent of C and for which marginal well-being declines with C. As classroom examples, iso-elastic U-functions are useful, but they are not believable. That's because any U-function that is unbounded at either end is vulnerable to St Petersburg Paradoxes. Arrow (1965) proposed that the elasticity of marginal well-being should be expected to be less than 1 for small values of C

but greater than 1 at large values of C. Therefore, at some intermediate value of C the elasticity of U_C would equal 1. Any such U-function would be bounded at both ends. The Sidgwick–Meade Rule (equation (3)) is valid quite generally and covers U-functions that satisfy Arrow's proposed conditions.[46]

SENSITIVITY OF C^O/C^S AND N^S/N^O TO ρ In letter #3, Arrow uses equation (9) to study the sensitivity of C^O/C^S to ρ. He notes that C^O/C^S is a declining function of ρ and tends to 1 as ρ tends to 1. Because ρ is a measure of labor productivity relative to the biosphere, the finding says that an increase in labor productivity lowers the optimum living standard and correspondingly raises the optimum population size. Arrow finds that disturbing.

But we can put the matter in reverse and say that C^O increases if ρ is reduced. Which is why it is hard to know what our prior intuitions should be on the matter. We know that, as a function of ρ, the range of C^O/C^S is bounded. Should we on intuitive grounds have expected the ratio to move non-monotonically within that range as ρ is made to increase? The key finding is equation (9), which says that the range within which C^O/C^S (equally, N^S/N^O) lies is narrow. That is another way of saying that the bounds on the optimum are tight. The finding had been a surprise to me as a graduate student, but I had no reason even then to expect the result to have been otherwise.

Arrow observes that C^O/C^S is discontinuous at $\rho = 1$. He notes that if $A > C^S$, then $C^O = A$ and N^O is infinity, but that $N^O = 0$ if $A < C^S$. In a world where the average product of labor is independent of population size ($\rho = 1$), the biosphere imposes no constraint on labor productivity. It seems to me this is so unusual a case to consider that no ethical theory should be discounted merely because it displays features there that are unexpected. In his famous paper on optimum saving in an economy facing an infinite future, Ramsey (1928) discovered that Total Utilitarianism is incoherent for the problem because it awards the well-beings of future generations the same weight as

---

46. I know of only one study of intertemporal public policy in which the U-function is taken to satisfy the above Arrow conditions and a further one that needs to be invoked so as to keep optimal consumption away from 0, namely, that $U_C \to \infty$ as $C \to 0$. That exception is Arrow and Priebsch (2014).

the weight awarded to the present generation. The incoherence is a reflection of the fact that infinite sums of well-beings do not converge in that setting (I discuss this further in Section 9.1). But the problem of optimum saving in the economic model Ramsey worked with has a solution if a positive rate is used to discount the well-beings of future generations. We can say that Total Utilitarianism's response to the question of optimum saving is discontinuous at zero discount rate.[47]

5.6. Critical-Level Utilitarianism

So as to avoid what Parfit regards as a Repugnant Conclusion of Total Utilitarianism (Sect. 6), Kavka (1982) and Parfit (1984) explored the idea that, other things equal, the creation of an additional person should be judged to be good by DM only if the additional person's well-being were to exceed a critical level $U^C > 0$. The proposal sidesteps in one move what Parfit (1984) called the Mere Addition Paradox, a close cousin of the Repugnant Conclusion. Blackorby and Donaldson (1984) arrived at the proposal from a set of normative axioms. The theory is called Critical-Level Utilitarianism.[48]

There is a problem with it. Suppose DM selects births sequentially. Suppose also that the well-being of each of the first N people is expected to be $2U^C/3$. Because this is a positive number, each person's life would be good by their own reasoned reckoning. Critical-Level Utilitarianism, however, tells DM that, other things equal, creating a further person whose well-being would also be $2U^C/3$ is a bad idea. I cannot imagine why DM should be persuaded it is a bad idea.

A possible interpretation of the theory was suggested to me at a workshop on population ethics. We are to imagine that the authors

---

47. The greatness of Ramsey's paper does not lie in that observation, but in showing how the Utilitarian criterion can be altered to allow for an answer to the question of optimum saving even when no discounting is permitted. Roughly speaking, Ramsey renormalized the Utilitarian aggregator by subtracting an infinity from the infinite utility sum in such a way that the reconstructed Utilitarianism had an answer to the question he had started with, which was, "How much of a nation's output should it save for the future?" (Ramsey, 1928: 543)

48. See also Blackorby, Bossert, and Donaldson (1997). Broome (2004: 199–202) provides a supportive account of the theory.

of Critical-Level Utilitarianism recalibrated the personal well-being function U so that their U^C is the hedonistic zero (i.e., Classical Utilitarianism's $U = 0$). In that interpretation, life is not good if U lies in the interval $[0, U^C)$. Under the recalibration, states of affair would be evaluated using $U(C) - U^C$ as the basis of comparison. But if Critical-Level Utilitarianism is a mere renumbering of Total Utilitarianism, it is the same theory as Total Utilitarianism and is therefore unable to serve as an escape route from Parfitian concerns.

In support of Critical-Level Utilitarianism, it has been suggested that a life in which a person's well-being is below U^C is not one she deserves as a human being (Feldman, 1995).[49] But in the present example, the first N people will enjoy $2U^C/3$. There will be no inequality even when there are $N + 1$ people. Moreover, DM knows they all will acknowledge that by their own reckoning their lives are good. Nevertheless, Critical-Level Utilitarianism requires DM to say they deserve better and to believe that the world would be a worse place should another person be born with the same quality of life as the N people who preceded that additional person. I know of no reason why DM should accept the evaluation.

Once a figure for well-being subsistence is reached on the basis of individuals' reasoned conception of their well-being, DM should acknowledge that life for a person is good at any standard of living exceeding it (the higher, the better, of course). And a person's life is good if she enjoys $2U^C/3$. Of course, it could be that the underlying economy is mismanaged and there are sufficient resources to enable people to enjoy a life in excess of U^C. But that's a different matter in that it points to bad governance, and it doesn't provide a reason for modifying Total Utilitarianism.

5.7. Socially Embedded Well-Being

There is room for the notion of desert in population axiology if we recognize that people are not egoists. It pays to study that.

We should not imagine that C^S is independent of society's experiences. Personal aspirations and what reads as success or failure are influenced by what is reachable—they are not entertained in vacuum. So too with what constitutes a life that goes neither well nor not-well.

---

49. I owe this reference to Krister Bykvist.

It appears to be deep in our psychology that our living standard relative to that of others, especially perhaps our peer group, matters to us. Veblen (1925) is a classic on this line of inquiry. He pointed to the competitive side of our nature. Douglas and Isherwood (1979) is another, more recent, classic in which the authors pointed to the sociability in us.[50] In either case, the higher is the general standard of living, the higher would C^S be. That means zero well-being in the distant past would have been calibrated at a lower standard of living than it would be today. It also means that, in today's poor societies, C^S can justifiably be taken to be lower by people there than it is by people in rich societies. And it means that if the overwhelming majority of a society's population are very well off, a new-born in a poor household can be acknowledged to deserve better.[51]

In the formal model in which I derived the Sidgwick–Meade Rule, people are egoists. The assumption makes for simplicity of analysis, which is why we will continue to study that world. But it is just as well to check that the Sidgwick–Meade Rule extends to cover worlds where personal well-being is socially embedded.

Let $C\circ$ denote the average living standard. We assume now that a person's well-being is a function not only of her consumption level C, but also of $C\circ$. Thus $U = U(C,C\circ)$. In a Veblenesque world, U would satisfy

$$\partial U/\partial C = U_C > 0 \tag{13a}$$

$$\partial U/\partial C\circ = U_{C\circ} < 0 \tag{13b}$$

---

50. Bourdieu (1984) is a deep sociological study of consumption behavior. The evidence suggests that others influence our choices in every sphere of consumption. We coordinate our activities by appealing to social norms. Those norms could be the average of what others in one's society do. The norms are therefore determined within the social system. Dasgupta et al. (2016) is a formal inquiry into the implications of Bourdieu's empirical findings for public policy.

51. Veblen's observation on human psychology found a telling expression in a remark attributed to Garry Feldman of Stamford, Connecticut, one of the wealthiest towns in the United States: "I might be in the top one percent, but I feel that I am in the bottom third of the people I know." (*The Guardian*, February 16, 2013).

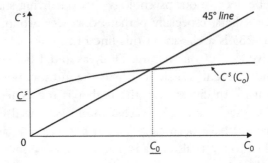

Figure 6 Well-Being Subsistence and Societal Living Standard

To have a meaningful problem for population ethics, we should also assume

$$\text{For all } C_\circ, \ U(C,C_\circ) < 0 \text{ for low enough values of } C \quad (13c)$$

$$\text{For all } C_\circ, \ U(C,C_\circ) > 0 \text{ for high enough values of } C \quad (13d)$$

Conditions (13c) and (13d) imply that for all $C_\circ$ there is a C^S such that

$$U(C^S,C_\circ) = 0 \tag{14}$$

It is immediate from conditions (13a)–(13d) and equation (14) that C^S is an increasing function of $C_\circ$. Write the function as $C^S(C_\circ)$. In Figure 6, $C_\circ$ is measured along the horizontal axis and C^S along the vertical axis. The curve $C^S(C_\circ)$, which is upward sloping, intersects the 45° line at $\underline{C}_\circ$. Empirically the interesting region in the quadrant is where $C_\circ$ exceeds $\underline{C}_\circ$.[52] It is an easy matter to confirm that the Sidgwick–Meade Rule (eq. 3) generalizes to read as

$$U(C,C_\circ) = [(AF(K,N)/N) - AF_N](U_C + U_{C_\circ}) \tag{15}$$

Equation (15) identifies the optimum living standard. The latter is above $\underline{C}_\circ$, but the Sidgwick–Meade Rule commends a large

---

52. $\underline{C}^S$ may be interpreted as a physical-subsistence level of consumption. Below that a person withers away. C^S is less than $C_\circ$ to the right of $\underline{C}_\circ$. The Sidgwick–Meade Rule commends a standard of living above $\underline{C}_\circ$.

population. It is large all the more so because a high consumption level doesn't amount much to the average person when all others also enjoy a high consumption level. Appendix 1 contains an explicit form of *U*-functions satisfying conditions (13a)–(13d).

We mustn't use the production function of equation (4) to study the implications of Veblenesque well-being functions for Total Utilitarianism. At an optimum in our model everyone consumes the average. Using equation (4) in equation (15) tells us that the optimum living standard is independent of A and K. Note though that equation (4) represents an extreme special case, useful for pen-on-paper calculations, which is why I will continue to use it here for studying population ethics. To understand the implications of Veblenesque well-being functions, however, we need to make use of more general production functions, consistent with equation (1). In general settings, the optimum living standard under Total Utilitarianism increases with A and K.

In contrast to conditions (13a)–(13d), the *U*-function in the world described by Douglas and Isherwood could be modeled as follows: Define $J(C,C\circ) = (C - C\circ)^2$ and assume that $U = U(C,J)$, with the properties $U_C > 0$ and $U_J < 0$. We now suppose that for all $C\circ$ there is a C such that $U(C,J) > 0$ and also a C such that $U(C,J) < 0$. Together they imply that there is a C^S such that $U(C^S, J(C^S, C\circ)) = 0$. Call the solution of this equation $C^S(C\circ)$. A reasoning similar to the one deployed in Appendix 1 then allows us to identify *U*-functions for which $C^S(C\circ)$ is upward sloping so long as $C\circ$ is not too small.[53]

5.8. Non-Archimedean Intuitions and Non-Additive Social Well-Being Functions

Parfitian concerns are directed at the tradeoffs that Total Utilitarianism advocates between population size (N) and average well-being

---

53. In the April 2016 version of this essay, I was tentative when remarking on socially embedded *U*-functions, even though Aisha Dasgupta and I had made use of it in analyzing the idea of fertility desires. I am grateful to Kenneth Arrow and Robert Solow for encouraging me to explore socially embedded *U*-functions in population axiology. For a study of the implications for optimum saving when consumption preferences are socially embedded, see Arrow and Dasgupta (2009) and Dasgupta et al. (2016).

(U) at large values of N. To explore alternatives to the theory, we imagine DM begins by expressing social well-being as V. We write the V-function as

$$V = V(N, U) \qquad (16)$$

Total Utilitarianism requires DM to value the world in terms of the function

$$V = NU \qquad (17)$$

In contrast, the economics literature in the first half of the twentieth century took J. S. Mill's Average Utilitarianism to be the basis for population ethics.[54] Average Utilitarianism says

$$V = U \qquad (18)$$

Average Utilitarians postulated a production function unlike equation (1). They assumed that the marginal productivity of population, AF_N, is an increasing function of N when N is small and a decreasing function of N when N is large, other things equal. Optimum population is at the point where average productivity equals marginal productivity (Gottlieb, 1945; see also Dasgupta, 2005a). Contemporary population ethicists have made convincing objections to the theory. Moreover, it recommends a vanishingly small population in the economic model we are working with here. So I ignore the theory.

As a way of avoiding the Repugnant Conclusion and related Parfitian puzzles such as the Reverse Repugnant Conclusion and the Mere Addition Paradox, population axiologists have inquired after tradeoffs between N and U that are intermediate between those that are reflected in equations (17) and (18). To avoid the Repugnant Conclusion, some scholars have appealed to a non-Archimedean intuition, which says that no number (no matter how large an N) of very small goods (U only just above zero) can exceed the value of a smaller number (small N) of greater goods (U greatly above zero). Parfit (2016) has an elaborate and largely sympathetic discussion of the intuition and develops a supporting idea that there is an ethical hierarchy of

---

54. Gottlieb (1945) is a well-known account of the literature.

the factors that give rise to U. The claim is that a world containing a population, no matter how small, enjoying only goods and engagements that are somewhere in the hierarchy is better than a world containing a population, no matter how large, enjoying only goods and engagements lower in the hierarchy. This amounts to a lexical ordering of the hierarchy of goods and engagements. We are told that virtuous activities are higher in the hierarchy than mere pleasurable ones, that reading Homer is superior to reading Spillane, that Mozart beats muzak, and so on.[55]

I may not be alone in reading the directives as finger-wagging from the Common Room window. Many of us aspire to a balanced life. A life of all Homer and no Spillane would be dull, and a life entirely of virtue is to be avoided if we want to maintain our sanity. Many people try to locate a combination of engagements that is ideal for their own reasoned projects and aims. And for nearly all of us, socio-economic constraints, misjudgments about our abilities, and bad throws of the die curb our ability to get there. More than 60 years of empirical research by sociologists and economists has shown that people choose on the basis of their personal tradeoffs between luxuries and necessities, work and leisure, "Giselle" (Live from the Royal Opera House, Covent Garden) and "Strictly Come Dancing" (the televised dance competition on BBC), and so on. And in democracies they vote in line with those tradeoffs in mind. For them the tradeoffs are embedded in their U-functions, which is why it pays to chase the non-Archimedean intuition as applied to $\{N, U\}$ pairs.

When we do that, the intuition requires the isoquants of $V(N, U)$ to asymptote to distinct values of U as larger and larger Ns are considered—the higher the isoquant, the greater the asymptotic value of U. Consider

$$V(N, U) = g(N)U$$

in which

$$\mathrm{d}g(N)/\mathrm{d}N \equiv g_N > 0;\, g(N) = \mathrm{o}(N) \text{ as } N \to 0;\, g(N) \to \pi > 0$$
$$\text{as } N \to \infty \tag{19}$$

---

55. Arrhenius (2005) contains a lucid discussion of the claim that there is a hierarchy of goods and engagements. Carlson (2007) constructed a mathematical formulation of the hierarchical structure of engagements but didn't put it to work on population axiology.

This can be read as Total Utilitarianism, but under the proviso that population numbers are measured using a non-linear scale that is based on the application of the operator g on N. An example is $g(N) = \tan^{-1} N$.

Let a be a real number. In equation (19), N and U are related on the isoquant of $V = a$ as

$$U = U_a(N) = a/g(N) \tag{20}$$

Figure 7 presents isoquants of V, which imagines for concreteness that $g(N) = \tan^{-1} N$. Equation (20) says that social well-being V is positive on isoquants in the upper panel and is negative in isoquants on the lower panel.[56]

The isoquants of V resemble the rectangular hyperbolae associated with $V = a$ in equation (17) in all essential ways but one. The exception is that $U_a(N) \to a/\pi$ as $N \to \infty$; which means the higher the isoquant, the greater its asymptotic value of U as N tends to infinity. DM can avoid both the Repugnant Conclusion and the Reverse Repugnant Conclusion by adopting the V-function in equation (19).[57]

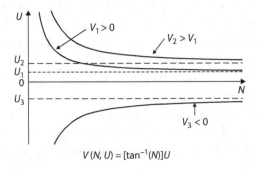

Figure 7 Isoquants of Social Well-Being Without the Repugnant Conclusion

---

56. Note also: (i) $U_{-a}(N) = -U_a(N)$, meaning that the isoquants on the upper panel are mirror images of those on the lower panel; (ii) $NU_a(N) = aN/g(N) \to a$ as $N \to 0$, which means $U_a(N)$ behaves like a/N for small N; and (iii) $dU_a(N)/dN = -[a/(g(N))^2]g_N$, which means the isoquants on the upper panel are negatively sloped, while those on the lower panel are positively sloped.

57. The Mere Addition Paradox (Parfit, 1984), which is related to RC, is also avoided.

On using equations (1) and (19), the rule that optimum population must satisfy in this modified version of Total Utilitarianism reads as

$$U(C) = g(N)[F(K,N)/N - F_N]U_C/Ng_N > 0 \qquad (21)$$

It is a simple matter to check that equation (21) is invariant to positive linear transformations of the U-function (Sect. 5.3). The equation also tells us that the question isn't whether we can avoid the Repugnant Conclusion or the Reverse Repugnant Conclusion in our ethical reasoning—we can. But there is a price to pay: the intuitive meaning of the V-function in equation (19) is unclear. In any case, I argue below that for us humans Total Utilitarianism's problems lie elsewhere.

6. Death

In a moving discourse on the place of autonomy and responsibility in personal well-being, Williams (1993: 50–102) drew attention to an aspect of personal responsibility that starts not from what others may demand of someone, but from what that someone demands of himself. Williams reminded readers that Sophocles had reported that Ajax, being slighted by the award of Achilles' arms to Odysseus, had intended to kill the leaders of the Greek army. To prevent the massacre, Athena put Ajax into a deluded state. It is significant that Ajax's condition didn't affect his purposes; rather, it altered his perception. Thinking that he was killing Odysseus and the others, Ajax slaughtered the army's flocks of sheep and cattle. In Sophocles' account the despair arising from the shame Ajax felt on awakening left no option open to him but to take his own life. And Williams observed that when Ajax says he must go, ". . . he means that he must go: period" (1993: 76).

Sidgwick in contrast offered a view of life that is at odds with Sophocles' account. In the chapter that introduces Utilitarianism to his readers, Sidgwick (1907: 414–415) wrote:

> . . . I shall assume that, for human beings generally, life on the average yields a positive balance of pleasure over pain. This has been denied by thoughtful persons: but the denial seems to me clearly opposed to the common experience of mankind, as expressed in their commonly accepted principles of action. The great majority

of men, in the great majority of conditions under which human life is lived, certainly act as if death were one of the worst of evils, for themselves and for those whom they love. . . .[58]

Nagel (1979) concluded that if death is an evil, it is the loss of life that is objectionable. The conclusion is incontrovertible to the secular mind, but there are at least three circumstances of death that should be distinguished, and they don't point in the same direction. There is death that comes naturally to one in the fullness of time; there is death that comes not from one's hands before one's time; and there is death that is brought on one by one's own deliberate action. Nagel contrasted the first two, but didn't speak to the third. And it is the latter that should make us pause before accepting Sidgwick's conclusion that life, all in all, is a positive good for most people.

Religious prohibition, fear of the process of dying (the possibility of suffering pain, the feeling of isolation), the thought that one would be betraying family and friends, and the deep resistance to the idea of taking one's own life that has been built into us through selection

---

58. Odysseus' tale of his encounter with Achilles in Hades' underworld gives striking expression to the thought that death is the worst evil that can befall someone. He reports having greeted Achilles by exclaiming that no one in the world will have been more blest than Achilles, and that, because Achilles now lords over the dead with all his powers, he has no cause to grieve at dying. To which, as Odysseus recounts, Achilles retorted,

> No winning words about death to *me*, shining Odysseus!
> By god, I'd rather slave on earth for another man—
> some dirt-poor tenant farmer who scrapes to keep alive—
> than rule down here over all the breathless dead.
>
> (*The Odyssey*, trans. Robert Fagels, Book 11 (lines 555–558),
> Penguin Books, 1996).

At the other extreme is the Chorus in *Oedipus at Colonus*, who were reported by Sophocles as having observed: "Not to be born is, past all prizing, best; but, when a man hath seen the light, this is next best by far, that with all speed he should go thither, whence he has come" (*Oedipus at Colonus*, trans. R. C. Jebb [lines 1225–1229], Cambridge University Press, 1917).

For a remarkable tour of visions of the after-life from ancient to modern times in literature and in religious teachings, see Casey (2009).

pressure would cause someone even in deep misery to balk. It may even be that no matter what life throws at us we adjust to it, if only to make it possible to carry on. But the acid test for Sidgwick's inference that "life on the average yields a positive balance of pleasure over pain" is to ask ourselves whether we shouldn't pause before creating a person so as to imagine the kind of life that is likely to be in store for the potential child.[59] The desire to procreate springs from our deep emotional needs, and the direct motivation we have to create children can be traced to a wide variety of reasons (we noted a few in Section 1; see also "Socially Embedded Preferences, Environmental Externalities, and Reproductive Rights"), but here we are concerned only with the life of the prospective child.

In the passage in which he presented the Repugnant Conclusion, Parfit (1984: 388) recognized Total Utilitarianism's pro-natalist character, but then interpreted it in the following way:

> For any possible population of at least ten billion people, all with a very high quality of life, there must be some much larger imaginable population whose existence, if other things are equal, would be better, even though its members have lives that are barely worth living.

The play on words in the passage has always baffled me. We are being asked to consider a figure for world population that will almost certainly be reached in the second half of this century (a figure that is unlikely to be sustainable at reasonable material comfort; Section 10), and are then made to imagine an Earth where, because of population pressure, people scramble for resources so as to eke out an existence, having *lives that are barely worth living*. But someone whose life is barely worth living doesn't enjoy a life of positive quality, she suffers from a life that is not only not good (as experienced by her), but is positively bad. In the contemporary world, more than a half billion people are malnourished and prone regularly to illness and disease, many of

---

59. Nagel (1979) acknowledges that the loss encountered when someone's life is cut short can't be balanced on a one-to-one basis by replacing that someone with a new birth. In my readings on the subject, I have found him (and Narveson, 1967, and Heyd, 1992) to be among the very few who (at least until recently) acknowledged the asymmetry. In Section 7, I make use of the asymmetry in developing population ethics.

whom are also debt-ridden, but who survive and tenaciously display that their lives are worth living by the fact that they persist in wishing to live. If you were to say that you would not wish the circumstances they endure on anyone, I wouldn't take you to mean their lives aren't worth living; I would take you to be saying that their circumstances are so bad that you wouldn't wish them on even your worst enemy, that something ought to be done to improve their lives, that if you were to disregard the countervailing needs you and your household may have, you wouldn't want to *create* children facing those circumstances.[60]

Death *relieved* the intolerable pain Ajax experienced on awakening from the madness Athena had inflicted on him. Ajax knew it would, which is why he chose it. It was better for him that he paid the price of death than that he carried on. The inference Sidgwick drew from the fact that death is generally thought to be one of the worst evils, namely, that life on the average yields a positive balance of pleasure over pain, is altogether unfounded, and I cannot imagine how so profound and careful a thinker could have made such an elementary arithmetical error. That death is a horror to most people doesn't imply that life is on balance pleasurable. On the contrary, the greater is the horror that taking one's own life poses to someone (i.e., betrayal of one's family and friends, revelation of one's misery to others when one wants it to remain undisclosed even after death), the *more* he would be willing to carry on in a state of misery.[61]

To illustrate Sidgwick's error, imagine that in the units chosen to measure U, the horror of suicide for someone is -300. The person would choose to continue to live so long as life offered her a value in excess of -300; and that could be as low as -299.99.

One way to interpret life in the range between the point at which a person takes his life and well-being subsistence is to view it as *bearable*

---

60. Parfit's interpretation of well-being subsistence hadn't changed over the years. On the Repugnant Conclusion, he wrote only a couple of years ago, "Compared with the existence of many people who would all have some very high quality of life, there is some much larger number of people whose existence would be better, even though these people would all have lives that are barely worth living" (Parfit, 2016: 110).

61. Suicide isn't that rare a phenomenon. Annually about three-quarters of a million people take their own life worldwide, and more than 20 million people attempt suicide.

but not good. The person would not contemplate suicide, but could wish he hadn't been born, that he didn't have to go through his life's experiences. Zero well-being is then the transition point from the bearable to the good.[62] That is why estimating well-being subsistence from people's behavior or responses to questionnaires would be a mistake.[63]

7. A Problem Like Sleeping Beauty

In the Genesis Problem, Earth is devoid of people. The domain of discourse consists only of potential persons. In any Actual Problem, Earth is inhabited. The question is whether further people should be created. The two settings are wildly different.

---

62. I owe this interpretation to Robert Solow.
63. The presumption that life on balance is inevitably good ($U > 0$) or that it is invariably bad ($U < 0$) precludes reasoned discussion on population policies. The former commends a large (even infinite) population; the latter commends an Earth devoid of people. That alone shows that, unlike decision theory, population ethics requires of us to specify the zero of the U-function.

   As far as I can tell, numerical measures of subjective well-being have been taken to be non-negative in all the large-scale surveys on happiness and life satisfaction that have been conducted in recent years (see Diener, Helliwell, and Kahneman, 2010; and Helliwell, Layard, and Sachs, 2013, for reviews of the findings). It would look as though designers of the questionnaires that have shaped the literature on empirical hedonism have also been greatly influenced by the thought that life satisfaction can never be negative (otherwise why do people continue to want to live?). I do not know whether people would respond differently to questionnaires on life satisfaction if, instead of a scale from, say 0 to 10, respondents were offered a scale from −5 to +5.

   Daly et al. (2011) found in one study that a major determinant of suicide is being at a well-being level significantly lower than others, thus implying that living in a country where well-being is high is a risk factor for committing suicide. This can be explained if the coefficient of variation in incomes in two countries, one rich and the other poor, is the same and personal well-being accords with Veblen (1925), so that, other things equal, U is a decreasing function of the average living standard relative to a person's own (Sect. 5.7 and Appendix 1).

Consider the problem of Sleeping Beauty. She is alive but in a state of total unconsciousness (Sidgwick would regard her state to be the hedonistic zero). What makes her an interesting case for us here is that her life expectation is the prevailing average, in that with a modicum of medical attention she can be expected to complete the natural lifespan in a state of total unconsciousness. A small expenditure can however revive her immediately and fully, in which case it is confidently expected her lifetime well-being will be $U^*(>0)$. That's option X for her parents. Option Y is for them to conceive another child who would enjoy a lifetime well-being equal to U^*. However, under Y Sleeping Beauty will remain unconscious. We suppose that the couple have no special feelings for Sleeping Beauty. She was born unconscious, so they have never got to know her. Assume now that in all other respects X and Y have the same consequences. What should Sleeping Beauty's parents do?

If, as in a literal interpretation of Sidgwick's Utilitarianism, agreeable consciousness is the sole good and if the fact that something good would be the result of one's action is the basic reason for doing anything (the two together give rise to agent-neutrality in ethical reasoning), the couple should be indifferent between X and Y. But there are a number of reasons X should be viewed as the right option. They all involve taming the Utilitarian-Consequentialist reasoning I have been following here with further considerations.

7.1. Imperatives

I first list four reasons that have been deployed by philosophers studying problems similar to that of Sleeping Beauty and discuss their extensions. I then develop the fourth reason, Parental Projects, by invoking arguments in Scheffler (1982) to apply agent-centered prerogatives to population axiology in Section 8.[64]

PARENTAL OBLIGATION TO SLEEPING BEAUTY X is the right option because Sleeping Beauty's parents have an obligation toward her which they don't have toward a potential child. They have an obligation toward Sleeping Beauty because they were responsible for conceiving her.

---

64. Nagel (1986: 164) sees the central problem of ethics thus: "(How) the lives, interests, and welfare of others make claims on us and how these claims, of various forms, are to be reconciled with the aim of living our own lives."

People don't have an obligation to become parents, but they acquire one if they choose to become parents. It can even be argued that parents have an obligation toward their offspring that no one else has. Parental obligation provides an argument for choosing X over Υ.[65]

SLEEPING BEAUTY'S CLAIM ON HER PARENTS Relatedly, Sleeping Beauty has claims on her parents. She is a person, it is *her* well-being that is subject to parental choice. She has a claim to be acknowledged by her parents, to be heard by them even though she is unconscious. The potential child has no comparable claims. Notice that this is not a neutral claim—that would be in the realm of deontology—the claim here is agent-relative (Sleeping Beauty's claims on her parents).[66]

THE VALUE OF LIFE'S EXPERIENCES Nagel (1979: 2) suggested that life has a value to the person living it that is independent of anything she may experience:

> The situation is roughly this: There are elements which, if added to one's experience, make life better; there are other elements which, if added to one's experience, make life worse. But what remains when these are set aside is not merely *neutral*: it is emphatically positive. Therefore life is worth living even when the bad elements of experience are plentiful, and the good ones too meager to outweigh the bad ones on their own. The additional positive weight is supplied by experience itself, rather than by any of its contents.

Experience has value to a person over and above its content. Call that stand-alone value Ω. When we say life is precious, even sacred, we probably point to Ω. Here we note that Ω gives content to the idea of

---

65. Simon Beard has pointed out to me that the example can be expanded to encompass a wider range of obligations; for example, if the chooser between X and Υ was Sleeping Beauty's friend (they would have no obligation to make a new friend).

66. Gosseries (2010) discusses this. He studies the obligations people have to one another, not simply parents toward their children. I am ignoring the obligation people may have (at least to themselves) to procreate in special cases, such as a population at risk of extinction from non-fecundity. See Section 13 on existential risks.

autonomy. That life has a stand-alone value Ω is not a sufficient reason for creating a person, but Ω provides a reason for awakening Sleeping Beauty. She has a claim to life's experiences that she will miss if she isn't revived. To deny her that option is to deny her autonomy.[67]

PARENTAL PROJECTS   In his comments on the population problem, Seabright (1989) spoke of the parental desire to promote their family. Sleeping Beauty is their child. Over and above her parents' obligation toward her, their own common project includes protecting the integrity of their family. Other considerations aside, responding to Sleeping Beauty's needs trump's option Υ. Choosing X is an agent-relative response on the part of her parents.

7.2. Wider Cases

A problem like Sleeping Beauty gives rise to a number of variations. Consider a case where X is not available, but X' is. In X' Sleeping Beauty is revived at a small cost, but her life will not be good. Even though she will be able to function, she will suffer from discomfort and pain and will not lead a fulfilling life. All in all, it is expected that her lifetime well-being will be U^{**}, a negative number whose absolute value is not large. Her parents can, as can others such as the physicians caring for her, point to Nagel's Ω and require that she be revived. That's one way to justify X'. Some would go a slightly different route and argue that Sleeping Beauty should be allowed to exercise her agency, her right to life's experiences.

Suppose even X' is not an option. Her parents, or for that matter anyone else, could argue that she should be released from the indignity of living in coma for the rest of her natural life. In that case they would give their consent to having her life-support system disconnected.[68]

Consider another variation. Option Υ remains, but in place of X we are faced with X'', which involves reviving Sleeping Beauty with the understanding that her lifetime well-being will be $U^* - \varepsilon$, where ε is a small positive number. Any one of the four imperatives described above is sufficient for her parents (or society, more generally) to choose X'' if ε was sufficiently small. Assuming her parents view states of affairs in a continuous manner, there is a value of ε, say ε^*, such that it is a matter

---

67. I am most grateful to Itai Sher and Krister Bykvist for helpful correspondence on this.

68. Removing Sleeping Beauty's life support system is not the same as killing her.

of normative indifference to them whether Υ is chosen, or whether Sleeping Beauty is revived with the understanding that her lifetime well-being will be $U^* - \varepsilon^*$. To acknowledge that ε^* is positive is to say that, other things equal, reviving Sleeping Beauty with an expectation of $U^* - \varepsilon$ (where $0 < \varepsilon < \varepsilon^*$) would have priority over creating a person with a lifetime well-being of U^*.

8. Generation-Centered Prerogatives in the Timeless World

The first three considerations in the Sleeping Beauty problem come close to what I am after, but don't quite get there. The fourth consideration, Parental Projects, gets there, but only in so tangential a form for my needs here that I am reluctant to use it. The general formulation is in Scheffler (1982), who uncovered agent-centered concerns that people can justifiably use as prerogatives over agent-neutral demands when deliberating on courses of action open to them:

> . . . a plausible agent-centered prerogative would allow each agent to assign a certain proportionately greater weight to his own interests than to the interests of other people. It would then allow the agent to promote the non-optimal amount outcome of his own choosing, provided only that the degree of its inferiority to each of the superior outcomes he could instead promote in no case exceeded, by more than the specified proportion, the degree of sacrifice necessary for him to promote the superior outcome. (Scheffler, 1982: 20)

In a society of N persons, those prerogatives would apply reciprocally, meaning that the state of affairs that would ensue would be the outcome of N choices, each having been guided by agent-relative concerns. In population axiology the force of those prerogatives works unidirectionally.[69]

---

69. Arrow (1981) used this reasoning to develop a theory of income distributions arising from voluntary contributions. He (personal communication) was moved to advance Agent-Relative Utilitarianism by the words of the first-century sage, Rabbi Hillel: "If I am not for myself, then who is for me? And if I am not for others, then who am I? And if not now, when?"

    Also recall (Sect. 6) Ajax's shame and the action he took to meet the obligation he had to himself.

We are to imagine that each generation reasons collectively and chooses the size of the next generation. Therefore, the "agent" in each generation is that "generation," not the set of all generations beginning with that one. Because generations enter sequentially, the prerogatives we study are unidirectional, not reciprocal. Moreover, the restrictions that I impose on account of those prerogatives are only a weak version of Scheffler's account; they only involve the place of potential well-beings in present people's moral considerations. I modify Total Utilitarianism by considering a weighted sum of personal well-beings, the weight awarded by existing people to potential well-beings being lower than the weight they award their own well-beings. But people in the modified theory display the same concern for actual future people (one's descendants) as they do for themselves (that requirement is the moral we took away from the case of Sleeping Beauty). We will call the modified perspective Generation-Relative Utilitarianism.

I first put the theory to work on the timeless model of Section 5. Stocks and flows are indistinguishable. In Section 9, the theory is extended to an economy moving through time. Stocks and flows have to be distinguished there.

8.1. The Two-Stage Decision

We imagine there are N_0 people, identical in every respect. They are the existing population. By assumption there are no environmental nor reproductive externalities. In that situation, an individual's choice reflects the choice of all. The biosphere is of size K.

Because the model we study here is timeless, each individual's life cycle is embedded in it. If C is someone's consumption level, his personal well-being is $U(C)$. The problem facing existing people is to determine the number of people to add to their world. We assume again that the world is thinly populated. It means K is large relative to N_0. It also means that if they were not to create further people, their standard of living would be high. Even though those further people will join them in production, adding to the numbers will cost the existing population some, because average product per person exceeds the marginal product (Fig. 2). But because they are Generation-Relative Utilitarians, the existing population decides how many to add by appealing to the theory's calculus.

The decision facing the existing population involves two stages. At the first stage, the number of additional people (N_1) is chosen. In making that choice, people know that, once born, the additional population will join them, both as producers and consumers, and enjoy the same status as they do. Production and consumption take place in the second stage.

Recall the production structure in equation (1). If N_1 people are born, total output will be $AF(K, N_0 + N_1)$. Because that output will be shared equally, each person's living standard will be $AF(K, N_0 + N_1)/(N_0 + N_1)$, which is C. That's the start of a backward induction, an essential requirement in Generation-Relative Utilitarianism.

Without loss of generality, the weight awarded by existing people to their own well-being is 1. The weight they award to the well-being of potential people is μ, where $0 \leq \mu \leq 1$. Let V be the representative person's conception of social well-being. Because her perspective plays a role in that conception, we will call V her *social valuation function*. Thus

$$V = N_0 U(AF(K, N_0 + N_1))/(N_0 + N_1)) \\ + \mu N_1 U(AF(K, N_0 + N_1))/(N_0 + N_1)) \qquad (22)$$

The problem before the existing population is to choose N_1 so as to maximize V in equation (22). To contrast it to the Genesis Problem, we will call the maximization of V in equation (22) an Actual Problem.[70] Routine calculations show that the optimum value of N_1 satisfies

$$\mu U(C) = [(N_0 + \mu N_1)/(N_0 + N_1)][(AF(K, N_0 + N_1)/(N_0 + N_1)) \\ - (\partial AF(K, N_0 + N_1)/\partial N_1)] U_C > 0 \qquad (23)$$

Equation (23) is the counterpart of the Sidgwick–Meade Rule in Generation-Relative Utilitarianism.

---

70. μ corresponds to ε^* in Section 7.2. Notice that the larger is ε^*, the smaller is μ.

   V in equation (22) is a direct extension of Total Utilitarianism and would reduce to it if $\mu = 1$. I have arrived at it by applying Scheffler's reasoning to population ethics. An alternative procedure would be to derive the formula from axioms on the way individual U-functions should be combined to yield the V-function. Welfare axiomatics do that. Blackorby and Donaldson (1982) applied welfare axiomatics to population ethics. Their techniques can be adapted to yield equation (22).

To contrast the two theories, it is simplest to return to the power functions in equations (4) and (5). Using them in equation (23) and labeling the optimum C as C^{OO} and the optimum N as N^{OO} yield

$$C^{OO}/C^S = (N^S/N^{OO})^{(1-\rho)} = 1 + \{[(N_0 + \mu N_1)/\mu(N_0 + N_1)](1-\rho)\sigma\}^{1/\sigma} \tag{24}$$

Compare equations (9) and (24). A simple calculation shows that the optimum standard of living (C^{OO}) in the Actual Problem is larger than in the Genesis Problem (C^O). This is shown in Figure 5.[71] Correspondingly, the optimum population is smaller in the Actual Problem (N^{OO}) than in the Genesis Problem (N^O). The smaller μ is, the lower are the additional numbers (N_1).[72]

In Figure 5, $\hat{C}$ is the consumption level at which average well-being equals marginal well-being. The magnitude of C^{OO} relative to $\hat{C}$ depends on μ, ρ, σ, and N_0. It is easy to confirm that if μ is not much less than 1, C^{OO} is less than $\hat{C}$, but that if μ is small, C^{OO} is greater than $\hat{C}$. In Figure 5, the two possibilities are identified by $C_1{}^{OO}$ and $C_2{}^{OO}$, respectively.

8.2. Reproductive Replacement

We now consider an extreme scenario that will prove useful when we come to study an economy moving through time in a stationary mode. Imagine that the optimum policy for the existing population is to replicate itself. That's when N_0 just *happens* to be a figure for which optimum N_1 equals N_0.

---

71. Proof: Use the fact that $(N_0 + \mu N_1)/\mu(N_0 + N_1) > 1$.

72. We may put the matter in a slightly more technical form: There exists a function $N(\mu)$, which decreases with μ, such that if $N_0 < N(\mu)$, equation (24) yields the optimum population. If $N_0 > N(\mu)$, the optimum policy is not to add to the existing population. Personal well-being in the latter case is $U(AK^{1-\rho}N_0{}^{(\rho-1)})$. If the existing population were to have the misfortune of being too many ($N_0 > N^S$), the personal well-being of each of the N_0 individuals would be negative—and *that* is over-population. (We are assuming that killing a fraction of the existing population to raise the well-being of those that remain to positive levels is forbidden.)

Define N by the equation $N_0 = N_1 = N$. $2N$ is total population, and N is the size of each of the two generations. Equation (22) then reduces to

$$C^{OO}/C^S = (2N^S/2N^{OO})^{(1-\rho)} = (N^S/N^{OO})^{(1-\rho)}$$
$$= [1 + (1 + \mu)(1 - \rho)\sigma/2\mu]^{1/\sigma} \qquad (25)$$

Equation (25) is the counterpart of the Sidgwick–Meade Rule in this model. As expected, equation (25) reduces to equation (9) if $\mu = 1$.[73]

Notice that C^{OO}/C^S is not bounded above by e. If μ is small, $C^{OO} > \hat{C}$ (Fig. 5). To obtain a quantitative sense of the optimum, we need numerical values of ρ, σ, and μ. As before, we set $\rho = 0.5$. σ has been estimated from consumption behavior under risk. $\sigma = 1$ is at the upper end of the range that has been found in empirical studies. For ease of computation I settle on that.

Stopping rules that are used by households to determine their family size could in principle be used to estimate μ, but I don't know of any study that has gone that route. No doubt household behavior isn't the exclusive source of ethical understanding (Section 1 drew attention to a number of reasons), but it would be wrong to ignore people's intentions altogether in reaching ethical directives. Casual empiricism on health and education expenditures in time and money on children in the West, especially perhaps on children with special needs, suggest that μ is considerably less than 1. People seem to place far greater weight on the well-being of their children than on the potential well-being of children who might have been born but weren't because couples chose not to have further children. I assume $\mu = 0.05$. This is to take a lunge in the dark, but I am using the figure only for illustrative purposes. Using the figures in equation (25) yields $N^S/N^{OO} \approx 39$, meaning that the biosphere's carrying capacity for humans is (approximately) 39 times optimum population. This is a far cry from the pro-natalism of Total Utilitarianism. Suppose C^S is taken to be below even the average annual income in the world's poorest countries; say 1,500 international dollars (Table 1).

---

73. Notice that C^{OO} is unboundedly large and N^{OO} vanishingly small if μ is infinitesimal.

In that case, equation (25) says $C^{OO} = 9{,}375$ international dollars. That's the average annual income in the World Bank's list of middle-income countries.

Even though equation (25) has been derived for a timeless world, it reflects Generation-Relative Utilitarianism in an economy moving through time in a stationary mode. We confirm that in Section 9.

Notice that I am unable to estimate N^{OO}. That's because we don't know N^S. In Part II we will make an attempt to estimate N^S from an ongoing research program of a group of environmental scientists.

8.3. Coherence

Total Utilitarianism requires people to award the same ethical weight to potential people as they do to and present and actual future people. That requirement has been questioned previously. Narveson (1967) noted difficulties in the requirement and recast Utilitarianism by observing that "we (utilitarians) are for making people happy, not for making happy people" (Narveson, 1973: 73). Narveson called his theory Person-Affecting Utilitarianism.[74]

Parfit (1976) observed that the theory yields an incoherent notion of goodness. Because his critique would apply equally to any theory that recognizes agent-centered prerogatives, no matter how attenuated they may be, here is an example of what he, and in endorsing the criticism Broome (2004), meant.

Consider individual A and a potential person B. In what follows, we apply the *ceteris paribus* clause on all other people. A's well-being is

---

74. Narveson (1967) argued that we are under no obligation to procreate, even if, other things equal, it was guaranteed that the person born would have an outstandingly good life. Obligation is a strong word. In this essay, I am exploring a particular way of evaluating states of affair, in which "well-being" serves as the coin with which states of affair are evaluated. Generation-Relative Utilitarianism is a lot closer to Total Utilitarianism than Narveson's theory. I have friends, however, who regard Generation-Relative Utilitarianism to be infested with ontological elitism. The criticism comes close to regarding potential persons as actual persons, a view that the problem of Sleeping Beauty asks us to reject.

expected to be 11 in the prevailing state of affairs, or "social state," X. But A has the option of creating person B. Two social states that include B are possible. In one (we label it Y), A's and B's well-beings would each be 6. In the other (we label it Z), they would be 8 and 4, respectively. Y and Z differ in the way A and B share resources, which is a feature of those states of affair that are taken into account by A when contemplating whether to create B. We re-label X, Y, and Z as $\{11\}$, $\{6,6\}$, and $\{8,4\}$, respectively. The problem is to rank them in a situation where A exists but B doesn't. We say that B, were he to be created, would be of a different generation from A (hence, "Generation-Relative Ethics").

Denote ethical dominance by ">" and ethical equivalence by "=." We imagine A to be a Generation-Relative Utilitarian. Suppose the weight that A awards to the well-being of a potential person is half the weight she awards her own well-being, the latter being set equal to 1. That means $\mu = 1/2$. It also means that, so long as B is a potential person, $X > Z > Y$. But if B were born, he would be an actual person. Person A recognizes that the ethical relation between Y and Z, the only remaining social states, would then be $Y = Z$. A's social valuation function is dependent on the state of affairs in which she constructs it. That's Parfit's criticism.

The trouble with the criticism is that it harks back to the Genesis Problem. As the name suggests, the Genesis Problem is viewed by someone residing nowhere. That is why Total Utilitarianism would say $Y = Z > X$ before B is conceived. Parfit took exception to Narveson's Person-Affecting Utilitarianism because the binary relation between social states is dependent on whether B is an actual person. Generation-Relative Utilitarianism has that same feature. In the present example, it is A who is evaluating social states. She does that from somewhere, that is, she is not nowhere (Nagel, 1986, is the classic on the significance of the distinction).

It is key to Generation-Relative Ethics that the ranking of the three social states X, Y, and Z is a function of the state of affairs in place when the ranking is determined. The ranking corresponds to A's social valuation function. The perspective is from the current state. The normative content of the pair $\{6,6\}$ in a world where B is only a potential person differs from the normative content of the pair $\{6,6\}$ in a world where B is an actual person. Denote the ranking of the triplet $\{X,Y,Z\}$ at X (the social state at which only A is present) under Generation-Relative Utilitarianism by the relationships "$>_X$" and "$=_X$", and define ("$>_Y$", "$=_Y$") and ("$>_Z$", "$=_Z$"), correspondingly, at Y and Z.

Because person A is a Generation-Relative Utilitarian, she would choose not to add to the population, because viewed from X,

$$\{11\} >_X \{8,4\} >_X \{6,6\} \tag{26}$$

If A were to view the triplet from Y, however, the ranking would be

$$\{6,6\} =_Y \{8,4\} >_Y \{11\} \tag{27}$$

and from Z, it would be

$$\{6,6\} =_Z \{8,4\} >_Z \{11\} \tag{28}$$

There is no contradiction here. Once X ceases to be an element of the set of possible outcomes (because B has come into existence), the place of X is reversed in the way the states of affairs are ranked.[75]

That a person's social valuation function could depend on the state of affairs in which she finds herself is at odds with a long-standing tradition in both moral philosophy and welfare economics. It has become common practice in both disciplines to seek a ranking of social states that is reached by the ethicist looking at states of affairs from the outside. The incoherence Parfit thought he had noted in someone's ethical reasoning when she views her actions from where she stands has been used by philosophers even to dismiss calibrating zero well-being by

---

75. Total Utilitarianism and General-Relative Utilitarianism are not the same normative theory. The binary relations over social states that are implied by the two are different. We should therefore distinguish them. Under Total Utilitarianism, the social state in which the ethics is conducted does not matter. The ranking of $\{X,Y,Z\}$ is the same ($Y=Z>X$), regardless of whether B exists. If a temporal structure were imposed on the example, X would not be reachable if either Y or Z were realized; nevertheless, the thought experiment that would give rise to inequalities (26)–(28) can still be conducted. I am grateful to Simon Beard and Shamik Dasgupta for clarifying the complexities of the example to me.

reference to non-existence (more accurately, to an absence of all experiential states). Broome (1999: 168), for example, has argued that it cannot ever be true that it is better for a person that she lives than that she should never have lived at all; because if it *were* better, then it would have been worse for her if she had never lived at all; but if she had never lived at all, there would have been no her for it to be worse for, so it would not have been worse for her.

The chain of reasoning is correct enough, but the premise reads as doctored. It is doubtful that anyone would acknowledge her life to be going well by saying it is better for her that she lives than that she were never to have lived. On those occasions when we express a sense of well-being, we tend to say that it is good to be alive, or that we are grateful to our parents for having conceived and nurtured us, or that we ought to do something for our society in return for our good fortune. But those are different thoughts, and they are meaningful. When one's well-being is compared with non-existence, the comparison is made from the perspective of the person herself, the comparison isn't made from a universal point of view. The person does not ask herself how she would have felt had she not been born. She knows that to ask that would be absurd.

The preference reversal displayed in inequalities (26)–(28) translates to intergenerational inconsistency. Each generation's ordering over possible future worlds differs from those of future generations over the possible future worlds they in turn will face. Nevertheless, it is possible for the generations to arrive at choices that are consistent with one another's perspective. We now confirm that each generation could both influence and affirm the choices to be made by those that are to follow. We do that by extending the timeless model to construct a world moving through time.

9. Generations Across the Indefinite Future

Generations may be relatively easy to define within dynasties, but because individuals of all ages live side by side, they are a slippery concept when we want to identify them from the demographic structure of an entire economy. What we mean by a generation depends on the purpose to which the notion is needed (e.g., year of birth, those of working age, retired people, and so on). In welfare economics, generations are often identified with time, as in, "the generation at time t." But justifying that move requires a number of demographic and normative assumptions. In Section 11, we will find a way to distinguish generations in a clean manner, but that will be in an economy in a stationary state. Matters become difficult outside stationary states, but the problems are not insurmountable.

Total Utilitarianism invites members of each generation to evaluate the choice of their successors' numbers on the basis of a weighted sum of well-beings across the generations. Here is Sidgwick (1907: 414) on the matter:

> It seems . . . clear that the time at which a man exists cannot affect the value of his happiness from the universal point of view; and that the interests of posterity must concern a Utilitarian as much as those of his contemporaries, except in so far as the effect of his actions on posterity—and even the existence of human beings to be affected— must necessarily be more uncertain.

Discounting for well-beings at future times differs from discounting the well-beings of future generations. An individual could choose to discount his own future well-being at a positive rate but feel that, in the choice of public policy, the well-being of future people should receive the same weight as his own. Frank Ramsey would appear to have held that view (see note 77 below). But to distinguish discounting for time from discounting for generations would be to make the models that follow untidy; more importantly, it would take us afield. So I conflate the two. Sidgwick in the passage just quoted spoke against the thought that it is ethically legitimate to discount the well-being of future generations merely on grounds that future generations will appear in the future. He spoke to future generations' futurity. Of course, Sidgwick (1907) was advancing a teleological theory.

We consider three reasons for applying generation-discounting: (i) discounting the well-beings of future generations on grounds that not to do so could lead a person to commend states of affairs with features that run counter to other values he may hold; (ii) discounting for risk of extinction of the human race (this is the case Sidgwick spoke of in the above passage); and (iii) exercising generation-centered prerogatives.[76] In Sections 9.1 and 9.2, we identify periods with generations so as to draw out sharply that generations arrive sequentially in time. But that means even adjacent generations don't overlap; rather, time and the generations coincide. That assumption is removed in Section 9.3, and in the rest of the Arrow Lecture we study population ethics in a world of overlapping generations. To keep generation-discounting from contaminating the force of generation-centered prerogatives, I eschew the futurity argument and assume from Section 9.3 onward that only the risk of extinction and generation-centered prerogatives matter. However, so as to expose the underlying structure of Generation-Relative Utilitarianism, even the risk of extinction is assumed to be negligible in Section 11, which is when we come to estimate globally optimum population size and the optimum standard of living. The risks, if not of extinction but of future catastrophes owing to our own actions, are discussed in Section 10 and in my Response to Commentaries that follows the Arrow Lecture.

Because I want to stay close to the literature on discounting future generations, we assume in Sections 9.1–9.2 that population is exogenously given (i.e., the future population is not subject to choice). Such a world gives rise to what Parfit (1984) called Same Numbers Choices. We return to population ethics in Section 9.3.

9.1. Discounting Future Generations

Sidgwick's formulation of Utilitarianism was the opening observation in Frank Ramsey's famous paper on the optimum rate of saving in a world shorn of risk (Ramsey, 1928). Ramsey regarded the practice of discounting future well-beings in such a world to be ethically indefensible and thought it "arises merely from the weakness of the imagination" (Ramsey, 1928: 543). In a book that laid the foundations of the modern theory of economic growth, Harrod (1948: 40) judged discounting future generations to be ". . . a polite expression of rapacity and the conquest of reason by passion." Strong words, and to many economists Ramsey's and Harrod's

---

76. Beard (2018) in unpublished notes discusses further reasons.

strictures read like Sunday pronouncements. Solow (1974a: 9) expressed the feeling exactly when he wrote, "In solemn conclave assembled, so to speak, we ought to act as if the [discount rate on future well-beings] were zero."[77]

Parfit (1984) applied sophisticated reasoning in support of the Sidgwick–Ramsey–Harrod view on discounting the well-being of future generations. That view has influenced one strand of the welfare economics of global climate change (Broome, 1992, 2012; Cline, 1992; Stern, 2006), but it appears to be a minority opinion among economists. Economists generally have adopted the attitude that, because people do in fact discount for time and, judging by their behavior, they would appear to discount the well-being of future generations as well, the (social) decision-maker (DM) should follow the practice

---

77. In a talk on February 28, 1925, before fellow Apostles (a secret, mostly-undergraduate discussion society in Cambridge University, known to its fraternity as "The Society"), with the title, "Is There Anything Left to Discuss?", Ramsey had expressed a different viewpoint:

> My picture of the world is drawn in perspective, and not like a model to scale. The foreground is occupied by human beings and the stars are as small as threepenny bits. I don't really believe in astronomy, except as a complicated description of part of the course of human and possibly animal sensation. I apply my perspective not merely to space but also to time. In time the world will cool and everything will die; but that is a long time off still, and its present value at compound interest is almost nothing. Nor is the present less valuable because the future will be blank. (Ramsey, 1931: 291).

Ramsey was of course speaking after dinner, behind closed doors, to his fraternity of Apostles. However, because the talk predated his famous 1928 paper in the *Economic Journal*, I couldn't tell for a long while whether he had changed his mind by the time he came to compose the paper, or whether he had just put on Sunday-best clothes for a journal publication (see also Arrow and Kurz, 1970: 12). Recently Ken-Ichi Akao suggested to me an entirely convincing, third explanation. Akao observed that in his talk to the Apostles, Ramsey was giving expression to his personal discount rate, whereas in his *Economic Journal* paper, concerned as he was there with socially optimum national saving, Ramsey was speaking of the public discount rate.

(Nordhaus, 1994, 2007).[78] And there are economists (e.g., Arrow and Kurz, 1970; Arrow, 1999; Dasgupta, 2005b, 2007b) who have questioned the Sidgwick–Ramsey–Harrod view because they have been persuaded by an equally sophisticated reasoning as Parfit's, which showed that to insist on *not* discounting the well-being of future generations can have deeply problematic implications. The argument was fashioned in a remarkable set of papers by Koopmans (1960, 1965, 1967, 1972, 1977).

We consider a deterministic world, for that's where the argument is simplest. There are two strands to Koopmans' reasoning, and they come at the question of time/generation discounting from different directions. One strand (Koopmans, 1965, 1967) begins by noting that the productivity of investment creates an asymmetry between the present and the future. Seedlings grow to become trees, fish stocks increase if fisheries are left alone, and so on; which is to say investment has a positive return (i.e., a foregone unit of consumption today can generate more than a unit of consumption in the future). The asymmetry is so built into the arrow of time that symmetric treatment of well-beings across the generations is questionable, or so it can be argued. We study that possibility first (the example is taken from Arrow, 1999: 14).

Time is divided into periods: $t = 0,1, \ldots$ ad infinitum. We are to imagine that population is projected to remain constant over time. Moreover, so as to focus on the distribution of well-being *across* the generations, we assume people are identical, and that generations coincide with periods. The latter assumption implies that we may speak of "generation-t" and "period-t" interchangeably. And because people

---

78. In their work on global climate change, the annual time discount rate chosen by Cline (1992) was 0 percent; by Nordhaus (1994), 3 percent; and by Stern (2006), 0.1 percent. Stern's 0.1 percent was attributed by the author to an annual risk of human extinction. Nordhaus' choice of 3 percent a year reflected his reading of consumer behavior in the United States and the private rate of return on investment there. We should note here though that inferring people's social values from their behavior in a world where much of the biosphere is free to all is unjustifiable. In a world where population is large relative to the biosphere, we each have a private incentive to rush and convert the open-access natural capital into private goods (see Dasgupta, Mitra, and Sorger, 2018). Preferences that are revealed in that kind of marketplace tells us little about our social values.

are identical, we may also speak of "generation-t" and "a person of generation-t" interchangeably. That same reasoning tells us that we can simplify our notation without loss of generality by assuming that each generation consists of a single person. Imagine now that output consists of a steady stream of a completely perishable good, and that generation-0 has an investment opportunity in which a unit of consumption foregone yields a perpetual stream of r units of the consumption good from $t = 1$ onward. The rate of return on the investment, r, is positive.

To not discount future well-beings would imply that the present-value of returns is infinite. That's because the infinite sum, $r + r + \ldots$, is unbounded. We are to understand then that generation-0 incurs a finite loss for a unit of consumption sacrificed, but that the investment yields an infinite gain to future generations, no matter how small r happens to be. It is obvious the investment should be undertaken, which means consumption should be reduced by generation-0.

Now suppose a similar investment project is also available. The same reasoning says the new project should also be accepted, further reducing current consumption. And so on, until current consumption is reduced to near-zero. Thus *any* consumption sacrifice by generation-0 (short of 100 percent of available consumption) is good. Many would regard that to be an unacceptable burden on the present generation.

The reasoning goes further. Generation-0, having sacrificed nearly everything for future generations, is followed by generation-1. Imagine that it too is faced with a string of investment projects of the same kind. An identical reasoning would come into play for generation-1, who also would be required to consume at a near-zero level. And so on, down the generations. But that means every generation is required to live in penury for the sake of a future that's always just beyond. Koopmans (1965, 1967) likened this consequence of Total Utilitarian reasoning to a "never-ending potlatch," which of course cannot be an optimum policy. But that only shows that Total Utilitarianism is incoherent under the circumstance of the model: there *is* no optimum policy.[79]

---

79. The flavor of the argument remains if the horizon is long but finite. The present value of a T-period consumption flow, r, without time discounting, is Tr. If T is large, Total Utilitarianism demands an attenuated form of consumption postponement: An optimum exists, but the overwhelming bulk of consumption is to be enjoyed by the last few generations. In the limit, if $T \to \infty$, the never-ending potlatch emerges, and there is no optimum policy.

The argument extends to models with durable capital goods. There are classroom models in which an optimum saving policy under Total Utilitarianism with zero discounting exists but which requires each generation, even if the early generations are very poor, to save nearly 100 percent of GDP so as to accumulate wealth for the generations that are to follow (Dasgupta, 2005a, 2007b). That's not a never-ending potlatch (despite the high saving rate, consumption grows with time and the generations), but it comes pretty close to it.

The moral would seem to be this: In such complex exercises as those involving the use of resources in a world with a long time horizon, it is foolhardy to regard any value judgement as sacrosanct. One can never know in advance what it may run up against. A more judicious tactic than Sidgwick's and Ramsey's would be to play one set of ethical assumptions against another in not-implausible worlds, see what their implications are for the distribution of well-being across generations, and appeal to our varied ethical senses before arguing over policy. Koopmans (1965, 1967, 1977) promoted this reasoning process when formalizing the idea of optimum economic development. In contrast to Sidgwick (1907), he adopted a value-pluralist viewpoint. In his contractual theory of justice Rawls (1972) called the end point of such iterative processes a "reflective equilibrium." The iterative procedure for conducting normative reasoning is the one I follow in Part II.

There is another strand to Koopmans' reasoning, which provides a further argument in favor of generation-discounting.[80] If U_t denotes generation-t's well-being, then $\{U_0, U_1, \ldots, U_t, \ldots\}$ is an infinite well-being stream. We suppose U_t is uniquely measurable up to positive affine transformations for all t and that the generations' well-beings are fully comparable (see Sect. 5.3). The decision maker (DM) is generation-0. Her problem is to compare alternative well-being streams.

We imagine that the set of possible well-being streams, let us call it G, is bounded and endowed with a suitable distance measure (or metric, as mathematicians would call it). G is taken to be closed as well. The elements of G are thus (infinite) well-being streams. Moreover, and this is crucial to the formal analysis, we assume there are

---

80. The exposition follows Dasgupta and Heal (1979: ch. 9) and Dasgupta (2005b).

well-being streams in G that are bounded away from zero for all sufficiently large t's. Let V_0 denote social well-being as evaluated by DM.
In Ramsey's model, V_0 is the sum of every generation's well-being:
$U_0 + U_1 . . .+ U_t + ...$ Ethical comparisons of infinite well-being
streams in G in Ramsey's theory are derived from their sums, which,
when they exist, are real numbers. But infinite sums don't necessarily
exist. That is a problem Ramsey faced squarely when investigating the
optimum rate of saving for a nation, and he found an ingenious way
around it for his model. The second strand in Koopmans' reasoning
flips the way deliberations are conducted. The primitive concept there
is a complete ordering (henceforth, ordering) by DM of the elements
of G, it is not a social well-being function from which an ethical ordering of the elements of G is to be inferred by her. Her tactic is to impose
ethical conditions on orderings on G so as to determine, if possible,
the mathematical structure of her social well-being function V_0.[81]

We say an ordering of the elements of G is "continuous" if, in an
appropriate mathematical sense, well-being streams that don't differ
much are close to one another in the ordering. It follows from our
assumptions that the ordering has a best and worst element in G. We
say an ordering is "monotonic" if one stream of well-beings in G is
regarded as better than another, if no generation enjoys less well-being
along the former than along the latter, and if there is at least one
generation that enjoys greater well-being in the former than it does
in the latter.

Both assumptions are intuitively attractive. Lexicographic orderings
notwithstanding, I know of no convincing argument against continuity. Of course, Rawls (1972) placed priority rules and the lexicographic
orderings that come with them at the center of his theory of justice,
but that's proved to have been one of his most contentious moves.
The richness and depth of his analysis would not be lessened if small
tradeoffs were admitted between the objects of justice by the chooser
in Rawls' thought experiment (see Appendix 3). And it's hard to find
reasons against monotonicity. Even Rawls, whose work was so pointed
toward distributive justice, insisted on monotonicity.

---

81. Let V be a numerical function on X, which is to say the V-function
awards a numerical value to each element of X. We say V is a numerical
representation of the ordering R if, for all x, y in X, $V(x) \geq V(y)$ if and
only if xRy.

But it can be shown that orderings of G that satisfy continuity and monotonicity have generation-discounting built into them. When giving expression to V_0, DM awards a lower weight to U_t than she does to U_0. It seems the real numbers are not rich enough to accommodate the infinite well-being streams in G in a manner that respects continuity and monotonicity even while awarding the well-beings of all generations equal weights.[82]

So far we have been considering a deterministic world. In contrast, Yaari (1965), Mirrlees (1967), and Dasgupta (1969) interpreted the time/generation discount rate they introduced in their models to be associated with the risk of extinction. (Yaari, 1965, studied an individual's optimum saving policy over his lifetime. The extinction risk in Yaari's model is the risk of death.) We assume, as previously, that DM is a member (in our model, the sole member) of generation-0. We call the probability of extinction in period t conditional on the world surviving until t the hazard rate at t. From the hazard rates it is simple to compute the probability that the world will survive until t. Denote that probability by θ_t. Clearly, θ_t is a monotonically declining function of t. We assume that the probability that the world will suffer extinction at some date is 1. It follows that as t tends to infinity, θ_t tends to 0 at a rate that is so fast, that the sum $(\theta_0 U_0 + \theta_1 U_1 + \cdots + \theta_t U_t + \cdots)$ converges no matter which well-being stream is chosen from G. The latter sum is of course, expected well-being, which would appear to be the ethical object of interest in the above passage from Sidgwick (1907). We have therefore been able to bypass Koopmans' reasons for discounting time and the generations; and we have been able to do that because the risk of extinction implies that the "conditional well-being streams" $\{\theta_0 U_0, \ \theta_1 U_1, \ldots, \theta_t U_t, \ldots\}$ all converge fast enough to 0 for large enough t.

It could then be thought that we can ignore Koopmans' reasoning altogether. In fact we can't. The reason is that by assumption the risk of extinction is exogenous in our analysis, and there is no a priori reason why hazard rates are not negligibly small for a long while. If they *are* negligibly small, DM is obliged to recall the example of investment

---

82. The result is in Diamond (1965) and was attributed by the author to Menahem Yaari. It strengthened a theorem on positive time discounting in Koopmans (1960).

opportunities that commend protracted potlatches. In that example early generations would be asked by her to sacrifice enormously for the sake of later generations. Koopmans' analysis showed that insisting on equity in the way well-beings across the generations are entered into normative reckoning can lead to deeply non-egalitarian treatment of the generations. To forestall that possibility, DM would wish to introduce a (possibly small) positive discount rate on the well-beings of future generations. She would abandon the equity principle in the construction of V_0. This mode of reasoning is a departure from Koopmans' axiomatization of Total Utilitarianism; it instead invokes value-pluralism, where a multiplicity of value judgments is held by DM, and she juggles them in such ways as to yield prescriptions that she is able to defend before herself.

Sidgwick (1907) applied teleological reasoning to suggest, even if not explicitly, that social well-being should be read as "expected well-being." Dasgupta and Heal (1979: Ch. 9) showed that Sidgwick's conclusion can also be reached by a route that relies on modern decision theory (see also Dasgupta, 2005b). Adopting the classic thought experiment in Harsanyi (1955), the authors asked of DM to place herself in every generation's circumstances with equal probability. Equi-probability over an infinite horizon isn't a meaningful concept, but because of extinction risk, the horizon is only conditionally infinite in extent. In the example we are studying here, the weight DM would award to generation-t under the assumption of equi-probability is θ_t. If the criterion adopted by DM for ranking the elements of G is expected well-being, she arrives at Sidgwick's prescription, but by a decision-theoretic route.

I have digressed into discounting for time and generations because it could be thought that the practice can only be justified by an appeal to agent-centered prerogatives or the risk of extinction. The reasoning deployed by Tjalling Koopmans not only shows otherwise, but shows also that it is vital for intergenerational ethics. So we should keep the three notions separate.

9.2. Dynastic Well-Being

It pays to see how Koopmans' axiomatic approach to intergenerational ethics can be used to study dynastic saving, not only national saving. That will ease the way in Section 9.3 to Generation-Relative

Utilitarianism in Actual Problems, as opposed to the Genesis Problem, in population ethics.

Imagine now that the economy consists of N identical households. Assume that household numbers remain constant over time and that each household gives birth to only one child. Suppose parental well-being is a function of parents' own consumption and the well-being of their children. Then parental well-being can be expressed as $U(C,U)$, where the former U is the well-being of parents, C is the consumption enjoyed by parents, and the latter U is the well-being of their children. But parents know that their children's well-being will in turn depend on the consumption they enjoy and the well-being of their children, and so on down the generations. By recursion we have $U = U(C,U(C,U(\ldots))$. The formula says the well-being of informed parents includes the well-being of all their descendants.

Now suppose the economy faces no risk of extinction. Koopmans (1972) imposed a set of ethical conditions on the recursive form $U(C,U(C,U(\ldots))$ for parents of generation-0 and showed that it reduces to

$$U(C,U(C,U(\ldots)) = U_0 + U_1/(1+\delta)^{-1} + \ldots$$
$$+ U_t/(1+\delta)^{-t} + \ldots, \quad \delta > 0 \qquad (29)$$

The conditions required to obtain equation (29) include, as previously, continuity and monotonicity, but they also include "independence" (which says, very roughly, that the tradeoff rate between the personal well-beings of any pair of generations should be independent of the personal well-beings of all other generations) and "stationarity" (which says, roughly, that the ordering of two well-being streams that start to differ in a designated way only from some period t onward is independent both of what that t is, and of what the common well-beings in the two streams up to t are). Equation (29) is thus a precise form of Koopmans' finding that continuity and monotonicity of DM's social well-being function V_0 has discounting built into it. The equation says that dynastic well-being as perceived by parents is the discounted sum of theirs and their descendants' personal well-beings, and that the discount rate is a positive constant, δ. Define $\theta = 1/(1+\delta)$. θ is called the discount factor associated with the discount rate δ. Equation (29) can now be rewritten as

$$U(C,U(C,U(\ldots)) = U_0 + \theta^{-1}U_1 + \ldots$$
$$+ \theta^{-t}U_t + \ldots, \quad 0 < \theta < 1 \qquad (30)$$

The post-Koopmans literature on the axiomatics of time and generation discounting is huge. It would take us afield to discuss it here because the literature has in large measure been confined to Same Numbers Choices. We note though that the subject of discounting for time and the generations has not been confined to Utilitarian thinkers. Rawls in his contractual theory of justice spoke to intergenerational saving and to Sidgwick's arguments against discounting (Rawls, 1972: Ch. V, Sects. 44–45). An account of the ties that bind the generations in Rawls' work is presented in Appendix 3.

9.3. Overlapping Generations

We return to population ethics, or what Parfit (1984) referred to as Different Numbers Choices. In doing that we shall stay close to the model in Section 8. That will facilitate comparisons between the timeless economy there and an economy moving through time in a stationary mode. Because I am adopting Generation-Relative Utilitarianism and trying it on for size, I eschew generation-discounting merely on the grounds of futurity.

The horizon is taken to be "conditionally infinite," that is, there is a positive risk of extinction at t should the economy have survived until then.[83] People live for two periods. In their first period (childhood), they are maintained by their parents. At the beginning of their second period (adulthood), should humanity survive until then, they choose how many children to have and how to share the output they produce. The way I have phrased matters could suggest that the society we are studying is authoritarian and centralized. It isn't. Rather, we suppose as previously that people of the same generation are identical in all respects. That means adults in any period have the same ethical motivation. So, even though it is individuals who do the choosing, it is as though each generation chooses the size of the next generation. That means in each period t, should the world survive until then, DM can be thought of as representing the adults at t. Normative restrictions arising from agent-centered prerogatives translate here into generation-centered prerogatives.

By assumption people die at the end of their second period, which means there are two overlapping generations in any period. That isn't

---

83. Lind (1982) is an early collection of essays on discounting for time and risk.

good demography, but it turns out not to matter. To include realistic life cycles would not add to the substance of population ethics—it would only add to the notation. Let $N(t)$ be the number of adults at t, should the world have survived until then. I will call them "generation-t." We now conduct backward induction.

Denote the number of children born at t by $N(t+1)$. Total population is therefore $N(t) + N(t+1)$. Only adults work; children are pure consumers. But adults and children have the same well-being function, $U(C)$.[84] That means total output at t is $Q(t) = AF(K,N(t))$ and consumption per capita is $Q(t)/(N(t)+N(t+1))$. The transfer of output is therefore from the old to the young (Lee, 2000, 2007).

We will study the economy in a stationary mode. K can then be interpreted to be an aggregate measure of all capital assets other than labor. It includes not only natural capital, but also produced capital such as roads, buildings, and machines. Appendix 4 shows how to break away from assuming an aggregate measure of produced and natural capital; but because I want to stress the significance of the constraints Nature imposes on population axiology, I once again refer to K as the biosphere.

Because marginal U declines with C, the allocation rule in each period is simple: everyone gets to consume the average. In period $t+1$, assuming humanity survives, the $N(t+1)$ children of the previous generation are adults (they constitute generation-$(t+1)$); and if they give birth to $N(t+2)$ children, they produce $Q(t+1)$ and share $Q(t+1)$ equally. And so on.

The probability that humanity will suffer extinction at t conditional on having survived until then (i.e., the "hazard rate" at t) is a constant, $\delta > 0$. As noted in Section 9.1, δ functions like a "time discount rate." Define $\theta = 1/(1 + \delta)$. θ assumes the role of a "time discount factor." The random process defined by δ should be interpreted as governing the possibility of a global catastrophe, such as the impact of a massive meteorite. We assume that, other than humanity's survival, there is no future uncertainty. In Part II and in my Response to Commentaries on the Arrow Lecture, we consider catastrophic risks that are brought about by our own activities.[85]

---

84. To assume otherwise would be to add further notation.
85. Bostrom (2002) and Rees (2003) discuss the possible causes of such a global disaster.

That the hazard rate is constant is not believable. We are reliably informed that the Sun will be a hospitable star only for a finite length of time, which means the hazard rate we should work with remains small for a long while but will rise toward infinity as the Sun runs out of sufficient fuel to serve life's needs. It can be shown, though, that optimum policies for a considerable number of periods into the future are insensitive to whether the hazard rate is a small positive constant or whether it is a small positive constant for a long stretch of time but then rises sharply toward infinity. But that is another way of saying that to model the extinction process in terms of a small constant hazard rate is not misleading, at least not for a long stretch of time.[86]

Total Utilitarianism regards social well-being (that is, well-being across the generations) to be the expected sum of each person's well-being from the date of evaluation, say t, to infinity. Denote that by $V^U(t)$. As $N(t) + N(t+1)$ is the number of people alive at t and $U(C(t)) = U(Q(t)/(N(t) + N(t+1)))$ is the flow of well-being per person at t,

$$V^U(t) = {}_{u=t}\Sigma^\infty[(N(u) + N(u+1))U(C(u))]\theta^{(u-t)} \qquad (31)$$

$({}_{u=t}\Sigma^\infty$ denotes summation as u goes from t to infinity.) Equation (31) is the Total Utilitarian DM's conception of social well-being at t.

The uncanny similarity in discounting between equations (30) and (31) is inescapable. The discounting is identical in form, but its content is different. Koopmans' representation of θ is to be interpreted as the discount factor for time. I touched on this in Section 9.2. However, in contrast to Koopmans' work, I have eschewed discounting for time in equation (31) and have invoked discounting for the risk of extinction. The equation of course can't tell the difference between the two.

Among the many reasons Koopmans' work on the representation of social well-being functions is of huge significance is that it has taught us that the mathematical structure of Total Utilitarianism can be supported by more than one interpretation of its contents. With suitable adjustment of Koopmans' axioms on the V-function, we can even arrive at Generation-Relative Utilitarianism (eq. (32) below).

---

86. In his study of the optimum price of annuities, Yaari (1965) constructed a model of individuals facing the hazard of death in very much the way we are modeling the extinction process.

9.4. Generation-Relative Utilitarianism

To formalize Generation-Relative Utilitarianism, let $V(t)$ be the social valuation function of a representative member of generation-t (i.e., DM at t). In our model, there are no actual future people for her to consider because all future people are potential. Generation-centered prerogatives are the reason that each generation awards a lower weight to potential well-beings than to their own well-being. So we have

$$V(t) = N(t)U(C(t)) + \mu N(t+1)U(C(t)) + \mu\{_{u=t+1}\Sigma^{\infty}[\theta^{(u-t)}[(N(u) + N(u+1))U(C(u))]\}, 0 < \mu, \theta < 1; t = 0,1, \ldots \quad (32)$$

where $V(t)$ is generation-t's social valuation function. $V(t) = V^U(t)$ if $\mu = 1$.[87]

Agent-relative theories could appear to advance self-indulgence and, worse, callousness toward others. So it is useful to note that in equation (32) the representative member of generation-t advances personal projects that are especially meaningful to her by assigning a smaller weight to her potential descendants. To be sure, the smaller weight serves to raise her personal well-being, but it does so only by lowering the number of new births (that's confirmed below), not by discriminating against the interests of others. The backward-induction we have used to arrive at equation (32) formalizes the intention of the potential parent to allocate resources between herself and her children in such a way (complete equality there) that they too will be able to advance projects that are especially meaningful to them.

$V(t)$ guides the choices of generation-t, and does so for all $t \geq 0$. Our analysis starts at $t = 0$. Because the economy has a stationary structure, the generation at any t can reason that future generations will have a

---

87. Almost all formal models of economic growth and development assume that population size is exogenously given; that is, all future people are actual future people. They give rise to what Parfit (1984) called Same Numbers Choices. Generation-Relative Utilitarianism in a world with a mix of actual future people and potential people comes in two forms. In the Weak version, present people award the same weight to actual future people but a lower weight to potential people; in the Strong version, all future people, whether actual or potential, are awarded a lower weight.

motivation like their own. Generation-0 is $N(0)$ in number; it is a datum. If previous generations hadn't been moved by Generation-Relative Utilitarianism, $N(0)$ would not have been chosen with that motivation. No doubt generation-0 will want to ask what their ancestors' intentions had been; they may even feel obliged to choose so as not to be entirely at odds with them, but such considerations would be a distraction here. So I assume generation-0 regards the past as past and is entirely forward looking. I imagine also that all generations starting at $t = 0$ adhere to Generation-Relative Utilitarianism. In that case, the motivation embodied in the notion of expected well-being across the generations in equation (32) binds members of each generation to all their descendants.

9.5. Intergenerational Consistency

The preference reversal displayed in inequalities (26)–(28) translates here into inconsistent ethical values across the generations. The analysis that follows is informal. Beyond supposing that $N(0)$ is small relative to K (otherwise generation-0 will choose not to reproduce), I avoid technicalities.

Consider an arbitrary $t(t \geq 0)$. The size of generation-t will have been chosen by the previous generation. That means $N(t)$ will not be subject to choice at t. But generation-t chooses $N(t+1)$, which is the size of the generation that follows. And so on. Why doesn't generation-t choose the size of all subsequent generations? It has a conception of well-being across the generations, which is $V(t)$; so why not choose the size of all subsequent generations?

There are two reasons; one practical, the other ethical. The practical problem has to do with implementation. Generation-t has no viable means of enforcing its will on future generations. Moreover, later generations will have every incentive not to reproduce in accordance with generation-t's bidding. Because $\mu < 1$, their grounds of binding reason will differ from that of generation-t, and in turn from those of subsequent generations. That's intergenerational inconsistency.[88]

---

88. The rate at which generation-t would be willing to trade the potential well-being of generation-$(t+1)$ against the potential well-being of generation-$(t+2)$ differs from the tradeoff generation-$(t+1)$ would be willing to make between their own well-being and the potential well-being of generation-$(t+2)$.

Turning to the ethical reason, there is the deontological requirement that generation-t will have no right to enforce its will on future generations even if a method were found to enforce it. Taken together, the two considerations imply that each generation chooses the size of the generation that is to follow by reasoning progressively into the future. An optimum demographic profile would then be self-fulfilling. We now formalize the idea.

Consider generation-t. Its evaluation of well-being across the generations is $V(t)$. We start with generation-0. An ideal population profile under Generation-Relative Utilitarianism is a stream of reproductive choices $\{N^*(1), \ldots, N^*(t), N^*(t+1), \ldots\}$ such that, for all $t \geq 0$, $N^*(t+1)$ maximizes $V(t)$ on the supposition that all generations following t (should humanity survive until then) will choose in accordance with that profile.[89]

The common supposition has the status of an implicit understanding. Because each generation has an understanding of the choices its descendants will face conditional on humanity surviving, it can anticipate the choices they will make. Its own choice is based on a forecast of its descendants' choices. The exercise need not be exclusively forward looking. Each generation in a sequence of Generation-Relative Utilitarians may wish to look back at the choices its ancestors had made, if only to reassure itself of the implicit understanding and to confirm that its own choice is guided by it.[90] The birth profile $\{N^*(1), \ldots, N^*(t+1), \ldots\}$ is intergenerationally consistent, even though the ethical motivations of the generations are not consistent with one another. Formally, the birth profile $\{N^*(1), \ldots, N^*(t+1), \ldots\}$ is a Nash equilibrium across the generations.

9.6. The Stationary Optimum

Characterizing the implicit understanding for arbitrary values of $N(0)$ is hard work. So it pays to study population and consumption profiles that are stationary. It is reasonable to conjecture that if the U-function is the one in equation (5), the stationary profile (we confirm presently that it is unique) is dynamically stable, meaning that the optimum population profile from any $N(0)$ near the stationary value converges

---

89. The corresponding consumption profile, $\{C^*(1), \ldots, C^*(t), \ldots\}$ is implied by the condition that at each t, $C^*(t) = AF(K, N^*(t))/(N^*(t) + N^*(t+1)))$.
90. I return to this point in Appendix 3 when exploring Rawls' principle of just saving.

to it. Very rough calculations suggest that the conjecture is correct, but I haven't been able to nail it down. But dynamic stability of non-stationary profiles is the reason we should be interested in the stationary profile. In a stationary profile, the generations replicate their numbers, conditional on the world surviving, of course. Let N^* be that number.

The idea underlying the profile $\{N^*, N^*, \ldots\}$ can be expressed in the following way: If $N(0)$ just happens to equal N^*, then N^* would be the reproductive choice of generation-t for all t if it were to suppose that all subsequent generations will in turn choose N^*. It follows that N^* is a self-enforcing reproductive policy for every generation. The understanding that implements the policy is only implicit; but because N^* is a self-enforcing choice for each generation, there is no call for a constitutional directive. We now study the condition that the profile $\{N^*, N^*, \ldots\}$ must necessarily satisfy.

In each period there are N^* adults and N^* children, making a total population of $2N^*$. Only adults work. So output $Q = Q^* = AF(K, N^*)$. (The dependency ratio—i.e., the ratio of dependents to the working population—is 1 in our model. Globally the figure is about 1.6 today.) As both adults and children consume the same amount, each person will enjoy $Q^*/2N^* = AF(K, N^*)/2N^*$ units of consumption. Write that as C^*.

Return once again to the laboratory we have been using, consisting of equations (4) and (5). It is simple to confirm that the optimum stationary profile satisfies

$$C^*/C^S = (N_S/N^*)^{(1-\rho)} = (1 + \sigma P)^{1/\sigma},$$
$$P = (1 + \mu + 2\mu\theta(1 - 2\rho))/2\mu(1 + \theta) \tag{33}$$

Equation (33) is the counterpart of the Sidgwick–Meade Rule in the stationary state commended by Generation-Relative Utilitariansim. In Part II, we study the sensitivity of the optimum values of consumption and population to the various parameters in equation (33), ethical presumptions (C^S), and the productivity of capital, $AK^{(1-\rho)}$.[91]

---

91. To obtain equation (33), note that generation-t has direct control over $N(t+1)$, and nothing else. However, $N(t+1)$ appears only in the first four terms of the infinite series in equation (32). Differentiate those four terms partially with respect to $N(t+1)$ and set the sum of the partial derivatives equal to zero. Now set $N(t) = N(t+1) = N(t+2)$. Because this operation is to be conducted recursively by all generations, we obtain the common value, say, N^*; but $C^* = AK^{1-\rho}N^{*(\rho-1)}/2$. Equation (33) follows.

9.7. Extreme Theories

Total Utilitarianism represents one extreme set of values. The theory says $\mu = 1$. At the other extreme is a theory that is easy to describe but is also questionable. It says $\mu = 0$. That viewpoint was explored by Enke (1966) in his study of social cost-benefit analysis of family planning programs in poor countries. Enke sought ways to measure the economic value of prevented births, and he took the measure to be the discounted sum of the differences between an additional person's consumption and output over his lifetime. Children in Enke's theory have value only if they pay their way.

Enke's is an extreme point of view, as is Total Utilitarianism. Generation-Relative Utilitarianism lies between two extremes and reflects the strength of each without giving in to the weaknesses of either. It prescribes neither a large population nor a small population. Instead, it offers a wide space in between, within which more detailed ethical considerations can be embedded. We should not expect an ethical theory to do more.

Part II

Applications

10. The Biosphere as a Renewable Natural Resource

Equation (33) gives the ratio of Earth's (human) carrying capacity to the optimum population size, but it doesn't say what the carrying capacity is. No doubt "carrying capacity" is a range of values, not a precise figure; but it helps to use formal, deterministic models so as to think of it as a specific number. Once we have done that, we can loosen the model to construct a range around the figure.[92] To obtain

---

As an exercise, suppose we apply Classical Utilitarianism to equation (33). With $\mu = 1$, $\rho = 0.5$, $\sigma = 1$, and θ very slightly below 1, $C^*/C^S = 1.5$. As another exercise, let $\mu = 1$, θ very slightly below 1, and $\rho = 0$. The latter implies there is no production, that manna can be consumed directly. In that case, equation (33) and equation (9) become identical.

92. I am using Earth and the biosphere interchangeably.

estimates, I first collate salient findings on the current state of the bio-sphere. I then use estimates of our aggregate demand for goods and services from the biosphere relative to its ability to supply them on a sustainable basis. The procedure won't allow us to nail down Earth's human carrying capacity, even as a range, but it's about as close we can get to it with the information I have been able to obtain.[93]

10.1. Open-Access Resources

Mutually adverse environmental externalities are of an acute form when, as is the case with much of the biosphere, Nature is an open-access resource; meaning that it is free to all to do as we like with it. Gordon (1954: 135) famously wrote that a resource that is every-body's property is nobody's property. Using the example of fisheries, he showed that the scramble to extract open-access resources dissi-pates all potential rents from them, and he used the dissipation of rents to explain why fishermen working on open waters are usually poor. Hardin (1968) even more famously called the rent dissipation associ-ated with open-access resources "the tragedy of the commons."

Gordon's and Hardin's analyses were limited to timeless worlds. A complete analysis of the problem of the commons in an economy moving through time, including a proof that population size is a factor influencing whether open-access resources *do* give rise to the tragedy of the commons, has recently been offered by Dasgupta, Mitra, and Sorger (2018). Population was taken to be exogenously given. In a canonical setting, the authors showed that open-access resources suf-fer from the tragedy of the commons only when human population is large, other things equal. Property rights to resources don't matter in a thinly populated world; they matter only when population is large relative to the size of the resource base. The finding is used in Section 12 to read the experiences of some past societies.

To the best of my knowledge, we do not yet have a theoreti-cal account of reproductive behavior in an intertemporal economy containing open-access resources. In Appendix 2, I use the timeless model in Section 8 to confirm that open access to natural capital offers

---

93. Cohen (1995a, 1995b) reports methods that have been deployed to esti-mate the biosphere's human-carrying capacity. The range he arrived at was wide, but Cohen didn't have at his disposal the ominous environmen-tal signatures that have been uncovered in recent years.

incentives to households to have too many children. In such a property-rights regime, households of greater size are permitted to access a larger fraction of the resource base. They respond by converting the commons excessively into private assets—in our model, household size. The analysis is more restrictive than I would ideally like it to be. Being timeless, the model takes Nature to be a fixed factor in production. The biosphere is of course nothing like that.

10.2. Ecosystem Services

The term "biosphere" is an all-encompassing construct. We may think of it as a mosaic of renewable natural resources, not a fixed factor in production. There is more to the biosphere than that (technically, it's the part of Earth occupied by living organisms), but it is a useful reduction for our purposes. Agricultural land, forests, watersheds, fisheries, fresh water sources, estuaries, wetlands, the oceans, and the atmosphere are interlocking constituents of the biosphere. I shall refer to them generically as "ecosystems" and, so as to draw attention to populations of species in their habitats, I shall speak of them also, more narrowly, as "biological communities."[94]

Ecosystems combine the abiotic environment with biological communities (plants, animals, fungi, and microorganisms) that form functional units. Individual actors in ecosystems include organisms that pollinate, decompose, filter, transport, re-distribute, scavenge, fix gases, and so on. Nearly all organisms that help produce those services are hidden from view (a gram of soil may contain as many as 10 billion bacterial cells), which is why they are almost always missing from popular discourses on the environment. But their activities enable ecosystems to maintain a genetic library, preserve and regenerate soil, fix nitrogen and carbon, recycle nutrients, control floods, mitigate droughts, filter pollutants, assimilate waste, pollinate crops, operate the hydrological cycle, and maintain the gaseous composition of the atmosphere.[95]

---

94. Tilman (1982) remains an excellent introduction to the processes by which competition among organisms for resources gives rise to the structure of biological communities.
95. Daily (1997) is an early publication of the role ecosystem services play in our lives. Cardinale et al. (2012) report more recent findings. Perrings (2014) is a treatise-length account of the economic value of biodiversity.

In a ground-breaking set of publications assessing the state of the world's ecosystems, the Millennium Ecosystem Assessment (MEA, 2005a–2005d) constructed a four-way classification of goods and services we enjoy from them: (i) provisioning services (e.g., food, fiber, fuel, fresh water), (ii) regulating services (e.g., protection against natural hazards such as storms, the climate system), (iii) supporting services (e.g., nutrient cycling, soil production), and (iv) cultural services (e.g., recreation, cultural landscapes, aesthetic or spiritual experiences). Cultural services and a variety of regulating services (such as disease regulation) contribute directly to human well-being, whereas others (such as soil production) contribute indirectly (e.g., by providing the means of growing food crops).

Ecosystems differ in composition and extent. They can be defined as ranging from the communities and interactions of organisms in your mouth to those in the canopy of a rain forest to all those in Earth's oceans. The processes governing them differ in speed. There are systems that turn over in minutes, and there are others whose rhythmic time extends to hundreds of years. Some ecosystems are extensive ("biomes," such as the African savannah), there are those that cover regions (river basins), many involve clusters of villages (micro-watersheds), while others are confined to the level of a single village (the village pond). In each example, there is an element of indivisibility. Divide an ecosystem into parts by creating barriers, and the sum of the productivity of the parts will typically be found to be lower than the productivity of the whole, other things equal (Loreau et al., 2001; Worm et al., 2006; Sodhi, Brook, and Bradshaw, 2009). Mobility of biological populations is a reason (Sect. 4.2). Safe corridors, for example, enable migratory species to survive.

Ecosystems can regenerate, but they suffer deterioration (worse, exhaustion) when human expropriation exceeds the rates at which they are able to supply us with goods and services or when they are converted directly into produced capital; this is why they can be thought of as renewable natural resources. Population extinctions disrupt essential ecosystem services. In tropical forests, for example, dung beetles play an essential role in recycling nutrients. Excessive hunting of mammals in the forests has been found to be a cause of local elimination of dung-dependent beetles (Brook, Sodhi, and Bradshaw, 2008). When subject to excessive stress, once flourishing ecosystems (e.g., biologically rich estuaries) flip into unproductive states (dead zones). The stress could be occasioned by an invasion of a foreign species or substance (as in the above example), it could be due to a loss of population diversity (see below), it could be triggered by the demise of a dominant species (see below), and so on. Ehrlich and Ehrlich (1981) likened the pathways by which an ecosystem can be tipped out of a stable regime into an unproductive state to a flying aircraft from which rivets are removed, one at a time. The probability that it will crash increases very slowly at first, but then at some unspecifiable number of rivets the probability rises sharply to 1. Rockstrom et al. (2009) and Steffen et al. (2017) have reviewed what is currently understood about the biosphere's limits and its potential tipping points into unchartered attractors. In Appendix 4, we construct a simple model to illustrate the dynamics of renewable natural resources with tipping points.

Broadly speaking, an ecosystem's productivity (i.e., the flow of goods and services they offer us and their ability to withstand shocks) increases with the diversity of the functional characteristics of its species populations; a mere headcount of species can mislead.[96] Mutual dependence among the species is a reason. For example, many trees produce large, lipid-rich fruits that are adapted for animal dispersal, which means the demise of fruit-eating birds can have serious consequences for forest regeneration. Relatedly, in a study in Costa Rica, Ricketts et al. (2004) found that coffee yield declined with distance from the forest edge because forest bees aid pollination. The authors reported that the bees increased coffee yield by 20 percent in fields within 1 km of the forest edge. Looking elsewhere, about one-third of the human diet in tropical countries is derived from insect-pollinated plants. But that means a decline in forest-dwelling insects has an adverse effect on human nutrition. And so on.

In food webs, the relationships are unidirectional. Primary producers in the oceans (e.g., phytoplanktons, sea weeds) are at the bottom of the food chain, while species at higher trophic levels consume those that are below. Species whose impact on a community structure is large and disproportionately large relative to their abundance are called "keystone" species (Power et al., 1996). They are usually at the top end of the food chain. When human consumption reduces their populations

---

96. Hooper et al. (2005) is a review of the issues. A classic on the subject is Tilman and Downing (1994). See also Tilman (1997), Hector et al. (1999), and Walker, Kinzig, and Langridge (1999).

sizably, the community flips to a different state, as prey populations explode. That reduces diversity of functional characteristics.

Biological communities can influence their abiotic environment. The Amazon, for example, generates about half of its own rainfall by recycling moisture five or six times as air masses move from the Atlantic Ocean across the basin to the west. Mathematicians call this a positive feedback. Deforestation of the Amazon would be expected to reduce rainfall and to lengthen the dry season in the region. One estimate says that 20–25 percent deforestation of the Amazon can be expected to flip the forests in the east to savanna vegetation (Lovejoy and Nobre, 2018). Palm oil trees are planted increasingly in the Amazon so as to provide substitutes for fossil fuels, only to contribute to a sharp decline in the ability of the Amazon forest to absorb carbon dioxide from the atmosphere. The irony will not escape readers. Simultaneously, rising carbon concentration in the atmosphere is altering the composition of species in the Amazon forest (big canopy trees now enjoy increasing competitive advantage over small trees; Laurance et al., 2004).

The view that the biosphere is a mosaic of renewable natural resources also covers its role as a sink for pollution. As noted in Section 3.1, pollutants are the reverse of natural resources. One way to conceptualize pollution is to view it as the depreciation of capital assets. "Resources" are "goods," while "pollutants" (the degrader of resources) are "bads." Polluting is the reverse of conserving.

In Part I, it was assumed that the biosphere (K) remains unchanged. That enabled us to model the global economy in a stationary mode, but it misleads us when we move to study imperfect dynamic economies. Ecosystems decline in quality or quantity (or both) if our demand for their goods and services and the rate at which they are transformed directly into produced capital (e.g., roads and buildings) exceed the rate at which they are able to provide a sustainable supply of those goods (e.g., water purification by wetlands). By the same token, restoration and conservation measures (e.g., creating protected areas for marine fisheries) help increase the biosphere's productivity as measured by quality or quantity (or both).

10.3. Erosion of Natural Capital

Humanity's success in the Modern Era (post-1500 CE) in raising the standard of living has in great measure involved mining and degrading the biosphere. Habitat destruction caused by rising demand for Nature's products are the proximate causes of the decline in the biosphere's ability to supply our needs on a sustainable basis. The conversion of land for the production of food, livestock, and plantation crops is a prime cause of that decline. Conversion of land into produced capital (e.g., buildings, roads) is another cause.[97]

Erosion of natural capital usually goes unrecorded in official economic statistics because GDP does not record depreciation of capital assets. Destroy an open woodland to build a shopping mall, and the national accounts will record the increase in produced capital (i.e., the shopping mall is an investment), but not the disinvestment in natural capital. The example is a commonplace. Even while industrial output increased by a multiple of 40 during the 20th century, the use of energy increased by a multiple of 16, methane-producing cattle population grew in pace with human population, fish catch increased by a multiple of 35, and carbon and sulfur dioxide emissions rose more than ten-fold. It has been estimated that 25–30 percent of the 130 billion metric tons of carbon that are harnessed annually by terrestrial photosynthesis is appropriated for human use (Haberl et al., 2007). Although the rise in the concentration of atmospheric carbon receives much the greater public attention, MEA (2005a–2005d) reported that 15 of the 24 ecosystems the authors had reviewed world-wide were either degraded or are being exploited at unsustainable rates.

Current extinction rates of species in various orders have been estimated to be 10–1,000 times higher than their average rate (about 1 per million species per year) over the past several million years (Sodhi, Brook, and Bradshaw, 2009; Pimm et al. 2014; Ceballos, Ehrlich, and Ehrlich, 2015). The figures are reached from field studies of the decline in numbers of specific groups of mammals, insects, and birds, and from empirically drawn relationships between the number of species in an area and the size of the area. But the relationships are known to vary substantially among communities and habitats, which is why, as the range shows, there are great uncertainties in the estimates. Despite the uncertainties, the figures put the scale of humanity's presence on the Earth system in perspective (Ehrlich and Ehrlich, 2008)

---

97. For an analytical framework that maps the processes by which habitat destruction leads to species extinction, see Tilman and Lehman (1997).

and explain why our current times have been recognized as the start of a new epoch, the Anthropocene.[98]

The statistics I have just summarized for sketching humanity's recent doings differs sharply from the one that has been on offer in a string of recent books, in which intellectuals have re-drawn our attention to the remarkable gains in the standard of living humanity has enjoyed over the past century (Micklethwait and Wooldridge, 2000; Ridley, 2010; Lomborg, 2014; Norberg, 2016; Pinker, 2018). The authors have collated data on growth in scientific knowledge and the accumulation of produced capital and human capital and argued that humanity has never had it so good. But with the exception of rising carbon concentration in the atmosphere, trends in the state of the biosphere accompanying those advances have gone unnoted by the authors. The problem is, global climate change is but one of myriad environmental problems we face today. And because it is amenable to technological solutions (e.g., innovating with cheap non-carbon sources of energy and, more speculatively, firing sulfur particulates into the stratosphere to reflect sunlight back to space; Pinker, 2018), it is not representative. Global climate change attracts attention among intellectuals and the reading public not only because it is a grave problem, but also because it is possible to imagine meeting it by using the familiar economics of commodity taxation, regulation, and resource pricing without having to forego growth in living standards in rich countries. The literature on the economics of climate change (e.g., Stern, 2006; Lomborg, 2014) has even encouraged the thought that, with but little investment in clean energy sources, we can enjoy indefinitely an annual growth rate in global per capita GDP of, say, 1.3 percent.

And that's a thought to be resisted. Our economic possibilities are circumscribed, even if several steps removed via technological progress,

---

98. The term "Anthropocene" was popularized by Crutzen and Stoermer (2000) to mark a new epoch that began with the Industrial Revolution some 250 years ago. Wilson (1992) is a classic on the value of biodiversity. Colbert (2013) is an outstandingly readable account of how stratigraphers uncover geological signatures of abundance and disappearance of species in the distant past. Dasgupta, Raven, and McIvor (2019) is a collection of essays, presented at a joint meeting of the Pontifical Academies of Science and Social Sciences, on contemporary biological extinctions, ranging from mammals and birds to microorganisms in the soil.

by the workings of the Earth system. We should ask whether, at the living standards we are today encouraged to seek, the biosphere could support a global population somewhere in the range of 9.6 to 13.2 billion, which is the error bar around the population projection of 11.2 billion for year 2100 by the United Nations' Population Division (see Fig. 2 in "Socially Embedded Preferences, Environmental Externalities, and Reproductive Rights"). In effect we are being asked to imagine that such population numbers as these can enjoy high living standards even while making smaller demands on the biosphere than we make currently. I know of no study on the economics of technological change that has explored that question, let alone the question of what lifestyles that would involve. As of now, we should be circumspect that the scenario is plausible, because at least as grave a danger facing humanity as global climate change is the unprecedented rate of biological extinctions now taking place.

Climate change contributes to the extinction process, but it is only one among several major factors that are contributing to it. Other factors include the deforestation and habitat destruction that accompany agricultural extension and intensification and our growing need for timber, and the direct transformation of natural capital into produced capital (e.g., roads, dams, ports). There are now a number of studies (e.g., Laurance, Sayer, and Cassman, 2013) that have offered estimates of the additional agricultural land that will be required for the projected global population of 11.2 billion in year 2100. Continued biological extinctions will damage the biosphere irreparably, involving unknown numbers of tipping points, which tells us that potential cascades of tipping points cannot be staved off by mere technological fixes. Politics has intervened to prevent even the relatively small global investment that economic experts only a few years ago suggested was required to contain climate change. So we should expect the problem of biological extinctions to remain off the table, at least until citizens take the matter seriously.[99]

---

99. The really hard problem in the political economy of global climate change involves using the latter's special features to frame the way we should explore the prospects for international agreements. Barrett (2003, 2012, 2013) and Barrett and Dannenberg (2012, 2014) are analytical and empirical studies on this.

10.4. Global Ecological Footprint

Studying biogeochemical signatures of the past 11,000 years, Waters et al. (2016) tracked the human-induced evolution of soil nitrogen and phosphorus inventories in sediments and ice. The authors reported that the now-famous figure of the hockey stick that characterizes time series of carbon concentration in the atmosphere are also displayed by time series of a broad class of global geochemical signatures. They display a flat trend over millennia until some 250 years ago, when they begin a slow increase that continues until the middle of the 20th century, when they show a sharp and continuing rise. Waters et al. (2016) proposed that mid-20th century should be regarded as the time we entered the Anthropocene.[100]

Their reading is consistent with macroeconomic statistics. World population in 1950 was about 2.5 billion and global output of final goods and services a bit over 8.7 trillion international dollars (at 2011 prices). The average person in the world was poor (annual income was somewhat in excess of 3,500 international dollars). Since then, the world has prospered beyond recognition. Life expectancy at birth in 1950 was 45; today it is a little over 70. Population has grown to over 7.5 billion, and world output of final goods and services is (at 2011 prices) above 110 trillion international dollars, meaning that world income per capita is now more than 15,000 international dollars. A somewhat more than twelve-fold increase in global output in a 70-year period helps explain not only the stresses to the Earth system that we have just reviewed, but it also hints at the possibility that humanity's demand for the biosphere's services has for several decades exceeded sustainable levels.[101]

In a review of the state of the biosphere, the World Wildlife Fund (2008) reported that although the global demand for ecological services in the 1960s was less than the biosphere's ability to supply them on a sustainable basis, it exceeded supply in the early years of the present century by 50 percent. The figure is based on the idea of

---

100. The Anthropocene Working Group has proposed that the immediate post-war years should be regarded as the start of the Anthropocene. See Vosen (2016).

101. This is a more accurate estimate of growth in world income over the period 1950–2015 than the one in Dasgupta and Dasgupta (2017). It has been taken from Barrett et al. (2018).

"global ecological footprint," which is the surface area of biologically productive land and sea needed to supply the resources we consume (i.e., food, fibers, wood, water) and to assimilate the waste we produce (i.e., materials, gases). The overshoot in our ecological footprint thus includes the overshoot in our carbon emissions into the atmosphere. The Global Footprint Network (GFN) updates its estimates of the global ecological footprint on a regular basis. A footprint in excess of 1 means demand for ecological services exceeds their supply. By GFN's reckoning, maintaining the world's average living standard at the level reached some ten years ago (roughly 12,000 international dollars) would have required 1.5 Earths.[102]

These are *really* crude estimates, and I feel nervous using them. Figures for such socio-economic indicators as GDP, population size, life expectancy, and adult literacy are reached by a multitude of national and global institutions, who exchange information and coordinate their work. They are practiced regularly and governments and international agencies use them routinely when advocating and devising policy. We all take note of their figures and trust them. In contrast, I am obliged here to rely on the estimates of a solitary research group (GFN), albeit one with a network of collaborators. Most people will look askance at their estimates. What matters though is not the exact figure but whether the footprint exceeds 1. On that there should be little question. That there is an overshoot in global demand for the biosphere's goods and services is entirely consistent with a wide range of evidence on the state of the biosphere, some of which I have reviewed here. Because the estimates from GFN are the only ones on offer, I make use of them. Readers who are even more nervous than me when using such crude figures should recompute the estimates I report in Section 11.2 by supposing that the global ecological footprint (GEF) is 1. But that's as low a figure as is believable, because we can be confident that GEF is not less than 1.

GFN's most recent estimate of the global ecological footprint is 1.6. Sustainable development would require that the footprint must on average equal 1 over time. Global demand for ecological services can exceed supply for a period, but not indefinitely (Appendix 4). Economic

---

102. For pioneering work on the idea of ecological footprint, see Rees and Wackernagel (1994) and Rees (2006). See also Kitzes et al. (2008). Wackernagel, who founded the Global Footprint Network (www.footprint network.org/public), was a lead author of World Wildlife Fund (2008).

development during the past 70 years has raised the average living standard beyond recognition even while the population has increased by an unprecedented amount; but we have enjoyed that success by leaving a substantially diminished biosphere for future generations. It would appear we are living at once in the best of times and the worst of times.

11. Estimates of Globally Optimum Population

Equation (33) expresses C^*/C^S and N^S/N^* in terms of four parameters: μ, θ, ρ, and σ. To appreciate what the numerical exercise on Generation-Relative Utilitarianism didn't display in Section 9, it helps to de-couple the equation and express it as

$$C^* = C^S(1 + \sigma P)^{1/\sigma} \qquad (34a)$$

$$N^S = N^*(1 + \sigma P)^{1/\sigma(1-\rho)} \qquad (34b)$$

$$P = (1 + \mu + 2\mu\theta(1 - 2\rho))/2\mu(1 + \theta) \qquad (35)$$

In our model, people live for two periods, but no mention has been made of the number of years that add up to make a period. I need to do that now because we will be applying annual global data to the model and because people live for more than two years. So suppose each period is of T years. That means people live for $2T$ years, the first T years as children (non-workers) and the latter T years as adults (workers). People reproduce the moment they enter adulthood.

We now imagine that equation (32) is the social valuation function of the member of a dynasty (Sect. 9.4). Some dynasties have an identical age structure, while others have a different age structure. For reasons that will become clear presently, suppose there are T sets of dynasties, with the property that those in any given set have the same age structure, but that dynasties not in the same set differ in their age structure. For example, in any calender year, τ, there would be a set of dynasties in which the adults are all $T + 3$ years old and the young are all 3 years old. And so on. That means dynasties in adjacent sets have age structures that are a year apart. There will be an adjacent set in which adults in every dynasty is $T + 4$ years old and the young are 4 years old. And so forth.

The sets are identical in size, say M. That will be shown presently to be a requirement of stationary models. M is determined within the model. If an economy governed by Generation-Relative Utilitarianism is in a stationary mode, we would have $M = M^*$, where $M^*T = N^*$. Similarly, if the economy's population is the biosphere's human carrying capacity, $2N^S$, the number of dynasties in each set would be M^S, where $M^S T = N^S$. Equations (34a and 34b) can now be used to solve for M^S and M^* in terms of N^S and N^*, respectively.

Equations (34a and 34b)–(35) represent the stationary state commended by Generation-Relative Utilitarianism in what may be called a "reduced form." They do not display the demographic structure of the population, but they are sufficient for us to determine optimum population and the optimum living standard. We now apply annual global data to estimate, very crudely, the optimum stationary state.

11.1. Earth's Human Carrying Capacity

Equation (35) says μ, θ, and ρ determine P, while equation (34a) says P, σ, and C^S (well-being subsistence) determine the optimum living standard C^*. There is no need to consult environmental scientists if we want to estimate C^*.

But when it comes to estimating N^*, even moral philosophers need environmental scientists. The reason is equation (34b), which says P, σ, and ρ determine N^*/N^S. The problem is, the equation doesn't yield N^*. To determine N^*, we need an estimate of N^S, and to obtain that we need data on the biosphere's productivity and its regenerative capabilities. The analysis in Appendix 4 tells us that the biosphere can support a range of human population numbers on a sustainable basis depending on the standard of living we want to enjoy. Well-being subsistence is a minimum living standard we should want to consider. That is why in Section 5 we defined the human carrying capacity as the largest population the biosphere can support on a sustained basis at well-being subsistence. But without consulting the environmental sciences, we can't tell what that population number is. And without that we wouldn't be able to tell what N^* is.

As of now we have little quantitative knowledge of the biosphere's dynamics. But we do know that expanding our stock of produced capital is likely to have environmental consequences. So, with both hands proverbially tied behind my back, I regard K to be an aggregate measure of the biosphere and produced capital. Next, I stop both A and K in their tracks and estimate $AK^{(1-\rho)}$ (eq. (4)) on the basis of figures for the global ecological footprint, the current size of the world economy, and our model of global production (eq. (4)). The estimate of $AK^{(1-\rho)}$ includes the social value not only of the biosphere, but also of produced capital, social institutions, and public knowledge. In short, I use equation (4) to estimate the social worth of all capital assets with the exception of labor. That enables me to estimate N^S. I realize that's applying an intellectual sledgehammer to a delicate problem (even if humanity were to disappear from the face of the earth, the biosphere's dynamics would be shaped by the human imprint of the past), but I have found no other way to get at N^S.[103]

The data being utterly crude, I confine myself to pen-on-paper computations. I assume that the value of the world's production of final good and services draws proportionately on ecosystem services at all levels.[104] World output is currently about 110 trillion international dollars. Using the model of production in equation (4), we therefore have

$$AK^{1-\rho} N^\rho = 110 \text{ trillion (international) dollars} \qquad (36)$$

World population today is approximately 7.6 billion. So as to remain in step with our demographic model, I assume that half our numbers are engaged in production. We continue to assume $\rho = 0.5$. And for simplicity we interpret the factor $AK^{1-\rho}$ in equation (4) as an aggregate measure of all assets other than labor.

Write $AK^{1-\rho}$ as $\mathbf{K}$. Equation (36) then says

$$\mathbf{K} = 110 \times 10^{12}/(3.8 \times 10^9)^{0.5} \text{ dollars per producer}^{0.5}$$

$$\approx 1.8 \text{ billion dollars per producer}^{0.5} \qquad (37)$$

---

103. That I am creating a short-cut to what should be a dynamic optimization exercise and not inventing an ad hoc method of analysis is shown in Appendix 4. Stopping the biosphere on its track amounts to imposing a global quota on its use (see Wilson, 2016).

104. This would be a crude assumption in non-stationary states because it ignores differences among economic sectors in the value labor adds in production. For assumptions other than proportionality, see Part II of "Socially Embedded Preferences, Environmental Externalities, and Reproductive Rights" (Dasgupta and Dasgupta, 2017).

To err on the conservative side of GFN's most recent estimate, I take the current global ecological footprint to be 1.5. This means that, if the biosphere and all other forms of capital assets barring labor were to be stopped in their tracks, their sustainable value would be $K/1.5$, which I denote by K^*. Using equation (37),

$$K^* = 1.2 \text{ billion dollars per producer}^{0.5} \qquad (38)$$

We have now calibrated the model. Because there are two generations in each period, optimum population is $2N^*$ and human carrying capacity is $2N^S$. So we have all the information we need to estimate $2N^*$.[105]

11.2. Parameter Values

The sticking points in determining C^* and $2N^*$ will almost certainly be C^S, μ, and the aggregate of capital assets, K^*. Our understanding of K^* at the global level is woefully inadequate, and equation (38) only offers a first cut into it.

C^S and μ involve value judgments in pristine form. Moreover, cultural norms enter both (Sect. 5.7). It would be possible in principle to

---

105. In "Socially Embedded Preferences, Environmental Externalities, and Reproductive Rights," Aisha Dasgupta and I took a different route for estimating the optimum global population number. We sought the number that could, under present technologies and institutions, be sustained at a living standard of 20,000 international dollars. We also assumed that the biosphere is a durable consumption good. Denoting the biosphere in that model by K_1 and the global population by $2N$, it meant $K_1 = 2NC = 73 \times 10^{12}$ international dollars. So, $2N = 73 \times 10^{12}/20 \times 10^3 \approx 3.6$ billion. Because the biosphere was assumed to be a pure consumption good in our essay, K_1 (which is expressed in dollars) has a different dimension from K^* (the latter is expressed in dollars per producer$^{0.5}$). If we now apply the numbers to the present model ($\rho = 0.5$) for estimating the global population that could be sustained at a living standard of 20,000 international dollars, we obtain $K^* N^{0.5}/2N = 20,000$ international dollars, which on using equation (32) yields a population size of $2N = 1.8$ billion. That was the global population circa 1925. For further discussion on how many people Earth can support in comfort, see Dasgupta and Dasgupta (2019).

obtain an intuitive feel for μ from the reproductive stopping rules that couples have been known to follow (e.g., "We intend to have only one child so that we can give our baby a good start in life."), but the sad truth is that population ethics has been so comprehensively neglected in the social sciences that we have developed no informed intuition about either C^S or μ. Economists and decision theorists have identified reasons for recommending that σ should be in the range $(0,1]$, and they have devised techniques for estimating income inequality, social discount rates, the cost of carbon in the atmosphere, and for identifying absolute and relative poverty lines; but on ethical parameters that are crucial to population ethics, we have developed little intuition.[106]

Notice that P (eq. (35)) is a decreasing function of μ. That means C^*/C^S $(= (N^S/N^*)^{1-\rho})$ increases as μ is reduced. To get a quantitative feel for C^*, I work with alternative values of C^S and μ.

Recall $\acute{C}$, which is the consumption level at which marginal well-being equals average well-being per unit of consumption (Fig. 5). Under Total Utilitarianism, $\acute{C}/C^S$ is the upper bound of the ratio of optimum consumption to well-being subsistence. It is the natural reference point for judging quantitative differences between the directives of Total Utilitarianism and Generation-Relative Utilitarianism.

11.3. Sensitivity Analysis

Studying the sensitivity of C^* to various parameters in equation (33) is about the best we can do today. But sensitivity analysis alone is not helpful. It informs but doesn't tell us how to proceed from there. One thought is to iterate: (i) start with an arbitrary pair of figures for C^S and P and derive C^* and $2N^*$; (ii) revise the figures and estimate the corresponding C^* and $2N^*$; and (iii) continue doing so until the evaluator (e.g., DM) reaches what Rawls would call a "reflective equilibrium" regarding C^* and $2N^*$. Of course, a pair of figures for C^* and $2N^*$ that "feel" right may still be very wrong, but we would then want to

---

106. Cowie (2016) has argued that we have no clear sense of what a minimally good life is, and that it makes it all too difficult to nail down C^S. The point I am making in the text is that econometricians haven't been asked to look for data that could point to C^S.

know why they are wrong. That would force us to think some more about the issues.

In what follows, I suppose θ is just a shade under 1 so as to ensure that $V(t)$ is a convergent series, but I then ignore the error that arises when setting $\theta = 1$. We continue to work with $\rho = 0.5$ in equation (4) and $\sigma = 1$ in equation (5). With these parameter values, equation (35) reduces to $P = (1 + \mu)/4\mu$, and equations (34a and 34b) together read

$$C^*/C^S = (N^S/N^*)^{0.5} = (1 + 5\mu)/4\mu \qquad (39)$$

For illustration I consider four sets of figures for C^S and μ. Using each pair of values in equation (39) yields C^*. C^S and K^* (eq. (38)) then yield N^S on the basis of the equation that says aggregate consumption equals aggregate output:

$$2N^SC^S = K^*[N^S]^{0.5}. \qquad (40)$$

For ease of comparison, recall that average world income per person today is 15,000 dollars and world population 7.5 billion.

(1) $\mu = 0.01$. Equation (35) then says $P = 25.25$ and $C^*/C^S = 26.25$. As a trial, we set $C^S = 1,500$ (international) dollars, which is less than the average annual income in the World Bank's list of low-income (read, "poor") countries (Table 1). Then $C^* = 39,375$ dollars, which is just below the living standard in the Bank's list of high-income (read "rich") countries. Equations (38)–(40) together imply $2N^S = 320$ billion (we haven't accounted for crowding!) and $2N^* \approx 464$ million.[107]

In contrast, Total Utilitarianism ($\mu = 1$) would commend $C^* = 2,250$ dollars and $2N^* = 142$ billion. The difference between the directives of Total and Utilitarianism and Generation-Relative Utilitarianism, respectively, is striking.

(2) $\mu = 0.05$. Equation (35) then says $P = 5.25$ and $C^*/C^S = 6.25$. Let $C^S = 1,500$ (international) dollars. Then $C^* = 9,375$ dollars, which is the per-capita income in the World Bank's list of low- to middle-income

---

107. A simple way to introduce crowding externalities would be to make the parameter B in equation (5) a declining function of N for large values of N. See Dasgupta (1969: sect. 4) for a study of the quantitative significance of crowding on Total Utilitarianism's prescriptions.

countries. As with the first set of figures, $2N^S = 320$ billion, but the optimum population is considerably larger at $2N^* \approx 8.2$ billion.

In contrast, Total Utilitarianism ($\mu = 1$) would commend $C^* = 2,250$ dollars and $2N^* \approx 142$ billion.

(3) $\mu = 0.05$. Equation (35) then says $P = 5.25$ and $C^*/C^S = 6.25$. As a trial, we set $C^S = 3,500$ (international) dollars, which falls within the range of per-capita incomes in the World Bank's list of low-income countries. Then $C^* = 21,875$ dollars, which is the standard of living in the World Bank's list of upper middle-income countries. Equations (38)–(40) imply $2N^S \approx 57.8$ billion and $2N^* \approx 1.5$ billion.

In contrast, Total Utilitarianism ($\mu = 1$) would commend $C^* = 5,250$ dollars and $2N^* \approx 25.7$ billion.

(4) $\mu = 0.1$. Equation (35) then says $P \approx 2.75$ and $C^*/C^S \approx 3.75$. As another trial, we set $C^S = 7,300$ (international) dollars, which is slightly above the per-capita income in the World Bank's list of lower middle-income countries. Then $C^* = 27,375$ dollars, which is at the lower end of per-capita incomes in the World Bank's high-income countries. Equations (38)–(40) imply $2N^S \approx 13.4$ billion and $2N^* \approx 1.9$ billion.

In contrast, Total Utilitarianism ($\mu = 1$) would commend $C^* = 10,950$ dollars and $2N^* \approx 5.9$ billion.

Four exercises can't reveal much, but they tell us that Generation-Relative Utilitarianism is most distinct from Total Utilitarianism when μ is small (thereby P is large) and C^S is large. I expected the former but didn't expect it would come tied to the latter.

12. Technology and Institutions

When communities face exceptional resource stress (droughts and pests are only two causes), they can be expected to seek new practices and fashion new institutions. If migration to better locations is a possibility, communities can be expected to try that if all else fails. We shouldn't imagine people taking impending disasters lying down. Boserup (1965) collated evidence from agrarian societies to argue that resource stress generates societal responses that not only fend off disaster but can even lead to prosperity. Exceptional scarcities may raise exceptional "problems," but as the saying goes today, they offer exceptional "opportunities" as well. Boserup's work countered a widespread fear in the early 1960s that our capacity to produce food was being overtaken by growth in human numbers. She saw population growth as a spur to innovations. The Green Revolution that came soon after her publication matched her narrative. Population was dropped from public discourse even as Boserup came to be seen as a counterpoint to Malthus.[108]

Boserup's case studies were about "organic economies" (Wrigley, 2004), where not only food but also most raw materials needed for manufacturing material artefacts are either animal or vegetable in origin. Inevitably, there was sample bias in her choice of examples. Societies that hadn't made the cut would have disappeared or moved to blend themselves among communities that survived; they would be absent from such records as those that Boserup studied. In a study of a modern-day society, Turner and Ali (1996) put together the contrasting concerns of Malthus and Boserup by demonstrating that, in the face of rising population and a deteriorating resource base, small farmers in Bangladesh expanded production by intensifying agriculture practices (i.e., by introducing multiple cropping and, with government help, collectively strengthening drainage systems and flood and storm defenses). The farmers haven't been able to thrive—they still live in poverty—but they staved off collapse (i.e., they haven't abandoned their villages *en masse* for cities), at least for now. Studies with a similar flavor for agricultural prospects in Africa have been reported in Christiaensen (2017).

If Boserup is a counterpoint to Malthus, Jared Diamond is a natural counterpoint to Boserup. Techniques for reading archaeological records have improved since the 1960s. In a series of case studies drawn from early-to-middle second millennium CE, Diamond (2005) found that a number of societies that had deforested their land had been able to develop successful forest-management practices and population measures, but that in contrast there were others, most notoriously Easter Island, that had failed to develop successful management practices and had collapsed as a result. Diamond also found a common pattern in past collapses: Population growth that followed access to

---

108. Economic historians refer to our need for energy to make the same point. Human societies have over millennia improved their living standard by finding new sources of energy in the face of rising costs of established resources. The succession of human sweat, animal power, rivers and streams, wind, timber, coal, oil and gas, and most recently the nucleus of radioactive matter is a frequently cited example of the global success in finding ways to harness energy.

an abundant resource base made people intensify the means of food production (irrigation, terracing, double-cropping) and expand into marginal land. Growing populations led to a mining of the resource base, which in turn left communities vulnerable to climatic variations, because there was little room left for either mistakes or bad luck.[109]

PNAS (2012) contains a Special Feature on historical collapses. Contributors reported twelve studies of past societies that had faced environmental stress. Seven were found to have suffered severe transformation, while five overcame the environmental stresses through changes in their practices. Butzer (2012) reported the ways in which a number of societies in 14th–18th-century Western Europe displayed resilience by coping with environmental stresses through innovation and agricultural intensification. Like Diamond, he concluded that collapse is rarely abrupt.

That collapse is rarely abrupt suggests that socio-ecological systems are not brittle, but that on facing continual stress they become less resilient in withstanding shocks and surprises. In a study of European Neolithic societies that began some 9,000 years ago, Downey, Randall Haas, and Shennan (2016) found that the introduction of agriculture spurred population growth, but societies in many cases experienced demographic instability and, ultimately, collapse. The authors also uncovered evidence of warning signs of eventual population collapse, reflected in decreasing resilience in socio-ecological systems. Scheffer (2016) has given further support to the thesis by reporting that there had been warning signs of reduced resilience prior to the great drought in the late 1270s that destroyed the communities that had built the iconic alcove sites of Mesa Verde.[110]

---

109. The present section is taken from Section 5 of Dasgupta, Mitra, and Sorger (2018), which contains a formal model of the socio-ecological processes identified by Jared Diamond in his study of the success and failure of organic economies.

110. That would happen if the resource stock were nearly depleted. Scheffer et al. (2012) is an excellent study of the loss of resilience in non-linear systems when they are near bifurcation points. Beach and Luzzader-Beach (2019) illustrate the idea by identifying the decline in soil productivity as a cause of loss of resilience in some societies that collapsed in the past. See Appendix 4 for an example of bifurcation points in non-linear systems.

Inevitably, these studies have been about societies with tight geographical boundaries. A community that failed because of population overshoot or poor resource-management practices no doubt destroyed their natural resource base, but it was their *local* resource base they destroyed; societies until modern times were incapable of affecting the Earth system as a whole. Matters are different today. Our presence is so dominant that the biosphere is no longer as modular as it was until recently. Disturbance in one location today is transmitted to other parts in short order. Movements of people and trade in goods have created a transmission mechanism with a long and quick reach. The mechanism's medium has, however, remained the same: Nature is mobile. We weaken the Antarctica ice sheet without ever going there; fish in the North Sea eat micro-plastic originating in markets in the Bahamas; phosphorus discharge from farms in Minnesota contribute to a deadening of the Gulf of Mexico; emissions of black carbon from kitchens in the Indian sub-continent affect the circulation patterns of the monsoons; the Green Revolution's demand for water, fertilizers, and pesticides pollute the rivers and ground waters of the Indo-Gangetic Plain; and so on.

Economic historians of the Industrial Revolution point to the role institutions played in creating incentives for entrepreneurs to find ways to work around natural-resource constraints.[111] The rate at which we are able to reduce our dependence on natural capital has to exceed the growth rate of humanity's consumption level. Otherwise our ecological footprint will not decline. The footprint currently exceeds 1 and is continuing to increase. We can be sanguine about the character of technological advances and consumption patterns we correspondingly adopt only if we personally experience the scarcity value of the biosphere, that is, if we have to pay for its use, in one way or another. Understandably, entrepreneurs economize on the expensive factors of production, not the cheap ones. So long as the biosphere's goods and services remain under-priced, technological advances can be expected to be rapacious in their use. Moreover, technological advances that are patently good can have side-effects that are not benign. The tightening

---

111. Landes (1998) is a classic on the subject. See also Mokyr (2002, 2016). In contrast, Barbier (2011) reports on the ways in which past societies moved away from the use of natural capital of growing scarcity to natural capital that had thus far had remained unexploited.

of links that bind the biosphere together has meant that economizing on the use of one resource is frequently at the expense of a greater reliance on some other resource (e.g., sinks for our waste products). The ability to use fossil-based energy at large scales has transformed lives for the better, but it has created the unintended consequence of global climate change. Bulldozers and chainsaws enable people to deforest land at rates that would have been unimaginable 250 years ago, and modern fishing technology devastates large swathes of sea beds in a manner unthinkable in the past. If technological progress is our hope, it either has to come allied with elimination of environmental externalities or must be directed by public investment in research and development.

The recent focus on global climate change has led us, even if imperceptibly, to concentrate on technological solutions. But, as noted in Section 10, climate change is not paradigmatic of environmental problems. Contaminating the oceans with materials in all probability requires collective behavioral change in parallel with research and development that is moved by public concerns. Advances in biotechnology will be an essential requirement if our increased demand for food and fibers is to be met. Restoration and conservation measures are ways by which we can reduce the global ecological footprint. Creating safe zones for migratory species is another needed measure. Reducing waste is yet another. But irreversible losses, arising, say, from biological extinctions, would act as constraints on the biosphere's ability to recover. Social moves toward consumption and production practices that make smaller demands on the biosphere would be a more direct approach to reducing our impact on the Earth system. That's the basis on which the numerical exercises were conducted in Section 11.

13. Existential Risks and Informed Ends

In a deep meditation on the significance of a possible nuclear holocaust in which humanity suffers extinction, Jonathan Schell (1982: 114–115) distinguished two types of death:

> It is of the essence of the human condition that we are born, live for a while, and then die . . . . But although the untimely death of everyone in the world would in itself be an unimaginably huge

loss, it would bring with it a separate, distinct loss that would be in a sense even huger—the cancellation of all future generations of human beings.

Schell's book was originally published as a three-part essay in *The New Yorker* in 1981, at a time the Cold War had created an especial chill. Schell was a writer, not a professional philosopher, but he made not one false move in philosophical reasoning in the crucial middle chapter, Second Death. Both Total Utilitarianism and Generation-Relative Utilitarianism measure the loss from the Second Death in terms of the well-being of all who would not exist on account of human extinction. The coin with which the loss would be measured is the Total Utilitarian social well-being function, V^U (eq. (31)). In Sections 9–11 we saw how those losses could be estimated.[112] Schell, however, made a different move. He spoke of the loss each of us alive today would suffer if we were to discover that there will be no one after we are gone. He located that loss not to any attachment we may have to humanity writ large, but to a devaluation of our own lives. And he used the artist and his art to make the point:

> There is no doubt that art, which breaks into the crusted and hardened patterns of thought and feeling in the present as though it were the prow of the future, is in radically altered circumstances if the future is placed in doubt. The ground on which the artist stands when he turns to his work has grown unsteady beneath his feet. (Schell, 1982: 163)

Schell spoke of the artist, but he could have made the same case for all who create ideas and objects. Future people add value to the creators' lives by making their creations durable. Here the fact of a general assumption that people desire to have children is significant. An artist may regard his work to be far more important than parenting, but he is helped by the presumption that there will be future generations to bestow durability to his work.

The examples Schell pointed to were works of art and discoveries in the sciences. Those creations are public goods, and most people don't

---

112. Sikora (1978) is an early exploration for a response to the question using Total Utilitarianism as the guide.

have the talent to produce them. Confining attention to public goods is not only limiting, it also raises an ethical dilemma: Suppose we all were indifferent to having children and stared only at the prospective costs of raising them. We would then free-ride, and the artist would be mistaken in his assumption that there will be future people to give durability to his work.

Nevertheless, the direction in which Schell was pointing is exactly right. Public goods aren't the only objects of ethical significance. Our values and practices are significant, too. Many are private, even confined to the family, and it is important to us that they are passed down to future generations. Procreation is a means of making one's values and practices durable. We imbue our children with values we cherish and teach them the practices we believe are right, not merely because we think it is good for them, but also because we desire to see our values and practices survive. Those values and practices are not public goods. On the contrary, we cherish them *because* they are intimate. They are stories we tell our children about their grandparents' foibles, of our own joys, sorrows, and discomfiture, and we instruct them on the family rituals we ourselves inherited from our parents. Our descendants do something supremely important for us: they add value to our lives that our own mortality would otherwise deprive them of. That is the reason we would not practice reproductive free-riding even if we found reproduction to be personally costly.[113]

The springs that motivate humankind to assume parenthood are deep and abiding. Their genetic basis explains the motivation but doesn't justify it. Justification is to be found elsewhere. Our children provide us with a means of self-transcendence, the widest avenue open to us of living through time, not merely in time. Mortality threatens to render the achievements of our life transitory, and this threat is removed by procreation. The ability to leave descendants enables us to invest in projects that will not cease to have value once we are gone, projects that justify life rather than merely serve it. Alexander Herzen's remark, that human development is a kind of chronological unfairness

---

113. I explored this viewpoint in Dasgupta (2005a). In a wide-ranging and moving essay on death and the afterlife, Scheffler (2013) has also observed that our own lives would be diminished if there were to be no future people.

because those who live later profit from the labor of their predecessors without paying the same price, and Kant's view that it is disconcerting that earlier generations should carry their burdens only for the sake of the later ones, that only the last should have the good fortune to dwell in the completed building—or in other words, that we can do something for posterity but it can do nothing for us—are a reflection of an extreme form of alienation.[114]

The motivation transmutes from the individual to the collective. Every generation is a trustee of the wide range of assets—be they cultural or moral, produced capital or natural capital—it has inherited from the past. Looking backward, it acknowledges an implicit understanding with the previous generation, of receiving the capital in return for its transmission, modified suitably in the light of changing circumstances and increasing knowledge. Looking forward, it offers an implicit proposal to the next generation, of bequeathing its assets that may in turn be modified suitably by it and then passed on to the following generation. This perspective is not at odds with either Total or Generation-Relative Utilitarianism. In our account of population ethics in a world moving through time, generation-t would be moved to internalize the potential well-being of its descendants, expressed in $V(t)$. Our descendants are not us, but they are not outside us either.[115]

---

114. Rawls (1972: 291) has a characteristically profound criticism of Kant's perspective.

115. The idea of stewardship would appear to be common among different cultures. On African conceptions of intergenerational ethics, Behrens (2012: 189) writes:

> African thought does not limit moral consideration to only the current generation. It conceives of a web of life that transcends generations, and of the environment as a resource shared by different generations. This entails a direct moral obligation to preserve the environment for future persons, since it is a communal good. Africans also expect that the current generation should develop an attitude of gratitude towards their predecessors for having preserved the environment on their behalf. This virtue of gratefulness ought to be realized by the current generation seeking to reciprocate by preserving the environment for future generations, in turn.

I am grateful to Simon Beard for this reference.

Schell's reflections point also to the intrinsic value of Nature. It's a mistake to seek justification for the preservation of ecological diversity, or more narrowly the protection of species solely on instrumental grounds; that is, on grounds that we know they are useful to us or may prove useful to our descendants. Such arguments have a role, but they are not sufficient. Nor can the argument rely on the welfare of the members of such species (it does not account for the special role that species preservation plays in the argument) or on the "rights" of animals. A full justification bases itself as well on how we see ourselves, on what our informed desires are. In examining our values and thus our lives, we are led to ask whether the destruction of an entire species-habitat for some immediate gratification is something we can live with comfortably. The idea of intergenerational exchange is embedded in the perspective of eternity, but the intellectual source of such exchange is a far cry from the conception that confounded Herzen in his effort to locate mutually beneficial terms of trade. The mistake is to see procreation and ecological preservation as matters of personal and political morality. They are at least as much a matter of personal and political ethics.

Socially-Embedded Well-Being Functions

STUDIES BY anthropologists and sociologists have established that personal well-being is socially embedded; in other words, personal well-being depends not only on one's circumstances but also on the circumstances of others. We compete with others in some spheres of life (Veblen, 1925) and conform with others in some other spheres (Douglas and Isherwood, 1979; Douglas and Ney, 1998). Veblen exposed conspicuous leisure in the Gilded Age in America, and Douglas and her co-authors returned to the ancient view of consumption as gift exchange to show that it still guides our consumption activities. In "Socially Embedded Preferences, Environmental Externalities, and Reproductive Rights," Aisha Dasgupta and I study the implications of conformism on reproductive behavior. Our analysis exploits the fact that conformist preferences give rise to social settings that game theorists know as "coordination games." Here I develop an account of well-being subsistence for a world where individual preferences are competitive. Such preferences give rise to social settings that have been widely studied by social scientists under the name of the Prisoners' Dilemma.

Let $C_\circ$ denote the average level of consumption in society. The U-function would now depend not only on C but also on $C_\circ$. We write this as $U(C, C_\circ)$ and note that the function has the following properties:

$$\partial U/\partial C = U_C > 0 \tag{A1.1a}$$

$$\partial U/\partial C_\circ = U_{C_\circ} < 0 \tag{A1.1b}$$

for all $C\circ$, $U(C,C\circ) < 0$ for low enough values of C (A1.1c)

for all $C\circ$, $U(C,C\circ) > 0$ for high enough values of C (A1.1d)

Conditions (A1.1a–d) imply that for all $C\circ$ there exists a C^S such that $U(C^S,C\circ) = 0$ and that C^S is an increasing function of $C\circ$, which is to say that welfare subsistence in Veblenesque societies increases with the general standard of living. We write that functional dependence as $C^S(C\circ)$.

If $U(C,C\circ)$ is applied to the production model of Section 4.2, the Sidgwick–Meade Rule is meaningful and reads as

$$U(C,C\circ) = [(AF(K,N)/N) - AF_N](U_C + U_{C\circ})   \quad (A1.2)$$

To illustrate the dependence of well-being subsistence on the average living standard in society, we consider a particular form of the U-function in equations (A1.1a–d)

$$U(C,C\circ) = C^\theta/(C\circ + M)^\eta - T, \quad M, T > 0, 1 > \theta > \eta > 0 \quad (A1.3)$$

Setting $U(C,C\circ) = 0$ in equation (A1.3) yields

$$C^S = T^{1/\theta}(C\circ + M)^{\eta/\theta} \quad\quad (A1.4)$$

Equation (A1.4) relates C^S to $C\circ$. To have a well-defined problem, we now assume

$$\theta M^{(\theta - \eta)/\theta} > \eta T^{1/\theta} \quad\quad (A1.5)$$

Condition (A1.5) ensures that the slope of $C^S(C\circ)$ is less than 1. It also means that $C^S(C\circ)$ cuts the 45° line in Figure 7 at a unique value of $C\circ$, labeled as $\underline{C}\circ$. Because people are identical in all respects, consumption is the same for everyone at the optimum. It is routine to confirm that optimum consumption exceeds $\underline{C}\circ$.

Common Property Resources
and Reproductive Choices

THROUGHOUT THE body of the Arrow Lecture, I have identified adverse environmental externalities as a common cause of natural capital depreciation. How do those externalities affect fertility choice? A commonplace intuition, stemming from Gordon (1954) and Hardin (1968), is that imperfectly managed natural resources—they don't have to be open-access resources—are overused because they can be converted into private capital. There is a similar informal intuition, among anthropologists studying rural poverty in the world's poorest countries, that households have an incentive to convert imperfectly managed local resources (e.g., grazing fields, water sources, local forests) into household numbers. Communal land tenure of the lineage in sub-Saharan Africa has been seen by anthropologists to offer an inducement for men to procreate, because a large family can (or, at least until recently, *could*) claim a greater amount of land than a small family. In "Socially Embedded Preferences, Environmental Externalities, and Reproductive Rights," Aisha Dasgupta and I list this as one of the forces driving sub-Saharan Africa's high fertility rate. To the best of my knowledge, though, there isn't a formal support for the intuition. Here I make use of the timeless model of Section 8 to confirm it.

Recall the production possibilities in equation (1). The assumption that the function $AF(K,N)$ is homogeneous of degree 1 in K and N means that it has the property of "self-similarity," which is a way of saying that every feasible mix of inputs in production can be applied at any scale of operation. This fact reveals itself most vividly when

F is a power function, as in equation (4), which is what I use in the analysis that follows. Assuming that access to *K* can be monitored and restricted, I first uncover (Sect. (A2.1)) the system of property rights to *K* that can implement the population optimum (eq. (25)) in a decentralized world. In Section (A2.2) I study fertility choice when a household's entitlement to *K* increases with household size. I show that this form of property rights motivates households to reproduce more than is socially optimal. To avoid additional notation, I assume reproduction is asexual.

A2.1. Decentralizing Population Optima

As in Section 8.2, the model is timeless. There are N_0 individuals. By mutual agreement, households are taken to be the social units irrespective of their size. Thus, each individual is restricted to the fraction $1/N_0$ of the common property resource *K*. We study the decisions of person i ($i = 1, \ldots, N_0$).

Let *n* be the number of children each of the remaining people intend to have, and let n_i be the number of children *i* intends to have. As in Section 8.2, we suppose children join the adults in the workforce. If intentions are realized, total population will be $[(N_0 - 1)(1 + n) + (1 + n_i)]$. In view of the entitlement rule we are studying, the quantity of *K* to which each household has access is K/N_0. I assume that production possibilities are given by equation (4). Without loss of generality, we set $A = 1$. That means person *i*'s valuation function V_i is

$$V_i = U((K/N_0)^{(1-\rho)}(1 + n_i)^{\rho-1}) + \mu n_i U((K/N_0)^{(1-\rho)}(1 + n_i)^{\rho-1})$$

Or

$$V_i = (1 + \mu n_i) U((K/N_0)^{(1-\rho)}(1 + n_i)^{\rho-1}) \qquad \text{(A2.1)}$$

It follows from equation (A2.1) that *i*'s optimum choice of n_i satisfies the condition

$$\mu U(C_i) = [(1 + \mu n_i)/(1 + n_i)](1 - \rho)C_i dU(C_i)/dC_i \quad \text{(A2.2)}$$

In a social equilibrium, i's optimum choice of n_i equals n. As in the replicating population in Section 8.2, we take it that N_0 just happens to be the number for which $n = 1$. Denote that number as N^*. Population size is then $2N^*$. Let C^* be average consumption per person in social equilibrium. From equation (A2.2) we know that C^* satisfies

$$\mu U(C) = [(1 + \mu)(1 - \rho)/2] C U_C \qquad (A2.3)$$

For vividness, suppose U satisfies equation (5). Then equation (A2.3) reduces to

$$C^*/C^S = (2N^S/2N^*)^{(1-\rho)} = (N^S/N^*)^{(1-\rho)}$$
$$= [1 + (1 + \mu)(1 - \rho)\,\sigma\,/2\mu]^{1/\sigma} \qquad (A2.4)$$

Comparison of equations (25) and (A2.4) confirms that $C^* = C^{OO}$ and $N^* = N^{OO}$.

A2.2 Open-Access Resources and Population Overshoot

We now consider a different property-rights regime. Imagine that the community takes household size into account when allocating rights to the commons. In that case, i's household would be entitled to $\{(1 + n_i)/[(N_0 - 1)(1 + n) + (1 + n_i)]\}$-th portion of K. To avoid clutter, write $H = (N_0 - 1)(1 + n)$. Then, in place of equation (A2.1), we have

$$V_i = (1 + \mu n_i) U\{[K/(H + 1 + n_i)]^{(1-\rho)}\} \qquad (A2.5)$$

In a social equilibrium, i's optimum choice of n_i equals n, and as in the replicating population studied in Section 8.2, I assume N_0 just happens to be the number for which $n = 1$. Denote that number as N^{**}. Population size is then $2N^{**} > 1$. Let C^{**} denote average consumption per person in social equilibrium. From equation (A2.5), it follows that C^{**} satisfies

$$\mu U(C) = [(1 + \mu)(1 - \rho)/2] C U_C / 2N^{**} \qquad (A2.6)$$

For vividness, suppose U satisfies equation (5). Then equation (A2.6) reduces to

$$C^{**}/C^S = (N^S/N^{**})^{(1-\rho)}$$

$$= \{[1+(1+\mu)(1-\rho)\sigma/2\mu]^{1/\sigma}\}/2N^{**} \qquad (A2.7)$$

Comparison of equations (25) and (A2.7) confirms that $C^{**} < C^{OO}$ and $N^{**} > N^{OO}$. The result confirms the suggestions in Sections 8 and 11 concerning population and the environment: Freedom on the commons leads to overpopulation.

Notes on Rawls' Principle of Just Saving

MOST WRITINGS on the ethics of intergenerational saving have been built on Utilitarian thinking, but Rawls (1972: 284–298) sketched a principle of saving in his contractual theory of justice. It will prove useful to see in which ways the reasonings differ from each other. For convenience, I quote the two principles of justice Rawls expounded (p. 302):

> *First Principle*: Each person is to have an equal right to the most extensive total system of equal basic liberties compatible with a similar system of liberty for all.

> *Second Principle*: Social and economic inequalities are to be arranged so that they are both: (a) to the greatest benefit to the least advantaged, consistent with the just saving principle; and (b) attached to offices open to all under conditions of fair equality of opportunity.

There are priority rules among the principles. They have been much discussed since the publication of *A Theory of Justice*. Far less attention has been paid to Rawls' Saving Principle, which is what binds the generations and is therefore of interest to us here.

Rawls argued that the Difference Principle (ranking infinite well-being streams in accordance with "greatest benefit to the least advantaged" generation) would not be reached by the parties behind the veil of ignorance because well-designed investment projects have a positive social return (p. 291):

> It is now clear why the Difference Principle does not apply to the saving problem. There is no way for later generations to improve the situation of the least fortunate first generation. The principle is inapplicable and it would seem to imply, if anything, that there be no saving at all. Thus, the problem of saving must be treated in another fashion.

A3.1 Parental Motivations

Rawls found a basis for the required treatment by drawing on the fact that parents care about their children. Here is how he states the Just Saving Principle (p. 287–288):

> The parties do not know which generation they belong to . . . . They have no way of telling whether it is poor or relatively wealthy, largely agricultural or already industrialized . . . . The veil of ignorance is complete in these respects. Thus the persons in the original position are to ask themselves how much they would be willing to save at each stage of advance on the assumption that all other generations would save at the same rates . . . . Only those in the first generation do not benefit . . . for while they begin the process they do not share in the fruits of their provision. Nevertheless, since it is assumed that a generation cares for its immediate descendants, *as fathers care for their sons*, a just saving principle . . . would be adopted. (Italics added)

Rawls (p. 292) tied this to the Difference Principle thus:

> We now have to combine the Just Saving Principle with the two principles of justice. This is done by supposing that this principle is defined from the standpoint of the least advantaged in each generation. It is the representative men from this group as it extends over time who by virtual adjustments are to specify the rate of accumulation . . . . Thus the complete statement of the Difference Principle includes the Saving Principle as a constraint.

Rawls was less than transparent in his formulation. "As fathers care for their sons" can be read to mean that a father's personal well-being depends not only on his own living standard but also on his sons' living standards. But it could also be read to mean that fathers care for their sons' well-being. In the latter case, parental well-being takes the recursive form we encountered in Section 9.2. The problem is, as Koopmans (1972) showed, a few normative moves reduce the recursive form to equation (29), which is Total Utilitarianism with a positive discount rate (Sects. 9.1–9.2). That appeared to me to be so contrary in spirit to the rest of Rawls' work that I took the link between adjacent generations to be the sons' living standard (Dasgupta, 1974b). That's a truncated view of what binds the generations, but as Rawls was reviving a contractual theory of justice, not a Utilitarian one, I felt I had interpreted him correctly.

Rawls' ideas on just saving weren't built on any specific population projection. The principles of justice pronounce on the basic structure of society, not population numbers. Instead, Rawls studied the pure saving problem. We may as well then assume that population, consisting of identical people, is constant. For simplicity, we identify each time period with a generation.

Time is taken to be discrete. Consider someone of generation-t, where $t \geq 0$. If $C(t)$ denotes his consumption level, we are to imagine that

$$U_t = U(C(t)) + \theta U(C(t+1)), \quad 0 < \theta \leq 1 \qquad \text{(A3.1)}$$

This is the motivation assumption made in Dasgupta (1974b). We now assume that the world is endowed with a single capital good that can be consumed or saved. Investment enjoys a positive return. Consumption takes place at the beginning of each period. Thus, if $K(t)$ is the stock at time t (time and generations are labeled identically), the accumulation process is defined by

$$K(t+1) = r(K(t) - C(t)), \quad r > 1 \qquad \text{(A3.2)}$$

The rate of return on investment is $r - 1$. The saving rate can now be defined as

$$s(t) = (K(t) - C(t))/K(t) \qquad \text{(A3.3)}$$

from which it follows that

$$K(t+1) = rs(t)K(t) \qquad \text{(A3.4)}$$

Notice that $s(t)$ lies in the unit interval $[0,1]$. Because consumption takes place at the beginning of each period, net saving is zero at t if $s(t) = 1/r$. Saving is positive if $s > 1/r$, and it is negative if $s < 1/r$.

Because Rawls rejected the Difference Principle for identifying the just saving rule, I studied equilibria that would emerge in a non-cooperative game among the generations with well-being functions (A3.1). I followed Rawls' wording of the saving principle and studied Nash equilibria when each generation chooses its saving rate. Arrow (1973) agreed with the way I had formulated parental motivations (eq. (A3.1)) and the accumulation process (eqs. (A3.2)–(A3.4)), but applied an intergenerational max–min principle to infinite well-being streams. That is why we published our papers separately.

The character of Rawls' saving policies under the two formulations were reviewed in Dasgupta (1974b). Each was found to have questionable features. Nash equilibrium saving rates were found to be intergenerationally inefficient (there are non-equilibrium saving rules under which all generations would enjoy higher levels of well-being). That would be found objectionable behind the veil of ignorance. I also found that, if refined versions of the concept of Nash equilibrium were deployed by the generations, there would be a plethora of equilibrium outcomes. Rawls would then require further normative directives for selecting one from among the multiplicity of refined Nash equilibria.

Arrow (1973) showed that if $\theta r < 1$, intergenerational max–min commends that there be no (net) saving (i.e., $s(t) = 1/r$), which means the stock of capital remains constant through time. Zero net saving per se is not to be rejected (Section 11 and Appendix 4 below show why); what is worrying for the theory, however, is that it commends zero net saving irrespective of the capital stock that society has inherited from the past. Arrow (1973) also showed that if $\theta r > 1$, the optimum saving behavior under intergenerational max–min is a sawtooth function of time (each period of positive saving is followed by a period of negative saving). Such a saving policy was shown by Dasgupta (1974b) to be intergenerationally inconsistent: the expectations of each generation are thwarted by the desired saving rate of the next generation.

Independently of us, Solow (1974b) put intergenerational max–min to work in a model in which a constant population produces output when working with produced capital and an exhaustible resource. But he was under no illusion that Rawls advocated max–min (p. 30):

> In this article I am going to be *plus Rawlsian que le Rawls*: I shall explore the consequences of a straightforward application of max–min principle to the intergenerational problem of capital accumulation.

In a canonical example of production possibilities (i.e., the power-function form in eq. (4)), Solow showed that, if the rents from the exhaustible resource used in production are saved and invested, the economy follows the max–min path of constant consumption. Along the path the exhaustible resource is depleted gradually, but produced capital is accumulated in such a way that inclusive wealth (Sect. 3.1) remains constant and net saving is zero.[1] Dasgupta and Heal (1979: Ch. 10) applied the production structure studied by Solow to a society wedded to Total Utilitarianism with zero discounting for time and the generations, demonstrating that the optimum saving rate is positive. Positive saving leads to rising living standards over time and the generations. The exhaustible resource is depleted gradually, but produced capital is accumulated at a sufficiently fast rate to ensure that inclusive wealth grows indefinitely.

Rawls' ideas of intergenerational justice in *A Theory of Justice* were unsuccessful. When modeled formally, they were found to have unsatisfactory saving behavior. Perhaps because of those findings (I can't be sure, of course) he offered a different reading in a later publication (Rawls, 1993: p. 274). There he wrote:

> . . . the correct principle is that which the members of any generation (and so all generations) would adopt as the one their generation is to follow and as the principle they would want preceding generations to have followed (and later generations to follow), no matter how far back (or forward) in time.

---

1. The result was generalized by Hartwick (1977) and Dixit, Hammond, and Hoel (1980) to wider production structures.

Unfortunately this gets Rawls nowhere; including past generations in the exercise makes no difference. If the motivation assumption in his previous work is retained, as in equation (A3.1), the saving behavior identified in Dasgupta (1974b) remains, with all its problems intact. On the other hand, if the motivation assumption is dropped, by which I mean the chooser in the original position cares only about his own prospects, an independent notion of fairness has to be introduced if generations are to be motivated to save on grounds of justice. Otherwise, in a world where people of the same generation have the same wealth, no saving can be expected to be forthcoming, no matter whether the chooser looks back or looks forward.

English (1977) had previously coaxed positive net saving out of Rawls' revised proposal (Rawls, 1993, acknowledges her priority over the idea), but she did it by arguing, on empirical grounds, that even in a growing economy some people of generation-$(t+1)$ will be less wealthy than some people of generation-t. The wealthier person in generation-t would then be motivated to save for the less wealthy person in generation-$(t+1)$. The problem is that, in a growing economy, the weighted average wealth of people of generation-$(t+1)$ would be greater than that of people of generation-t. There is thus every likelihood that the worst off person in generation-$(t+1)$ would be better off than the worst off person in generation-t. The Difference Principle would now kick in from the opposite direction. Generation-$(t+1)$ will reason that justice would have been better served had the previous generation saved less. Generation-t will have anticipated that reasoning. That reasoning is always implementable, because saving can be made negative by depreciating assets (i.e., by setting $s(t) < 1/r$), or more generally, by mining natural capital (Sect. 10). We should conclude that Rawls didn't have a principle of just saving after all.

I am a theoretical economist, not a moral philosopher. I don't have the facility to resuscitate Rawls' theory of just saving. But it seems to me that one does disservice to the idea of personhood if our deep-rooted concern and affection for our children is not acknowledged to be an integral part of what defines us. Thus, it seems to me that we would not wish to shed those concerns of ours when entering the original position. Even if we are not fortunate enough to meet our grandchildren, we will have met our children and will know they will meet and care about their children, and so on, through all our descendants. That's a deep fact of our motivation, and to discard it would be to imagine that we enter the original position with a truncated conception of the self. So I now think I was wrong in 1973 to dismiss the recursive form of personal well-being when modeling Rawls' motivation assumption in *A Theory of Justice*. Following the lead of equation (29), we could push the consideration and even imagine that the well-being function of someone of generation-t would be

$$U_t = U(C(t), U(C(t+1), U(\ldots))$$

$$= {}_{u=t}\Sigma^\infty [U(C(u))/(1+\delta)^{-(u-t)}], \delta > 0 \qquad (A3.5)$$

where $C(u)$ is the living standard of the person's descendant in generation-u. In standard economic models, the intergenerational Nash equilibrium saving behavior of interest would be the one that maximizes U_t for each t subject to all other generations complying with their roles in fulfilling the saving policy. The policy would thereby be self-enforcing, which is a crucial requirement of a contractual theory of justice. But the just saving rule would be indistinguishable from Utilitarian solutions to the optimum saving problem.

Fertility choice is not of direct concern in Rawls' thought experiment. But under the "present time of entry" interpretation of the original position, it is tempting to ask whether citizens behind the veil could reach a view that is consistent with the character of population ethics as envisaged in Generation-Relative Utilitarianism. Dasgupta (1974a) contains a model that could be used to test the idea. When I constructed it, I was so unsure that Rawls' thought experiment was a suitable basis for developing population ethics that I didn't go down that route. I still haven't, but would be less hesitant today to try it on for size.

A3.2 Inclusive Wealth as Rawlsian Primary Goods

The principles of justice in Rawls (1972) address the basic structure of society, but Rawls needed a way to bind the generations together, and he found exactly the right objects with which to do the binding. Rawlsian "primary goods" are the ingredients of a society's *productive base*. His saving principle addresses the transmission of (inclusive) *wealth*.

If this reads as a bizarre interpretation of what is probably the most intensively scrutinized treatise on political philosophy in the last hundred years, recall the wealth/well-being equivalence theorem (Sect. 3.2). An economy's inclusive wealth is the social worth (or accounting value) of its stock of capital goods (i.e., produced capital, human capital, and natural capital). That worth is shaped by the social environment in which people try to realize their projects and purposes. A society where citizens lack opportunities to meet one another freely and develop institutions that protect and promote trust among themselves will not prosper. This is why the social environment includes various forms of personal liberties and access to opportunities (Rawls' First Principle and part (b) of the Second Principle). An economy's social environment imbues its capital goods with their social worth, large or small depending on its character, implying that it is composed of the economy's *enabling* assets (Sect. 3.2). Other things equal, an economy's stock of capital goods has lower social worth if society is dysfunctional than if it is well-ordered.[2]

The claims of justice relate to the citizens' ability to create and access their productive base. Inclusive wealth is a measure of the productive base. An economy's inclusive wealth is not the same as social well-being, but the equivalence theorem says it moves in tandem with social well-being, which is why it is the object of interest in both policy analysis and in analyses of sustainable development (Appendix 5).

In stating the general conception of justice he was putting forward, however, Rawls (1972: p. 62) spoke of the distribution of "income and wealth," an unexpected carelessness in a towering work:

All social values—liberty and opportunity, income and wealth, and the bases of self-respect—are to be distributed equally unless an unequal distribution of any, or all, of these values is to everyone's advantage.

---

2. Rawls limited his analysis to economically advanced, well-ordered societies, but I am concerned here with the spirit of his inquiry, not whether his priority rules would be found attractive behind the veil of ignorance in poor societies.

Wealth is a stock; income is a flow. The two amount to the same object in a stationary economy, because in that world one is proportional to the other. But they are not proportional to each other in any other world. In the former you don't need both; in the latter there is no principle to which one could appeal for combining them in an aggregate measure.

Income has no place in Rawls' principles of justice because, being a flow, it is unable to reflect anything about an economy's future prospects and the corresponding prospects of its citizens. To be sure, many of the claims a Rawlsian citizen is entitled to make on her fellow citizens will be in the form of flows (e.g., medical care, unemployment benefits, child maintenance allowance, and so on), but they are claims to a share of national wealth. For administrative convenience it may be that she is also taxed on her income, not her wealth; but the real object of interest is (inclusive) wealth. The notion of wealth that was sketched in Section 3.2 is far more expansive than the one Rawls had in mind, but it is the inclusive notion that responds to the Rawlsian citizen's needs, no matter what kind of society she happens to inhabit. Because inclusive wealth is a measure of an economy's productive base, it is able to reflect her society's future prospects, no matter how functional or dysfunctional that society happens to be (Appendix 5). It follows that so long as inclusive wealth is distributed in accordance with the choice made behind the veil of ignorance, it reflects citizens' prospects in the Rawlsian world.

A3.3 Wealth and Materialism

But wealth, even inclusive wealth, smacks of materialism, a worry that lies behind not only the criticism of Rawls' theory by Communitarians (Sandel, 1982), but also the one lodged by Bernard Williams. After giving a favorable report on *A Theory of Justice*, Williams (1985: 80) wrote:

The list of primary goods does not plausibly look as if it had been assembled simply from the consideration that they are uniquely necessary for pursuing anything. From that consideration we are not likely to derive more than liberty. It is hard to see, also, how the parties could avoid the reflection (available to them from their knowledge of general social facts) that some of these primary goods, notably money, are more important in some societies than in others.

Rawls included wealth among primary goods (we have already seen why income should not have entered the list), not money, unless the economy in question is monetized. I don't know whether the misconception Williams suffered from about wealth is common, but as it is Williams who had that misconception, I imagine it is not uncommon.

The wealth/well-being equivalence theorem holds in all societies, not just in monetized ones. For a hunter-gatherer society, the list of capital goods would include the amount of territory the tribe commands, the supply of water it can count upon, the surrounding vegetation, the extent of game within reach, the quality of their hunting equipment, the infant survival rate, the number of able-bodied men and women, the number of old people (as the repositories of tribal knowledge), and so forth. It doesn't matter whether the economy is monetized or whether exchanges are conducted through barter, social custom, or the dictates of the tribal elder: assets matter to people in all societies. Their worth, whether it is expressed in monetary units or in cowrie shells, reflects the contributions they make (at the margin!) to the well-being of tribal members. Whatever else a person needs, he needs capital goods and the enabling assets that bestow value to capital goods. This is so, regardless of whether the capital goods are owned and managed collectively or they are privatized.

Behind the Rawlsian veil of ignorance, the citizen does not, of course, know the worth of those capital goods. For one thing, there is insufficient knowledge about the social environment (i.e., the enabling assets) that will prevail in the later stages of Rawls' thought experiment (e.g., whether it will be a property-owning democracy). The veil is so thick that the chooser doesn't even possess a sense of his good. But choice behind the veil is only the first stage of political engagement. Citizens know that, once the veil lifts gradually and they learn more and more about themselves and the world, they will probably want to establish the law of limited liability and institutions such as banks, charities, cooperatives, and mortgage and insurance companies, at the very least a monetized economy. Choices over matters such as whether a natural monopoly is to be located in the private or public sector are made at later stages of the thought experiment, when the veil has been lifted sufficiently. As the Rawlsian veil is lifted, inclusive wealth comes to have a more concrete magnitude, but even behind the veil citizens know they will want primary goods if they are to pursue their projects and purposes, whatever they may happen to be.

I have heard it suggested over the years that Rawlsian choice behind the veil of ignorance is the same as the one to which Harsanyi (1955) appealed for deriving Utilitarianism. The difference between the theories as expressed in the authors' publications, it is often observed, lies in differences in the chooser's reasoned aversion to risk. In fact, the difference is far greater. It is to misread Rawls entirely not to recognize the centrality of the temporal structure of the thought experiment he used to identify the principles of justice. The Rawlsian citizen is invited to identify the principles she would choose when they are to guide the allocation of resources in a world where, with the passage of time, she learns more and more about herself and the world. This is why she is seen as making commitments to herself of varying strengths, the strongest (i.e., the principles of justice) being the ones she makes when the veil is thickest. We are thus encouraged to think of a hierarchy of commitments, those made in a given stage being less firm than those in any previous stage. To me, this reading puts into perspective the phenomenal opening pair of sentences of Rawls' treatise: "Justice is the first virtue of social institutions, as truth is of systems of thought. A theory however elegant and economical must be rejected or revised if it is untrue; likewise laws and institutions, no matter how efficient and well-arranged, must be abolished if they are unjust."

One reason the Rawlsian citizen *wants* to choose the principles behind a thick veil is that, by so doing, she is able to tie her hands so as to better exercise her options as and when her ignorance is lifted. The principles of justice serve as a commitment device for future flexibility of choice. Current uncertainty about future circumstances and the fact that many of the choices she makes, or are made on her behalf, are irreversible (e.g., whether to learn to read and write in the early years of one's life; Sect. 3.3) gives value to keeping her options open for as and when occasions arise. The priority rules that Rawls thought he had arrived at can be questioned, but that should not detract from the truth that Rawls' primary goods point to a society's productive base, nor that the distribution of primary goods reflects the distribution of inclusive wealth, and thereby the distribution of personal well-being. Choosing to commit oneself to the principles of justice behind the veil of ignorance serves the same purpose (though, to be sure, it is toward a far greater matter) as purchasing options in contemporary markets for securities. A formal model that illustrates the argument is presented in Appendix 6.[3]

---

3. Rawls' views on the substance of the original position in political discourse underwent a shift in his later writings (Rawls, 1993), but that doesn't affect my comments on *A Theory of Justice*. I am grateful to Ira Katznelson for an illuminating conversation on Rawls' later views on the content of liberalism.

Modeling the Biosphere

TO DISPLAY the workings of dynamical systems, it helps to simplify human demography by imagining that people are both producers and consumers throughout their life. In Section 10, the biosphere was viewed to be a gigantic renewable natural resource. To illustrate that in formal terms, we model human activities in a simple ecosystem. The mathematics is easier to deal with if we regard time to be a continuous variable, $t \geq 0$. That is what we do here. (For a more complete study of coupled socio-ecological systems, see Brock and Xepapadeus, 2018.)

A4.1 Pure Resources

In the text, we denoted the aggregate measure of capital goods as K. Because the model we construct here includes all three categories of capital goods, we alter the notation and denote the biosphere as S. Now we must distinguish stocks from flows. Let $S(t)$ be the state of the biosphere at time t. $S(t)$ is a stock and is measured in, say, tons of biomass. In this section, we study the biosphere (natural capital) as the sole object of interest to the human population. In subsequent sections, we combine natural capital with produced capital.

The net output of goods and services produced by the biosphere at t is denoted as $G(S(t))$. $G(S(t))$ is a flow (i.e., biomass per unit of time). The most common form of G in the empirical literature on forests and fisheries is quadratic. A generalized form is

$$G(S) = -T + rS(1 - S/L), \qquad \text{if } S > 0, \qquad r, T, L > 0;$$

$$= 0 \qquad\qquad\qquad\quad \text{if } S = 0 \qquad\qquad\qquad (A4.1)$$

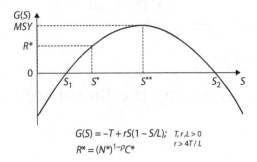

$$G(S) = -T + rS(1 - S/L); \quad T, r, L > 0$$
$$R^* = (N^*)^{1-P}C^* \qquad r > 4T/L$$

Figure 8 Natural Capital's Regeneration Rate

To ensure that Earth can support a biosphere, we assume

$$r > 4T/L \qquad (A4.2)$$

Otherwise, $G(S) = 0$ for all S. Figure 8 displays the G-function in equation (A4.1), in which the parameters of G satisfy condition (A4.2).

We imagine first that there is no human predation. In that situation, $S(t)$ changes over time in accordance with the dynamical equation

$$dS(t)/dt = -T + rS(t)[1 - S(t)/L], \quad S(t) > 0 \qquad (A4.3)$$

Equation (A4.3) has three stationary points (Fig. 8):

$$S = 0; \; S = S_1 = [r - (r^2 - 4rT/L)^{1/2}]L/2r;$$
$$S = S_2 = [r + (r^2 - 4rT/L)^{1/2}]L/2r \qquad (A4.4)$$

In Figure 8, $G(S)$ is shown to attain its maximum value at S^{**}. $G(S^{**})$ is the ecosystem's maximum sustainable yield (MSY). From equation (A4.1) and Figure 8, it is apparent that, of the three stationary points, $S = 0$ and $S = S_2$ are stable, whereas $S = S_1$ is unstable. We imagine for vividness that the system rested at S_2 before human predation.

The ideas underlying the dynamical system in equation (A4.3) are as follows: (1) S has to be of a minimum size S_1 (read minimal biodiversity) if the biosphere is to flourish; (2) at values of S greater than S_1 (but less than S_2) the stock grows in size, but the growth rate declines at large values of S because the system is constrained by a finite planet;

(3) the Earth system is incapable of sustaining a biosphere of size greater than S_2.[1]

Now introduce human predation. Let $N(t)$ be population size at t. Producing the consumption good requires labor and the use of the biosphere's services. Denote by $R(t)$ the rate at which humanity draws on the biosphere at time t. It is conceptually simplest if we think of $R(t)$ as the rate of extraction of biomass at t. We can now express the socio-ecological system as

$$dS(t)/dt = -T + rS(t)[1 - S(t)/L] - R(t) \qquad (A4.5)$$

The purpose behind extracting R is to produce consumption goods. As previously, write global output (GDP) as Q. Using the production structure of equation (4), we have

$$Q(t) = AR(t)^{1-\rho}[N(t)]^{\rho}, \qquad A > 0, 0 < \rho < 1 \qquad (A4.6)$$

Equation (A4.6) is the dynamic counterpart of equation (4) in the text. In the timeless world of Sections 5 and 8, stocks and flows amount to the same thing. In the text we had denoted the aggregate measure of produced capital and natural capital by K and had assumed

---

1. A simplified form of $G(S)$ that ecologists use to model a wide variety of ecosystems (e.g., fisheries, trees), assumes $T = 0$. In that case, equation (A4.3) becomes

$$dS(t)/dt = rS(t)[1 - S(t)/L], \ r, \ S > 0 \qquad (F4.1)$$

Here r is the "intrinsic growth rate" of S (r at small values of S is the percentage rate of growth of S), and S is the ecosystem's carrying capacity for life forms barring humans ($G(S) = 0$). Integrating equation (F4.1) yields

$$S(t) = S(0)Le^{rt}/[L + S(0)(e^{rt} - 1)] \qquad (F4.2)$$

If $S(0) < L/2$, $S(t)$ assumes the classic sigmoid shape. It follows from equation (F4.2) that $S(t) \to L$ as $t \to \infty$. That's the stable stationary point of the system. The stable stationary point of equation (A4.3) that corresponds to L in equation (F4.1) is S_2.

The growth of trees from their seedling stage has been modeled by forestry experts as $S(t)$ in equation (F4.2).

that the aggregate output was $Q = AK^{1-\rho}N^\rho$. But even in the world of Section 9 the biosphere was assumed not to be a dynamic entity. Instead we assumed that the world enjoys a constant supply of the biosphere's goods and services and that the stock of produced capital is constant. That constant stock of produced capital and natural capital (the biosphere) was denoted by an aggregate index K. Matters are different here. The rate at which we appropriate goods and services from the biosphere can be as large as we like, but at the cost of a degraded biosphere, that is, of a reduced K.

To model those possibilities, let $C(t)$ be consumption per capita at date t. As in Section 9, we assume for illustrative purposes (but see Sect. A4.2) that what is produced is consumed. It follows from equation (A4.6) that

$$N(t)C(t) = AR(t)^{1-\rho}[N(t)]^\rho \qquad (A4.7)$$

Using equation (A4.7), equation (A4.5) reads

$$dS(t)/dt = -T + rS(t)[1 - S(t)/L] - N(t)[C(t)/A]^{1(1-\rho)} \quad (A4.8)$$

Equation (A4.8) can be interpreted as the balancing of biomass across time:

$$dS(t)/dt > 0 \text{ if } -T + rS(t)[1 - S(t)/L] > N(t)[C(t)/A]^{(1-\rho)} \quad (A4.9a)$$

$$dS(t)/dt < 0 \text{ if } -T + rS(t)[1 - S(t)/L] < N(t)[C(t)/A]^{(1-\rho)} \quad (A4.9b)$$

In keeping with the notation of Sections 9 and 11, Figure 8 draws attention to a stock S^* at which $-T + rS^*(1 - S^*/L) = N(t) [C(t)/A]^{(1-\rho)}$. The quartet of variables $\{S^*, C^*, R^*, N^*\}$ denotes a stationary state. The stock is maintained at the level S^* by drawing biomass at each moment at the rate R^*.

To contrast this with the route we followed when conducting numerical exercises in Sections 9 and 11, recall that we stopped all capital goods except labor on their tracks and denoted the aggregate of those capital goods as K^*. The pair $\{C^*, N^*\}$ was obtained in Section 8 by an optimization exercise in Generation-Relative Utilitarianism, while holding K^* fixed.

A4.2 Prototype Capital Model

We can extend the previous model to include produced capital. To see how, let $M(t)$ be the stock of a non-deteriorating, all-purpose commodity that can be consumed or set aside as investment for enhancing future consumption. Suppose the output of the all-purpose commodity is given by

$$Q = AR^a M^b N^{(1-a-b)}, \quad A > 0, 0 < a, b, (1 - a - b) < 1 \quad (A4.10)$$

I have specified the output function in equation (A4.10) in the form of a power function only for convenience, nothing more. A power function is unrealistic because it says that, no matter how small a value of R you care to choose, output can be as large as you like provided there are enough people and/or enough produced capital to work with. But the Q-function in equation (A4.10) isn't overtly restrictive because we will settle our discussion here on stationary states, which doesn't require us to consider extreme substitution possibilities among the factors of production.

The dynamics of the socio-ecological system now reads to include, in addition to equations (A4.5) and (A4.10), an equation that says that at each date t the society's intended saving equals its intended investment in the all-purpose consumption good. Using equation (A4.10), we have

$$dM(t)/dt = AR^a(t)M^b(t)N(t)^{(1-a-b)} - N(t)C(t) \quad (A4.11)$$

Stocks of capital goods are state variables in dynamic socio-ecological models, whereas control variables are subject to immediate choice. In the present case, the dynamics of the state variables are given by equations (A4.5) and (A4.11).

We now re-introduce the Decision-Maker (DM), who is a Total Utilitarian. The Genesis Problem is solved at date $t = 0$. Social well-being is the integral of the discounted flow of well-beings from $t = 0$ to ∞. Then

$$V(0) = {}_0\!\int^\infty [N(t)U(C(t))]e^{-\delta t}dt, \delta > 0 \quad (A4.12)$$

In equation (A4.12), δ can be thought of as either the hazard rate of extinction or the discount rate for time, or a combination of both (Sect. 8.1). We make the same assumptions on the U-function as we did in Section 5.[2]

$C(t)$ and $R(t)$ are control variables. They are subject to DM's choice at each t. That leaves us with population profiles over time. There are two ways to model this. One is to suppose, as would seem natural when DM is the chooser (i.e., the Genesis Problem), that $N(t)$ is a choice at each moment t (including the present, $t = 0$). The world pictured there would be, to use the terminology in Arrow and Kurz (1970), *fully controllable*. The other is to suppose that the rate of change in $N(t)$ is a choice, but $N(t)$ is not a choice. The world pictured there is only partially controllable. In the former case, even the present stock of people is a choice for DM, whereas in the latter case the stock of people only in the distant future are subject to choice by DM. I realize that in the latter case Total Utilitarianism is being applied to the world we live in, and that's a long after Genesis, but I want to see how Total Utilitarianism fares in a dynamic model. Because the two cases differ in the extent to which the socio-ecological system is controllable by DM, they point to differences in their long-run optima. We study them in turn.

A4.3 Population Size as Choice

DM's choice variables at each moment t are $C(t)$, $R(t)$, and $N(t)$. The two state variables of the socio-ecological system are $S(t)$ and $M(t)$. As this is the Genesis Problem, it is reasonable to imagine that $S(0) = S_2$ (eq. (A4.1)); Fig. 8). So as to give the economy a kick start, we suppose that $M(0) > 0$. The dynamics of the economy are governed by equations (A4.5) and (A4.11).

I avoid technicalities here because it calls for the use of the variational calculus. Instead I use the findings in Dasgupta (1969; Sect. 3) to sketch the optimum policy. It can be shown that if $\delta < r^*$, where r^* is the derivative of $G(S)$ at S_1 (eq. (A4.1)), the solution of DM's

---

2. The corresponding analysis for Generation-Relative Utilitarianism is more difficult, especially characterizing the approach path to the optimum stationary state. I have the general formulation, but I haven't been able yet to nail the details.

optimization problem converges to a stationary state. If $M(0)$ is large relative to the other factors, $U(C(t)) > 0$ for all t. If $M(0)$ is small relative to the other factors, there is a finite initial period when $U(C(t)) < 0$, during which produced capital is accumulated for future prosperity. In due course, $U(C(t)) > 0$.

In the long-run stationary state (and our assumptions say that there is a unique optimum stationary state), let p and q be the social scarcity prices of produced capital M and natural capital S, respectively. In Section 3, we referred to p and q also as accounting prices. It can be shown that the stationary state to which the Total Utilitarian optimum tends is given by the solution to the following equations:

$$U_C = p \tag{A4.13a}$$

$$pa AR^{a-1} M^b N^{1-a-b} = q \tag{A4.13b}$$

$$U(C) = p[\,C - (1 - b - c)AR^a M^b N^{-(a+b)}\,] \tag{A4.13c}$$

$$\delta = bAR^a M^{b-1} N^{1-a-b} \tag{A4.13d}$$

$$\delta = G_S(S) \tag{A4.13e}$$

$$G(S) = R \tag{A4.13f}$$

$$AR^a M^b N^{1-a-b} = NC \tag{A4.13g}$$

Equations (A4.13a–A413g) are seven in number and there are seven unknowns to determine: p, q, R, M, N, S, C. Given our assumptions, the solution is unique and represents the optimum stationary state. The equations are derivable from the optimization techniques of Pontryagin, and they have an intuitive rationale:

Equation (A4.13a) says that marginal well-being equals the accounting price p of the all-purpose produced capital.

Equation (A4.13b) says that the social value of the marginal productivity of natural capital equals the accounting price q of natural capital.[3]

---

3. In an exceptional paper, Fenichal and Abbott (2014) used a prototype of the model here and applied it to fisheries data to estimate the accounting price of reef fish in the Gulf of Mexico.

Equation (A4.13c) is the Sidgwick–Meade Rule. Like equation (3) in the text, it says that average well-being U at the optimum stationary state equals the social value of the difference between average consumption and the marginal person's productivity.

It is simple to establish from equation (A4.12) that, in a stationary state, the social rate of discount is δ. Equation (A4.13d) says that, in the optimum stationary state, δ equals the social value of the marginal productivity of produced capital.

(A4.13e) says that δ also equals the social value of the marginal regeneration rate of natural capital.

Equations (A4.13.d) and (A4.13e) are fundamental to intergenerational welfare economics. They reflect the balancing act that Total Utilitarianism accomplishes between well-being at one moment and well-being at another.

(A4.13f) says that at each moment the rate at which natural capital is extracted (R) equals Nature's regeneration rate $G(S)$.

(A4.13g) says that aggregate consumption at each date equals aggregate output of the consumption good. In a stationary state, net investment is zero.

Denote all economic variables in the optimum stationary state by a dagger ($\dagger$). Equations (A4.13c) and (A4.13g) tell us that $U^\dagger = U(C^\dagger) > 0$. In Section 3 it was noted that the coin with which we should judge the performance of economies is their (inclusive) wealth. Write wealth as W. Our model economy contains two assets: produced capital (M) and natural capital (S). It could rightly be thought that population (N) is also a capital asset, but as we are studying the Genesis Problem, N has been taken to be a choice variable at all dates, meaning that it is on par with consumption. Wealth in the optimum stationary state is

$$W^\dagger = p^\dagger M^\dagger + q^\dagger S^\dagger \tag{A4.14}$$

Conditional on the economy surviving, social well-being (eq. (A4.12)) remains constant over time, as does wealth (eq. (A4.14)). Denote social well-being at the stationary optimum by $V^\dagger$. As the economy is at the optimum, any move away from it by changing the variables would reduce V to a figure below $V^\dagger$. Simultaneously, any such move would reduce W to a figure below $W^\dagger$. That's an application of the wealth/well-being equivalence theorem, which was sketched in Section 3.2 and will be developed further in Appendix 5. Social well-being and inclusive wealth are two sides of the same evaluative coin.

A4.4 Birth Rate as Choice

Now suppose that $N(0)$ is not a choice variable for DM, nor is the death rate a choice variable. We take it though that the birth rate is a choice variable. Let $x(t)$ be DM's choice of the birth rate at t per unit population (usually expressed by demographers as "per 1,000"), and let ξ be the natural death rate per unit of population. We suppose that $x(t)$ can't exceed some positive number, say λ, which represents the maximum fecundity rate. It is natural to suppose that $\lambda > \xi$. Then the relevant dynamical equation governing population is

$$dN(t)/dt = (x(t) - \xi)N(t), \qquad \lambda \geq x(t) \geq 0 \quad (A4.15)$$

Being a state variable, $N(t)$ is a capital good. Let $v(t)$ be the accounting price of $N(t)$.

DM's problem is to choose the time profiles of $R(t)$, $x(t)$, and $C(t)$ so as to maximize $V(0)$, subject to the dynamical equations (A4.5), (A4.11), and (A4.15). The initial conditions for the optimization problem for DM are $S(0)$, $M(0)$, and $N(0)$. Because DM enjoys only partial control in the present case (unlike the model in Sect. A4.3), $N(0)$ here is not a choice variable for DM), the maximum value of $V(0)$ that is attainable here is smaller than the maximum value of $V(0)$ that is achievable in the model economy of Section A4.3.

We assume, as in the previous exercise, that $G_S(S_1) > \delta$, that $S(0) = S_2$, and that $M(0)$, $N(0) > 0$. It can be shown that, conditional on the economy surviving, the optimum policy tends in the long run to a stationary state.[4] The stationary optimum satisfies equations (A4.13a), (A4.13b), and (A4.13d-g), but not equation (A4.13c). In the latter's place, we have two equations:

$$x = \xi \qquad\qquad (A4.16a)$$

$$\delta = \{U(C) - p[C - (1 - b - c)AR^a M^b N^{-(a+b)}]\}/v \quad (A4.16b)$$

Equation (A4.16a) says that in a stationary state the birth rate equals the death rate. Equation (A4.16b) is a generalization of the

---

4. The transition to the stationary state may involve holding $x(t)$ at one of its two extreme values, λ and 0, for a period of time.

Sidgwick–Meade Rule. Population is a stock here, which means that to identify the right balance of population at different moments of time, the social discount rate must equal the rate of return on population in its role as a capital good. The equation says that, at the optimum stationary state, δ equals the social value of the marginal productivity of population number (human capital here; but see Sect. A4.5). Unlike equation (A4.13c), population isn't allowed by DM to rise to the point where average well-being equals the difference between average consumption and the marginal productivity of human capital. It is kept larger than the difference because of the discounting that is applied to future well-being. Denote all economic variables in the optimum stationary state by a double dagger (††). It follows that the expression for inclusive wealth in the optimum stationary state is

$$W^{\dagger\dagger} = p^{\dagger\dagger}M^{\dagger\dagger} + q^{\dagger\dagger}S^{\dagger\dagger} + v^{\dagger\dagger}N^{\dagger\dagger} \qquad (A4.17)$$

In a stationary state, net accumulation of produced capital is zero and the size of the population remains constant. The net regeneration rate of natural capital is also zero. Nature, $S^{\dagger\dagger}$, appears as a fixed factor in production in the optimum stationary state. That completes our justification for using the model of Section 9 to global estimates of optimum population (Sect. 11).[5]

A4.5 Qualifications and Extensions

In this appendix, we have assumed that resources are managed in a socially optimum manner. Our findings there are meant only to be a benchmark against which to evaluate the world as we know it. We recognized in the text of this essay that the biosphere remains in large measure an open-access resource, and we have seen why and how population can overshoot under these circumstances (Appendix 2). But when population grows large relative to the size of other capital goods, demand for goods and services produced by open-access resources

---

5. A formal proof of the equivalence between inclusive wealth and social well-being when population change is endogenous was constructed by Arrow, Dasgupta, and Mäler (2003b). The proof is reproduced in Appendix 5.

becomes greater than their ability to supply them (Dasgupta, Mitra, and Sorger, 2018). In the context of the biosphere, the ecological footprint rises above 1. In time, the productivity of natural capital begins to diminish. In Section 10, we read evidence that in recent decades the biosphere has indeed been diminishing in its productivity. Interpreted in terms of Figure 8, the stock of natural capital should be read as now being to the left of S^{**}, even while moving further to the left. Unless collective action is taken by citizens in our model economy, the stock of natural capital would be expected in time to cross S_1, which is a tipping point. Citizens would fervently wish to avoid crossing that. (In Appendix 5, we sketch an imperfect economy with those features.) Mathematicians call S_1 a separatrix, meaning that opportunities open to the society when the stock of natural capital falls below S_1 are very different from those that are open to it when the stock of natural capital is above S_1. Above S_1 the biosphere is resilient; if permitted, it is able to regenerate, but it loses resilience once the stock falls below S_1.

Our model economy is stylized, but it displays possibilities of societal catastrophes in a simple manner. The Earth system is vastly more complex. It is a mosaic of dynamical systems of differing spatial reach and speed, and it harbors a variety of separatrices. Steffen et al. (2018), for example, have offered a sketch of the sequence of tipping points that probably lie in wait for humanity if carbon emissions are not abated.

There are, however, further problems in modeling the biosphere. Even two thousand years ago, when the global population was under 250 million and per-capita income was only a bit above a dollar a day, it would have been reasonable to treat humanity as a separate entity from the biosphere. Today it is no longer possible to do so. We are significantly engaged in transforming the biosphere, by both creating biomass and by destroying it. We have to imagine humanity as at once a constituent of the biosphere and an entity separate from it. No doubt that's a stretch, but it is possible to do it without running into contradictions. The way to avoid contradiction while retaining equation (A4.3) is to postulate that the parameters of the regeneration function $G(S)$ are themselves functions of S. For example, we could suppose that the parameter T, in equation (A4.1), is a declining function of S, making the biosphere a more fragile entity for human needs even as it declines. Under this reckoning, the fact that the global ecological footprint has exceeded 1 for some decades means the G

function has shrunk to the point where we have unleashed the Sixth Extinction. That puts in perspective the proposal by Wilson (2016) that we should leave a vital half of the biosphere alone.

There is deficiency also in the production side of our prototype model. The dynamical system represented by equations (A4.5), (A4.10), (A4.11), and (A4.15) does not include the production and dissemination of knowledge, nor does it include health. Both are features of human capital. Our model needs to be augmented by knowledge and health sectors. Two kinds of knowledge may be distinguished. First, there are the knowledge and skills that are embodied in the individual person. Second, there is publicly available knowledge (i.e., the arts and sciences), which can be accessed by anyone with the requisite knowledge and skills. Both have been much studied in the economics literature, as has health. Regarding publicly available knowledge, we can imagine that the factor A in the production function in equation (A4.10) is not a parameter but a function of human capital (scientists), produced capital (laboratories), and natural capital (raw materials from Nature). Extending our model in that direction is then a routine exercise.

Regarding the knowledge and skills embodied in a person and the person's state of health, we could combine education and health by an aggregate index h, interpreted as the per-capita human capital in the economy. It follows that if N is the population size, hN is the aggregate human capital in the economy. Equation (A4.10) would now read as $Q = AR^a M^b (hN)^{(1-a-b)}$.

A person's human capital h is itself a function of human capital (teachers), produced capital (schools and teaching material), and natural capital (raw materials from Nature). Extending our model in that direction is also a routine exercise.

Inclusive Wealth and Social Well-Being

TO CONFIRM that inclusive wealth is the basis on which we should both evaluate policies and assess whether the economy is on a sustainable development path, consider an arbitrary date $t \geq 0$. We call the person conducting the exercise the "social evaluator," or "evaluator" for short, rather than the "decision-maker" because we are to regard the person like a civil servant, who is charged with recommending policies that promote social well-being. The model economy is that of Appendix 4. The birth rate is a choice variable (Sect. A4.4). Our analysis extends to Generation-Relative Utilitarianism, but because it would involve additional notation, we construct the wealth/well-being equivalence theorem by supposing that the evaluator is a Total Utilitarian. The future consists of all dates $u > t$.

Let $V(t)$ denote social well-being at t. Extending equation (A4.12) to the arbitrary initial date t, we have

$$V(t) = {}_{u=t}\!\int^{\infty}[\, N(u)\, U(C(u))]\, e^{-\delta(u-t)}\mathrm{d}u, \quad \delta > 0 \qquad (\text{A5.1})$$

The evaluator recognizes that the economy is governed by equations (A4.10), (A4.11), and (A4.15). We assume she has an understanding of the motivations of the various agents in the economy, which means she can forecast consumption $C(u)$, the birth rate $x(u)$, and the rate at which natural capital is used, $R(u)$; we also assume she can do that for all $u \geq t$. $C(u)$, $x(u)$, and $R(u)$ are "control variables," to borrow terminology from control theory. The evaluator is thereby able to make a forecast of the pair of functions $\{C(u), N(u)\}$ in equation (A5.1). She needs to make a forecast of the pair for all $u \geq t$

because $\{C(u), N(u)\}$ are factors determining $V(t)$. We now need to know what data she needs and what assumptions she needs to make in order to make a forecast.

The welfare economics we develop here has a wide reach. It is *not* assumed that $\{C(u), N(u)\}$ maximizes $V(t)$. The following analysis includes the possibility that the economy suffers from all manner of institutional distortions and normative weaknesses. People as they go about their lives suffer from biases in their judgments. The social evaluator is aware of those biases that have been unearthed by behavioral psychologists. She is aware too that the economy suffers from any number of externalities and other imperfections. She makes an economic forecast on their basis. Her forecast is the "status quo" around which she studies small changes to the economy. Let us see how she can do that.

There are three capital goods: produced capital (M), natural capital (S), and population (N). They are the state variables of the dynamical system, namely, equations (A4.10), (A4.11), and (A4.15). For ease of notation, we write the triplet as $\underline{K}$. Thus $\underline{K} = \{M, S, N\}$. Because the social evaluator's forecast is based on her understanding of the dynamics governing the economy and the motivations of the various agents of the economy, she is able to reason with counterfactuals (otherwise her forecast wouldn't be backed by an understanding of the economy, it would be entirely arbitrary). She can make a forecast of the economy's future if the capital goods inherited by the economy at t had been other than what they are. Her knowledge and beliefs about the economy enable her to make a forecast of $\{C(u), N(u)\}$ for every value of $\underline{K}(t)$ she can imagine. We call forecasts based on all counterfactuals a resource allocation mechanism (RAM).

Definition 1: A *resource allocation mechanism* (RAM) is a many-one mapping from the set of all possible $\underline{K}$s at t into the set of possible pair of functions $\{C(u), N(u)\}$ for all $u \geq t$, satisfying equations (A5.5), (A5.10), (A5.11), and (A5.15).[1]

---

1. Defining RAM as a many-one mapping isn't restrictive here because production possibilities in our model define a convex set and individuals are assumed to be identical. If either assumption is dropped, RAM should be defined as a many-*many* mapping. As an example, imagine RAM is the mapping from $K(t)$s to the set of intertemporal competitive equilibria. Those equilibria cannot be guaranteed to be unique. Note though that if RAM is a many-many mapping, its definition should be accompanied by a rule that selects from the multiple outcomes.

$V(t)$ is a function of both the prevailing RAM and the initial stock of capital goods $\underline{K}(t)$. That's because, by Definition 1, the social evaluator's forecast $\{C(u),N(u)\}$ is a function of the prevailing RAM and the initial stock of capital goods $\underline{K}(t)$. The quality of the economy's social environment, what we have called *enabling assets* (Sect. 3.2) are thus reflected in the RAM.

To denote the dependence of $\{C(u),N(u)\}$ on both $\underline{K}(t)$ and the prevailing RAM would make the notation cumbersome. Therefore, in what follows we suppress the fact that $\{C(u),N(u)\}$ is also a function of the prevailing RAM. Moreover, to keep the account to its bare essentials, we assume also that the prevailing RAM is time autonomous.[2] That means $V(t)$ is not an explicit function of t. That means

$$V(t) = V(\underline{K}(t)) \tag{A5.2}$$

Combining equations (A5.1) and (A5.2) yields

$$V(\underline{K}(t)) = {}_{u=t}\!\int^{\infty}[\,N(u)\,U(C(u))\,]e^{-\delta(u-t)}du \tag{A5.3}$$

We confirm in Sections A5.2 and A5.3 that the expression for $V(t)$ on the right-hand side of equation (A5.3) is most suitable for policy evaluation, while the expression on the left-hand side is most suitable for assessing the sustainability of economic performance.

The RAM is the most significant item in the reasoning underlying the wealth/well-being equivalence theorem. The social evaluator uncovers RAM from the dynamical equations driving the economy. To illustrate, consider the socio-ecological system governed by equations (A4.5), (A4.10), (A4.11), and (A4.15) in Appendix 4. The state variables of the system are S (the stock of renewable natural resources), K (the stock of produced capital), and N (population size). The social evaluator would be expected not only to be familiar with the equations, but she would also be expected to uncover the behavioral rules that govern the choice of the control variables R (harvest rate), C (per-capita consumption), and x (birth rate). For simplicity of exposition, we imagine that consumption is subject to the behavioral rule postulated in the Keynesian "consumption function,"

---

2. In its general form, the wealth/well-being equivalence theorem includes non-autonomous RAMs. See Dasgupta and Mäler (2000).

which says that aggregate consumption is an increasing function of gross output, or GDP. (In applied work, aggregate consumption is frequently taken to be proportional to GDP.) A possible behavioral rule for harvesting natural capital would be $R(t) = R(Q(t))$, in which the harvest rate is an increasing function of GDP (which is, of course, a function of the harvest rate itself).[3] Finally, she could appeal to models in economic demography which assume that the birth rate is a declining function of the value of time, which in turn could be regarded as an increasing function of GDP. In that, case $x(t)$ is a decreasing function, $x(Q(t))$.

Introducing these behavioral rules on equations (A4.5), (A4.10), (A4.11), and (A4.15) gives us, for all $u \geq t$,

$$Q(u) = AR^a(u)\, M^b(u) N(u)^{(1-a-b)}, \; A > 0,$$

$$0 < a, b, 1 - a - b < 1 \qquad \text{(A5.4)}$$

$$dS(u)/du = -T + rS(u)(1 - S(u)/L) - R(Q(u)) \qquad \text{(A5.5)}$$

$$dM(u)/du = AR^a(u)M^b(u)N^{(1-a-b)}(u) - N(u)C(Q(u))/N(u)) \quad \text{(A5.6)}$$

$$dN(u)/du = (x(Q(u))/N(u)) - \xi)N(u), \; \lambda \geq x(u) \geq 0 \quad \text{(A5.7)}$$

Equations (A5.4)–(A5.7) define a fully determined system. The state variables at date u are $S(u)$, $M(u)$, and $N(u)$. The social evaluator can unravel the economy's RAM at t by using the dynamical equations (A5.4)–(A5.7). Applying the behavioral rules to the economy's dynamics, she is able to make a forecast of its future trajectory.

Definition 2: A RAM is *ideal* if it maximizes $V(\underline{K}(t))$.

In the theory of dynamic programming, $V(\underline{K}(t))$ under the ideal RAM is called the value function. The ideal RAM in Appendix 4 (Sect. A4.3) is time autonomous. Recall from Appendix 4 (Sect. A4.2) that the ideal RAM tends in the long run to the stationary state satisfying equations (A4.13a–b), (A4.13d–g), and (A4.16).

---

3. The circularity in the causal chain is not a cause for worry because we are looking at equilibrium harvest rates. National carbon emission rates, for example, have been found to be proportional to GDP.

A5.1 Two Types of Change

Let Δ denote a *small change*, or perturbation, to the economy. By "small" we mean small relative to the economy's size, say, in relation to GDP. We are interested here in a small change to $\underline{K}(t)$.[4] We write the perturbation to $\underline{K}(t)$ as $\Delta\underline{K}(t)$. $\Delta\underline{K}(t)$ should be interpreted as a reassignment of capital goods among the economy's activities. The altered stock, $\underline{K}(t) + \Delta\underline{K}(t)$, gives rise to a perturbed future, which the social evaluator is able to forecast. Her task is to study the perturbation's contribution to social well-being.

We write the perturbation to $V(t)$ as $\Delta V(\underline{K}(t))$. In the calculations that follow, I assume that the economy is at a value of $\underline{K}(t)$ at which $V(\underline{K}(t))$ is differentiable. This is certainly a false assumption to make if $\underline{K}(t)$ happens to be a separatrix of the dynamical system being tracked by the RAM. But the risk we are going wrong is nil because in familiar socio-ecological systems, such as the one represented by equations (A5.4)–(A5.7), separatrices are contained in a manifold of a smaller dimension than that of space of $\underline{K}(t)$. If, on the other hand, by pure fluke the economy is at a separatrix at t, the social evaluator will have to read from the RAM which stability regime the socio-economy will move into at t.

From equation (A5.2) we have

$$\Delta V(t) = \Delta V(\underline{K}(t)) = V(\underline{K}(t) + \Delta\underline{K}(t)) - V(\underline{K}(t)), \quad (A5.8)$$

which on using equation (A5.1) yields

$$\Delta V(\underline{K}(t)) = {}_{u=t}\int^{\infty} \{\Delta[\,N(u)\,U(C(u))]\}e^{-\delta(u-t)}du \quad (A5.9)$$

The perturbed integral in equation (A5.9) can be decomposed to yield

$$\Delta V(\underline{K}(t)) = {}_{u=t}\int^{\infty} [\,U(C(u))\Delta N(u)$$
$$+ N(u)\Delta U(C(u))]e^{-\delta(u-t)}du \quad (A5.10)$$

---

4. In the text we show how the wealth/well-being equivalence theorem, which we prove presently, should be restated if the change being considered is not small.

Because the change is small and V is differentiable, equation (A5.10) can be expressed as

$$\Delta V(\underline{K}(t)) = {}_{u=t}\int^{\infty}[\,U(C(u))\Delta N(u) + N(u)U_C(C(u))\Delta C(u)\,]e^{-\delta(u-t)}du$$
$$(A5.11)$$

Also note that

$$\Delta V(\underline{K}(t)) = [\partial V(\underline{K}(t))/\partial M(t)]\Delta M(t) + [\partial V(\underline{K}(t))/\partial N(t)]\Delta N(t)$$
$$+ [\partial V(\underline{K}(t))/\partial S(t)]\Delta S(t) \qquad (A5.12)$$

As you can see, equations (A5.11) and (A5.12) are equivalent ways of expressing $\Delta V(\underline{K}(t))$.

Define

$$\partial V(\underline{K}(t))/\partial M(t) = p''(t) \qquad (A5.13a)$$

$$\partial V(\underline{K}(t))/\partial S(t) = q''(t) \qquad (A5.13b)$$

$$\partial V(\underline{K}(t))/\partial N(t) = v''(t) \qquad (A5.13c)$$

where $p''(t)$, $q''(t)$, and $v''(t)$ are accounting prices of $M(t)$, $S(t)$, and $N(t)$, respectively. They reflect the marginal contribution of the respective capital goods to social well-being under the prevailing RAM.

Using equations (A5.13a–A5.13c) in equation (A5.12),

$$\Delta V(\underline{K}(t)) = p''(t)\Delta M(t) + q''(t)\Delta S(t) + v''(t)\Delta N(t) \quad (A5.14)$$

Define

$$W(t) = W(\underline{K}(t)) = p''(t)M(t) + q''(t)S(t) + v''(t)N(t) \quad (A5.15)$$

where $W(t)$ is the worth of the economy's capital goods when valued at their accounting prices. That's inclusive wealth. Equation (A5.15) says that the change to inclusive wealth due to the perturbation to $\underline{K}(t)$ is

$$\Delta W(\underline{K}(t)) = p''(t)\Delta M(t) + q''(t)\Delta S(t) + v''(t)\Delta N(t) \quad (A5.16)$$

Combining equations (A5.14) and (A5.16), we have

$$\Delta V(\underline{K}(t)) = \Delta W(\underline{K}(t)) \qquad \text{(A5.17)}$$

Equation (A5.17) gives us the

Wealth/Well-Being Equivalence Theorem: A perturbation to an economy that increases social well-being raises inclusive wealth. Similarly, a perturbation that decreases social well-being lowers inclusive wealth.

We may now distinguish two types of perturbations to $\underline{K}(t)$ and use the wealth/well-being equivalence theorem to show that each has a favored method of analysis. One of them (policy analysis) makes use of the left-hand side of equation (A5.17), while the other (sustainability analysis) makes use of the right-hand side of equation (A5.17).

A5.2 Policy Analysis

Imagine that a small policy change is proposed at t. We interpret the proposal to be an investment project. If accepted, the project would require a reallocation of capital goods among various activities at t (e.g., deploying drills for cutting earth from other uses to the project). The future trajectory of the economy will be slightly different from what it would be if the project were not to be undertaken. The social evaluator's task is to evaluate the project. This is the arena of social cost-benefit analysis. The evaluator recommends the project if $\Delta V(\underline{K}(t)) > 0$ (unless a project variant were found to be even better), but she rejects it if $\Delta V(\underline{K}(t)) < 0$.

For notational ease, we now write the base of the natural logarithm (e) interchangeably with "*exp*" (for "exponential"). Thus, for any number y, we write e^y and $exp(y)$ interchangeably. From equation (A4.15) of Appendix 4,

$$N(u) = N(t)exp\{{}_t\!\int^u[x(\tau)d\tau]\} \qquad \text{(A5.18)}$$

This means

$$\Delta N(u) = \Delta\{N(t)exp\{{}_t\!\int^u[x(\tau)d\tau]\}$$

$$= N(t)(\Delta x(t))exp\{{}_t\!\int^u[x(\tau)d\tau]\} \qquad \text{(A5.19)}$$

Equations (A4.4), (A5.17)–(A5.19) imply

$$\Delta V(\underline{K}(t)) = {}_{u=t}\int^{\infty}\{[\,N(t)(\Delta x(t))exp[{}_t\int^u[x(\tau)d\tau]\,U(C(u))]$$
$$+ N(t)exp\{{}_t\int^u[x(\tau)d\tau]\}\,U_C(C(u))\Delta C(u)\}e^{-\delta(u-t)}du \quad (A5.20)$$

Equation (A5.20) is the social cost-benefit rule that should be applied for evaluating the project. Large projects can be evaluated by integrating the right-hand side of equation (A5.20) over changes in C and N that would be occasioned by the project.

Ideally, the social evaluator will continue her search for investment projects until $\underline{K}(t)$ has been so reallocated among various activities that no further project could enhance social well-being. Imagine then that the economy is so well governed that it enjoys the ideal RAM. Using equation (A5.6), we express the optimality condition as

$${}_{u=t}\int^{\infty}\{[\,N(t)(\Delta x(t))exp[{}_t\int^u[x(\tau)d\tau]\,U(C(u))$$
$$+ N(t)exp[{}_t\int^u[x(\tau)d\tau]\,U_C(C(u))\Delta C(u)\}e^{-\delta(u-t)}du = 0\,(A5.21)$$

Equation (A5.21) is the Sidgwick–Meade Rule in a fully dynamic setting.

Equation (A5.21) is the present-value rule (Sect. 3.2). It says the evaluator should use two social discount factors—one to evaluate the perturbation to the birth rate at t (for which the discount factor for date u is $N(t)U(C(u))exp[-\delta(u-t)+{}_t\int^u[x(\tau)d\tau])$, and the other to evaluate the perturbation caused by the project to consumption (the discount rate at date u for which is $N(t)exp\{-\delta(u-t)+{}_t\int^u[x(\tau)d\tau]\,U_C(C(u)))$. The corresponding social discount rates are the percentage rates of change of the two discount factors, and they are related by the optimality conditions of the ideal RAM.

Assume the prevailing RAM is ideal. Equations (A4.25a–c) and (A5.13a–c) say that $p^{\dagger\dagger}(t) = p''(t)$, $q^{\dagger\dagger}(t) = q''(t)$, and $v^{\dagger\dagger}(t) = v''(t)$.

A5.3 Sustainability Analysis

Consider a short interval of time Δt that begins at t. We write the change in $\underline{K}(t)$ over the interval as $\Delta\underline{K}(t)$. Equation (A5.15) then says

$$\Delta W(\underline{K}(t)) = p''(t)[dM(t)/dt]\Delta M(t) + q''(t)[dN(t)/dt]\Delta N(t)$$

$$+ v''(t)[dS(t)/dt]\Delta S(t) \qquad (A5.22)$$

Equations (A5.16) and (A5.22) say that social well-being increases in the short interval of time $[t, t+\Delta t]$ if and only if inclusive wealth increases in that same short interval of time. Equation (A5.22) is the criterion that the social evaluator should use to assess the economy's performance over the period $[t, t+\Delta t]$. She can extend her assessment to any interval of time by integrating the small perturbations over the interval.

A5.4 Inclusive Wealth and Substitutibility of Capital Goods

An economy's inclusive wealth is a weighted sum of the stocks of all the capital goods it possesses (eq. (A5.15)). The weights are their respective accounting prices. The index is a linear function of the stocks. That feature may give the impression (e.g., Daly et al., 2007) that the wealth/well-being equivalence theorem is built implicitly on the hypothesis that the various capital stocks are perfect substitutes for one another in production.

The impression is mistaken. Nowhere in the derivation of the wealth/well-being equivalence theorem was there any mention of the substitutability of one capital good for another. But as equations (A5.13a–c) make clear, accounting prices are themselves functions of the stocks of capital goods. The extent to which various capital goods substitute for one another in production are reflected in the structure of accounting prices. And there may be little to no substitution possibilities between key forms of natural capital and produced capital, or for that matter any other form of capital. Suppose, to use the socio-ecological system of equations (A5.4)–(A5.7) as an example, the resource base is near its tipping point T. Crossing it would be very costly in terms of social well-being, because output in due course would perforce decline to zero. It follows from equation (A5.13c) that the accounting price of natural capital, $v''(t)$, would be so large that any further diminution of its stock would reduce inclusive wealth dramatically. The index would signal the precariousness of the situation. This and several other common misconceptions of the wealth/well-being equivalence theorem are discussed in Arrow et al. (2007).

A5.5 GDP and the Short Run

We have confirmed that economic evaluation involves wealth comparisons, over time and in the choice of policies. Economic progress should be read as growth in inclusive wealth. Nevertheless, in national economic accounts, the measure most commonly taken to correspond to social well-being is GDP, which is the market value of the flow of final goods and services in a country in a given year. The index is a measure of economic activity. In any given year, if Z is aggregate private consumption (i.e., total consumer spending), I is gross investment in produced capital, G is the sum of government expenditures, and Ex and Im are the market value of exports and imports, respectively, then

$$GDP = Z + I + G + Ex - Im \qquad (A5.23)$$

In a market economy, GDP is also the sum of domestic wages, salaries, profits, interests, rents, and government income net of taxes (the output has to reach *somebody's* hands!). That means GDP and gross domestic income are two sides of the same coin.

If the economy is closed to trade with the outside world, $Ex = Im = 0$, and equation (A5.23) reduces to

$$GDP = Z + I + G \qquad (A5.24)$$

Equation (A5.24) is a reasonable approximation for economies that trade little and is exact for the world economy, which has no outside world with which to trade.

GDP shouldn't be used to evaluate long-run prospects. Among other things, GDP ignores the depreciation of capital assets. The measure was created and designed for a different purpose from economic evaluation. Estimating the magnitude of economic activity became necessary in the Great Depression of the 1930s, when some 25 percent of working-age people in Europe and the United States of America were recorded as being unemployed and a corresponding proportion of factories and resources lay idle (Kuznets, 1941). In the years following the Second World War, when reconstruction of Europe and the Far East and economic development in what were previously European colonies became a matter for economic policy, GDP assumed its role as the measure of economic progress. I don't know why that transfer of purpose from the short to the long run came about.[5]

But even as you go beyond GDP, you find yourself returning to it. The index remains essential in short-run macroeconomics. It allows economists to estimate the gap between the economy's potential output and its actual output, and it is useful for studying household and corporate behavior. Because public goods and services are typically supplied by the government (local or national), the government requires funds to finance them. If the resources are to be obtained from taxes, there has to be sufficient income in the economy *to* tax. Therefore, finance ministers are drawn to GDP for revenue. As a criterion for evaluating short-run economic policy, GDP has served admirably, but ignoring capital depreciation is indefensible in economic evaluation involving the long run.

Here is a sectoral illustration of what goes wrong. Repetto et al. (1989) and Vincent et al. (1997) estimated the decline in forest cover in Indonesia and Malaysia, respectively. They found that when the decline is included, national accounts look different: net domestic saving rates turn out to have been some 20–30 percent lower than recorded saving rates. In their work on the depreciation of natural resources in Costa Rica, Solorzano et al. (1991) found that the depreciation of three resources—forests, soil, and fisheries—amounted to about 10 percent of GDP and over a third of domestic saving.

That GDP can mislead severely when it is put to use in sustainability and policy analyses is now well known, which is why the measure has a hard time these days among the general public and non-governmental organizations. Hardly a month goes by before another publication bearing the title "Beyond GDP" makes an appearance. Nevertheless, GDP growth is likely to remain a measure of economic progress in official eyes, for two reasons: global competition and employment.

---

5. Lewis (1988) offers an account of the historical roots of modern development theory but doesn't question that GDP is the object of normative interest. Coyle (2014) contains a history of the evolution of the ways in which GDP has been measured. She explains why seemingly small changes in the way GDP is measured can and have brought about large changes in estimates.

GDP and Global Competition

GDP is the market value of final goods and services. Those goods and services can be deployed to gain advantage in the international sphere. Never mind that a country may be enjoying a large GDP by depleting its natural resources, ruining the environment, or even running rough-shod over indigenous populations for access to land and minerals; GDP can be (and is) used by governments as a strategic weapon in a world where nations compete against one another for economic and political influence. Not only does a nation's status in the world rise if it enjoys high rates of growth of GDP, a large GDP enables a nation to tilt the terms of trade with the rest of the world to its advantage. History is replete with examples that demonstrate the strategic advantages of GDP growth.

GDP and Employment

There is another systemic problem in modern industrial societies that makes GDP pivotal. Economists have yet to discover ways to manage the macroeconomy in which GDP is de-linked from recorded employment. That GDP needs to keep rising if employment is not to decline is a view that appears to be shared by economists and decision makers, be they Keynesians or otherwise. Politicians and media commentators become deeply anxious when spending on consumer goods shows signs of stalling. We are encouraged to think that to consume is to contribute to the social good. It is more than an irony that short-run macroeconomic reasoning is wholly at odds with accumulation of inclusive wealth.

Valuing Freedom of Choice

IT WAS shown in Section 3.2 that Capabilitarianism is an expression of Utilitarianism. The argument drew on the commonality between choosing capabilities and purchasing options in the market for securities. Such choices reflect a desire for flexibility in the face of uncertainty about what the future holds. Freedom to choose cannot discriminate among alternative choice sets unless there is a machinery for valuing the objects of choice. Utilitarianism provides that machinery.

In Appendix 3, Rawlsian primary goods were interpreted as objects that best serve to protect and promote an individual's well-being, no matter what the state of the world turns out to be. To commit oneself behind the veil of ignorance to a fair allocation of primary goods is to promote choice once the veil is lifted. The wealth/well-being equivalence theorem tells us that Rawlsian primary goods should be regarded as the ingredients of inclusive wealth. In this Appendix, I construct a formal model to illustrate the value of freedom, using expected well-being as the criterion of choice. It is a simple exercise to extend the analysis to include the case where freedom of choice has intrinsic value as well.[1]

Imagine that people are to choose their individual life plans. We call a set of life plans an opportunity set. Consider a person who is

---

1. Kreps (1979) calls the value of freedom a preference for flexibility of choice. He notes that the analysis below remains valid if expected well-being is replaced by state-dependent well-beings, but he observes that informed justification of that desire would require a lot more than axioms on the way opportunity sets are to be ordered.

faced with a *set* of opportunity sets. He may choose a life plan from any of them, meaning that he compares life plans from the union of opportunity sets available to him. He could, of course, choose a life plan that appears to him to be the best. We are interested in situations where he will not want to do that, so we study situations where he chooses his life plan from the available set of opportunity sets of life plans in a two-stage setting. In the first stage, the individual chooses an opportunity set from those available to him. In the second stage, he chooses a life plan from the opportunity set he had selected in the first stage. The reason the person may not necessarily want to commit himself in the first stage to a life plan is that he knows he will acquire information in the second stage about the value (to him) of the various life plans available to him. He knows life plans can go awry if chosen too early; they can prove to be bad bets. Choosing an opportunity set is a way of keeping his options open. For the moment, we imagine that the available set of opportunity sets is exogenously given. Once we study that situation, we can extend the model to include the more interesting case where an investment or binding commitment made before the first stage determines the available set of opportunity sets in the first stage.

Consider then someone deliberating over alternative sets of life plans. Without loss of generality, we suppose that there are two opportunity sets available to him. He may choose at most one. The sets are indexed by a and b and are labeled as Υ_a and Υ_b. The sets need not be disjoint (i.e., there may be common elements among them), but cases of interest are those where neither set is a subset of the other. Let y_a, a life plan, be a generic element of Υ_a. Similarly, let y_b, also a life plan, be a generic element of Υ_b.[2]

That future contingencies are uncertain means that the worth of a life plan to the individual is uncertain. So we let the random variable $\tilde{\varepsilon}$ reflect that uncertainty, and we imagine that the person is to choose an opportunity set before observing the realization of $\tilde{\varepsilon}$. That's the first

---

2. This very stylized version can be extended in any number of ways: The sets can be imagined to evolve over time (with later additions being constrained by earlier choices; Appendix 3); the choices are made by others at the earliest stages of one's life (hopefully on the person's behalf!); and so on. The analysis in the text holds.

stage. For simplicity, assume that after he has chosen an opportunity set, the uncertainty resolves itself (the true value of $\tilde{\varepsilon}$ is revealed) and the individual then proceeds to select a life plan from the opportunity set he chose. That's the second stage.

Consider Υ_a. Let $U(y_a,\varepsilon)$ be the person's well-being if he were to choose y_a from Υ_a, and ε is the realization of $\tilde{\varepsilon}$. In the second stage, the value of $\tilde{\varepsilon}$ is realized. Denote by $y_a^*(\varepsilon)$ the person's best life plan in Υ_a should ε be realized; that is, $y_a^*(\varepsilon)$ is the best life plan conditional on ε being the realization of $\tilde{\varepsilon}$.[3] Thus he values Υ_a in terms of his uncertain well-being under the optimum life-plan function $y_a^*(\varepsilon)$. For concreteness, we imagine that choice under uncertainty involves maximizing expected well-being.[4] In that case, the value he would attach to Υ_a is $E[U(y_a^*(\varepsilon),\tilde{\varepsilon})]$, where E is the expectation operator. In contrast, if he were to choose a life plan from Υ_a at the first stage, he would choose a life plan in ignorance of the true value of $\tilde{\varepsilon}$. We denote the optimum choice in that case by y_a^*. Thus y_a^* maximizes $E[U(y_a,\tilde{\varepsilon})]$ on Υ_a. Notice that y_a^* is not conditioned on ε. Where $y_a^*(\varepsilon)$ is a life plan as a function of ε, y_a^* is a life plan, period.

The key point to note now is that

$$E[U(y_a^*(\varepsilon),\tilde{\varepsilon})] > E[U(y_a^*,\tilde{\varepsilon})] \qquad (A6.1)$$

Inequality (A6.1) says that by keeping his options open, the individual raises his expected well-being. The difference between the two figures, $E[U(y_a(\varepsilon),\tilde{\varepsilon})] - E[U(y_a^*,\tilde{\varepsilon})]$, is the value to him of keeping his options open.

The inequality holds regardless of the individual's attitude to risk. To confirm, note that risks are not being compared in the example. The risk remains the same whether the person keeps his options open or chooses not to. The inequality rests on the fact that the individual can make a more discriminating choice if he waits to receive relevant information before choosing his life plan.

Write $H(a) = E[U(y_a(\varepsilon),\tilde{\varepsilon})]$. $H(a)$ is the value the individual attaches to the opportunity set Υ_a. An identical reasoning yields $H(b)$, which

---

3. Formally, $y_a^*(\varepsilon)$ is any element in Υ_a that maximizes $U(y_a,\varepsilon)$. In many contexts, $y_a^*(\varepsilon)$ would be unique. If it isn't, the individual would be indifferent between options and may as well choose any one of them.

4. It may be that the probabilities in the exercise are entirely subjective.

is the value the person attaches to the opportunity set Υ_b. In contrast to Capabilitarianism, he is able to rank Υ_a and Υ_b no matter what life plans they contain. This means they are comparable by the person even if neither is a subset of the other. Υ_a is worth more to the person than Υ_b if and only if $H(a) > H(b)$. An abiding attraction of the broad class of Utilitarian theories is that it traces the overall value of freedom of choice to the objects over which that freedom is to be exercised.

Waiting can be costly, however, so the cost of waiting until the second stage has to be compared to the benefit of keeping options open. From inequality (A6.1) we conclude that if the cost is Π, it is worth keeping options open if $E[\,U(y_a{}^*(\varepsilon),\tilde{\varepsilon})\,] - \Pi > E[\,U(y_a{}^*,\tilde{\varepsilon})\,]$, but not otherwise.

Investments create opportunities. We now extend the model to a three-stage setting. In stage 0, the individual chooses whether to make an investment (or a choice is made on his behalf) that will enhance his opportunity sets.[5] There follow stages 1 and 2 as above. It is now a trivial matter to extend the line of reasoning we have followed to include the decision to invest, followed by the choice of an opportunity set, which in turn is followed by the choice of a life plan from the opportunity set that was chosen in the first stage. In Rawls' theory, choosing the principles of justice are commitments citizens would rationally make behind the veil of ignorance. The veil is the setting of stage 0.

---

5. The economics of human capital, for example, studies situations where the investment is in education or health.

References

Agliardi, E. (2011), "Sustainability in Uncertain Economies," *Environmental and Resource Economics*, 48(1), 71–82.

Arrhenius, G. (2000), "An Impossibility Theorem for Welfarist Axiologists," *Economics and Philosophy*, 16(2), 247–266.

Arrhenius, G. (2005), "Superiority in Value," *Philosophical Studies*, 123(1), 97–114.

Arrhenius, G., J. Ryberg, and T. Tännsjö (2017), "The Repugnant Conclusion," *Stanford Encyclopedia of Philosophy*, Online (revised January 16, 2017).

Arrow, K. J. (1965), *Aspects of the Theory of Risk-Bearing* (Helsinki: Yrjö Jahnssonin Säätiö).

Arrow, K. J. (1973), "Rawls' Principle of Just Savings," *Swedish Journal of Economics*, 75(4), 323–335.

Arrow, K. J. (1981), "Optimal and Voluntary Income Distribution," in S. Rosefielde, ed., *Economic Welfare and the Economics of Soviet Socialism: Essays in Honor of Abram Berson* (Cambridge: Cambridge University Press).

Arrow, K. J. (1995), "A Note on Flexibility and Freedom," in K. Basu, P. Pattanaik, and K. Suzumura, eds., *Choice, Welfare, and Development* (Oxford: Clarendon Press).

Arrow, K. J. (1999), "Discounting, Morality, and Gaming," in P. R. Portney and J. P. Weyant, eds., *Discounting and Intergenerational Equity* (Washington, DC: Resources for the Future).

Arrow, K. J. (2000), "Observations on Social Capital," in P. Dasgupta and I. Serageldin, eds., *Social Capital: A Multifaceted Perspective* (Washington, DC: World Bank).

Arrow, K. J., and P. S. Dasgupta (2009), "Conspicuous Consumption, Inconspicuous Leisure," *Economic Journal*, 119(541), F497–F516.

Arrow, K. J., P. Dasgupta, L. H. Goulder, G. Daily, P. R. Ehrlich, G. M. Heal, S. A. Levin, K.-G. Mäler, S. Schneider, D. A. Starrett, and B. Walker (2004), "Are We Consuming Too Much?" *Journal of Economic Perspectives*, 18(3), 147–172.

Arrow, K. J., P. Dasgupta, L. H. Goulder, G. Daily, P. R. Ehrlich, G. M. Heal, S. A. Levin, K.-G. Mäler, S. Schneider, D. A. Starrett, and B. Walker (2007), "Consumption, Investment, and Future Well-Being," *Conservation Biology*, 21(5), 1363–1365.

Arrow, K. J., P. Dasgupta, L. H. Goulder, K. J. Mumford, and K. Oleson (2012), "Sustainability and the Measurement of Wealth," *Environment and Development Economics*, 17(3), 317–355.

Arrow, K. J., P. Dasgupta, L. H. Goulder, K. J. Mumford, and K. Oleson (2013), "Sustainability and the Measurement of Wealth: Further Reflections," *Environment and Development Economics*, 18(4), 504–516.

Arrow, K. J., P. Dasgupta, and K.-G. Mäler (2003a), "Evaluating Projects and Assessing Sustainable Development in Imperfect Economies," *Environmental and Resource Economics*, 26(4), 647–685.

Arrow, K. J., P. Dasgupta, and K.-G. Mäler (2003b), "The Genuine Savings Criterion and the Value of Population," *Economic Theory*, 21(2), 217–225.

Arrow, K. J., and A. Fisher (1974), "Preservation, Uncertainty and Irreversibility," *Quarterly Journal of Economics*, 88(3), 312–19.

Arrow, K. J., and M. Kurz (1970), *Public Investment, the Rate of Return, and Optimal Fiscal Policy* (Baltimore: Johns Hopkins University Press).

Arrow, K. J., and M. Priebsch (2014), "Bliss, Catastrophe, and Rational Policy," *Environmental and Resource Economics*, 58(4), 491–509.

Atkinson, A. B. (1970), "On the Measurement of Inequality," *Journal of Economic Theory*, 2(3), 244–263.

Baland, J.-M., and J.-P. Platteau (1996), *Halting Degradation of Natural Resources: Is There a Role for Rural Communities?* (Oxford: Clarendon Press).

Balasubramanian, R. (2008), "Community Tanks vs. Private Wells: Coping Strategies and Sustainability Issues in South India," in R. Ghate, N. S. Jodha, and P. Mukhopadhyay (2008), *Promise, Trust and Evolution: Managing the Commons of South Asia* (Oxford: Oxford University Press).

Barbier, E. B. (2011), *Scarcity and Frontiers: How Economies Have Developed Through Natural Resource Exploitation* (Cambridge: Cambridge University Press).

Barrett, S. (2003), *Environment and Statecraft: The Strategy of Environmental Treaty Making* (Oxford: Oxford University Press).

Barrett, S. (2012), "Credible Commitments. Focal Points, and Tipping: The Strategy of Climate Treaty Design," in R. W. Hahn and A. Ulph, eds., *Climate Change and Common Sense* (Oxford: Oxford University Press).

Barrett, S., and A. Dannenberg (2012), "Climate Negotiations Under Scientific Uncertainty," *Proceedings of the National Academy of Sciences*, 109(43), 17372–17376.

Barrett, S., and A. Dannenberg (2014), "Sensitivity of Collective Action to Uncertainty About Climate Tipping Points," *Nature Climate Change*, 4, 36–39.

Barrett, S., A. Dasgupta, P. Dasgupta, N. Adger, J. Anderies, J. von den Bergh, C. Bledsoe, J. Bogaarts, S. Carpenter, F. S. Chapin, A.-S. Crepin, G. Daily, P. Ehrlich, C. Folke, N. Krautsky, E. Lambine, S. A. Levin, K.-G. Maler, R. Naylor, K. Nyborg, S. Polasky, M. Scheffer, J. Shogren, P. S. Jorgensen, B. Walker, and J. Wilen (2018), "Shifting Fertility and Consumption Norms to Safeguard the Global Commons," Discussion Paper, Beijer Institute of Ecological Economics, Stockholm.

Barry, B. (1990), "Introduction," in *Political Argument* (Berkeley: University of California Press), a re-issue of Barry (1965) with a new introduction.

Beach, T., and S. Luzzader-Beach (2019), "Out of the Soil: Soil (Dark Matter Biodiversity) and Societal "Collapses" from Mesoamerica to the Mesopotamia and Beyond," in P. Dasgupta, P. H. Raven, and A. McIvor, eds., *Biological Extinction: New Perspectives* (Cambridge: Cambridge University Press).

Beard, S. (2018), "Why Fairness May Require the Use of a Pure Time Discount Rate," Unpublished Notes, Centre for the Study of Existential Risk, University of Cambridge.

Behrens, K. G. (2012), "Moral Obligations Towards Future Generations in African Thought," *Journal of Global Ethics*, 8(2–3), 179–191.

Blackorby, C., and D. Donaldson (1982), "Ratio-Scale and Translation-Scale Full Interpersonal Comparability Without Domain Restrictions: Admissible Social-Evaluation Functions," *International Economic Review*, 23(2), 249–268.

Blackorby, C., and D. Donaldson (1984), "Social Criteria for Evaluating Population Change," *Journal of Public Economics*, 25(1–2), 13–34.

Blackorby, C., W. Bossert, and D. Donaldson (1997), "Critical-Level Utilitarianism and the Population-Ethics Dilemma," *Economics and Philosophy*, 13(2), 197–230.

Bledsoe, C. (1994), "Children are Like Bamboo Trees: Potentiality and Reproduction in Sub-Saharan Africa," in K. Lindahl-Kiessling and H. Landberg, eds., *Population, Economics Development and the Environment* (Oxford: Oxford University Press).

Bohn, H., and C. Stewart (2015), "Calculation of Population Externality," *American Economic Journal: Economic Policy*, 7(2), 61–87.

Bongaarts, J., and J. Casterline (2013), "Fertility Transition: Is Sub-Saharan Africa Different?," *Population and Development Review*, 39(1), 153–168.

Boserup, E. (1965), *The Conditions of Agricultural Growth: The Economics of Agrarian Change Under Population Pressure* (London: Allen & Unwin).

Bostrom, N. (2002), "Existential Risks: Analyzing Human Extinction Scenarios and Related Hazards," *Journal of Evolution and Technology*, 9(1).

Bourdieu, P. (1984), *Distinction: A Social Critique of the Judgement of Taste* (London: Routledge and Kegan Paul).

Brander, J. A., and M. S. Taylor (1998), "The Simple Economics of Easter Island: A Ricardo-Malthus Model of Renewable Resource Use," *American Economic Review*, 88(1), 119–138.

Brock, W. A., and A. Xepapadeus (2018), "Modeling Coupled Climate, Ecosystems, and Economic Systems," in P. Dasgupta, S. K. Pattanayak, and V. K. Smith, eds., *Handbook of Environmental Economics, Vol. 4* (Amsterdam: Elsevier).

Brook, B. W., N. S. Sodhi, and C. J. A. Bradshaw (2008), "Synergies Among Extinction Drivers Under Global Change," *Trends in Ecology and Evolution*, 23(8), 453–460.

Broome, J. (1992), *Counting the Cost of Global Warming* (London: White Horse Press).

Broome, J. (1996), "The Welfare Economics of Population," *Oxford Economic Papers*, 48(2), 177–193.

Broome, J. (1999), *Ethics Out of Economics* (Cambridge: Cambridge University Press).

Broome, J. (2004), *Weighing Lives* (Oxford: Oxford University Press).

Broome, J. (2012), *Climate Matters: Ethics in a Warming World* (New York: W. W. Norton).

Butzer, K. W. (2012), "Collapse: Environment and Society," *Proceedings of the National Academy of Sciences*, 109(10), 3632–3639.

Caldwell, J. C. (1981), "The Mechanisms of Demographic Change in Historical Perspective," *Population Studies*, 35(1), 5–27.

Caldwell, J. C. (1982), *The Theory of Fertility Decline* (New York: Academic Press).

Cardinale, B. J., J. E. Duffy, A. Gonzalez, D. U. Hooper, C. Perrings, P. Venail, A. Narwani, G. M. Mace, D. Tilman, D. A. Wardle, A. P. Kinzig, G. C. Daily, M. Loreau, J. B. Grace, A. Larigauderie, D. S. Srivastave, and S. Naeem (2012), "Biodiversity Loss and Its Impact on Humanity," *Nature*, 486, 59–67.

Carlson, E. (2007), "Higher Values and Non-Archimedean Additivity," *Theoria*, 73(1), 3–27.

Casey, J. (2009), *After Lives: A Guide to Heaven, Hell, and Purgatory* (Oxford: Oxford University Press).

Cavendish, W. (2000), "Empirical Regularities in the Poverty-Environment Relationships of Rural Households: Evidence from Zimbabwe," *World Development*, 28(11), 1979–2003.

Ceballos, G., A. H. Ehrlich, and P. R. Ehrlich (2015), *The Annihilation of Nature: Human Exhaustion of Birds and Mammals* (Baltimore, MD: Johns Hopkins University Press).

Chichilnisky, G., and G. M. Heal (1998), "Economic Returns from the Biosphere," *Nature*, 391, 629–630.

Cline, W. R. (1992), *The Economics of Global Warming* (Washington, DC: Institute for International Economics).

Cochrane, S. H., and S. M. Farid (1989), "Fertility in Sub-Saharan Africa: Analysis and Explanation," World Bank Discussion Paper No. 43, World Bank, Washington DC.

Cohen, G. A. (1989), "On the Currency of Egalitarian Justice," *Ethics*, 99(4), 906–944.

Cohen, J. E. (1995a), "Population Growth and Earth's Human Carrying Capacity," *Science*, 269(5222), 341–346.

Cohen, J. E. (1995b), *How Many People Can the Earth Support?* (New York: W. W. Norton).

Colbert, E. (2013), "The Lost World: Parts I and II," *The New Yorker* (December 16 and December 23–30 Issues).

Cowen, T. (1989), "Normative Population Theory," *Social Choice and Welfare*, 6(1), 33–44.

Cowie, C. (2016), "Does the Repugnant Conclusion Have Any Probative Force?," *Philosophical Studies*, https://doi.org/10.1007/s11098-016-0844-7.

Coyle, D. (2014), *GDP: A Brief but Affectionate History* (Princeton, NJ: Princeton University Press).

Crist, E., C. Mora, and R. Engelman (2017), "The Interaction of Human Population, Food Production, and Biodiversity Protection," *Science*, 356(6335), 260–264.

Christiaensen, L. (2017), "Agriculture in Africa—Telling Myths from Facts: A Synthesis," *Food Policy*, 67, 1–11.

Crutzen, P. J., and E. F. Stoermer (2000), "The Anthropocene," *Global Change Newsletter*, 41, 17–18.

d'Aspremont, C., and L. Gevers (1977), "Equity and the Informational Basis of Collective Choice," *Review of Economic Studies*, 44(2), 199–209.

Daily G, ed. (1997), *Nature's Services: Societal Dependence on Natural Ecosystems* (Washington, DC: Island Press).

Daly, H. E., B. Czech, D. L. Trauger, W. E. Rees, M. Grover, T. Dobson, and S. C. Trombulak (2007), "Are We Consuming Too Much—For What?," *Conservation Biology*, 21(5), 1359–1362.

Daly, M. C., A. J. Oswald, D. Wilson, and S. Wu (2011), "Dark Contrasts: The Paradox of High Rates of Suicide in Happy Places," *Journal of Economic Behaviour and Organization*, 80(3), 435–442.

Dasgupta, A., and P. Dasgupta (2017), "Socially Embedded Preferences, Environmental Externalities, and Reproductive Rights," *Population and Development Review*, 43(3), 405–441.

Dasgupta, A., and P. Dasgupta (2019), "Population Overshoot," in K. Bykvist and T. Campbell, eds., *Oxford Handbook of Population Ethics* (Oxford: Oxford University Press).

Dasgupta, P. (1969), "On the Concept of Optimum Population," *Review of Economic Studies*, 36(3), 295–318.

Dasgupta, P. (1974a), "On Optimum Population Size," in A. Mitra, ed., *Economic Theory and Planning: Essays in Honour of A. K. Dasgupta* (Delhi: Oxford University Press).

Dasgupta, P. (1974b), "On Some Alternative Criteria for Justice Between Generations," *Journal of Public Economics*, 3(4), 405–423.

Dasgupta, P. (1982), *The Control of Resources* (Cambridge, MA: Harvard University Press).

Dasgupta, P. (1989), "Population Size and the Quality of Life," *Proceedings of the Aristotelian Society, Supplementary Volumes*, 63, 23–40.

Dasgupta, P. (1993), *An Inquiry into Well-Being and Destitution* (Oxford: Clarendon Press).

Dasgupta, P. (1994), "Savings and Fertility: Ethical Issues," *Philosophy and Public Affairs*, 23(2), 99–127.

Dasgupta, P. (1995), "Population, Poverty, and the Local Environment," *Scientific American*, 272(2), 40–45.

Dasgupta, P. (2000), "Economic Progress and the Idea of Social Capital," in P. Dasgupta and I. Serageldin, eds., *Social Capital: A Multifaceted Perspective* (Washington, DC: World Bank).

Dasgupta, P. (2004), *Human Well-Being and the Natural Environment* (Oxford: Oxford University Press), 2nd ed.

Dasgupta, P. (2005a), "Regarding Optimum Population," *Journal of Political Philosophy*, 13(4), 414–442. Reprinted in J. Fishkin and R. Goodin, eds., *Population and Political Theory—Philosophy, Politics and Society* (Chichester: Wiley-Blackwell), 2010.

Dasgupta, P. (2005b), "Three Conceptions of Intergenerational Justice," in H. Lillehammer and D. H. Mellor, eds., *Ramsey's Legacy* (Oxford: Clarendon Press).

Dasgupta, P. (2007a), *Economics: A Very Short Introduction* (Oxford: Oxford University Press).

Dasgupta, P. (2007b), "Comments on the Stern Review's Economics of Climate Change," *National Institute Economic Review*, No. 199, 4–7.

Dasgupta, P. (2008), "Discounting Climate Change," *Journal of Risk and Uncertainty*, 37(2–3), 141–169.

Dasgupta, P. (2010), "The Place of Nature in Economic Development," in D. Rodrik and M. Rosenzweig, eds., *Handbook of Development Economics, Vol. 5* (Amsterdam: North Holland).

Dasgupta, P. (2014), "Measuring the Wealth of Nations," *Annual Review of Resource Economics*, 6, 17–32.

Dasgupta, P. (Chair), T. C. A. Anant (Member Secretary), K. Basu, K. Chopra, N. Desai, H. Gundimeda, V. Kelkar, R. Kolli, K. Parikh, P. Sen, P. Shyamsundar, E. Somanathan, and K. Sundaram (2013), *Green National Accounts in India: A Framework* (Report of an Expert Group convened by the Prime Minister of India. Issued by the Government of India), http://www.mospi.gov.in/sites/default/files/publication_reports/Green_National_Accouts_in_India_1may13.pdf.

Dasgupta, P., and P. Ehrlich (2013), "Pervasive Externalities at the Population, Consumption, and Environment Nexus," *Science*, 340(6130), 324–328.

Dasgupta, P., and G. M. Heal (1979), *Economic Theory and Exhaustible Resources* (Cambridge: Cambridge University Press).

Dasgupta, P., and K.-G. Mäler (2000), "Net National Product, Wealth, and Social Well-Being," *Environment and Development Economics*, 5(1), 69–93.

Dasgupta, P., S. Marglin, and A. Sen (1972), *Guidelines for Project Evaluation* (New York: United Nations).

Dasgupta, P., T. Mitra, and G. Sorger (2018), "Harvesting the Commons," *Environmental and Resource Economics*, https://doi.org/10.1007/s10640 -018-0221-4.

Dasgupta, P., P. H. Raven, and A. McIvor, eds. (2019), *Biological Extinctions* (Cambridge: Cambridge University Press).

Dasgupta, P., and I. Serageldin, eds. (2000), *Social Capital: A Multifaceted Perspective* (Washington, DC: World Bank).

Dasgupta, P., D. Southerton, A. Ulph, and D. Ulph (2016), "Consumer Behaviour with Environmental and Social Externalities: Implications for Analysis and Policy," *Environmental and Resource Economics*, 65(2), 191–226.

Diamond, J. (2005), *Collapse: How Societies Choose to Fail or Survive* (London: Allen Lane).

Diamond, P. A. (1965), "The Evaluation of Infinite Utility Streams," *Econometrica*, 33(1), 170–177.

Diener, E., J. F. Helliwell, and D. Kahneman, eds. (2010), *International Differences in Well-Being* (Oxford: Oxford University Press).

Dixit, A., P. J. Hammond, and M. Hoel (1980), "On Hartwick's Rule for Regular Maximin Paths of Capital Accumulation and Resource Depletion," *Review of Economic Studies*, 47(3), 551–556.

Douglas, M., and B. Isherwood (1979), *The World of Goods: Towards an Anthropology of Consumption* (New York: Basic Books).

Douglas, M., and S. Ney (1998), *Missing Persons: A Critique of Personhood in the Social Sciences* (Berkeley: University of California Press).

Downey, S. S., W. Randall Haas Jr., and S. J. Shennan (2016), "European Neolithic Societies Showed Early Warning of Population Collapse," *Proceedings of the National Academy of Sciences*, 113(35), 9751–9756.

Dworkin, R. (1981a), "What is Equality? Part 1: Equality of Welfare," *Philosophy and Public Affairs*, 10(3), 185–246.

Dworkin, R. (1981b), "What is Equality? Part 2: Equality of Resources," *Philosophy and Public Affairs*, 10(4), 283–345.

Edgeworth, F. Y. (1881), *Mathematical Psychics: An Essay on the Application of Mathematics to the Moral Sciences* (London: Kegan Paul).

Ehrlich, P. R., and A. H. Ehrlich (1981), *Extinction: The Causes and Consequences of the Disappearance of Species* (New York, NY: Random House).

Ehrlich, P. R., and A. H. Ehrlich (2008), *The Dominant Animal: Human Evolution and the Environment* (Washington DC: Island Press).

Ehrlich, P. R., and J. P. Holdren (1971), "Impact of Population Growth," *Science*, 171(3977), 1212–1217.

English, J. (1977), "Justice Between Generations," *Philosophical Studies*, 31(2), 91–104.

Enke, S. (1966), "The Economic Aspects of Slowing Population Growth," *Economic Journal*, 76(1), 44–56.

Feeny, D., F. Berkes, B. J. McCay, and J. M. Acheson (1990), "The Tragedy of the Commons: Twenty-two Years Later," *Human Ecology*, 18(1), 1–19.

Feldman, F. (1995), "Justice, Desert, and the Repugnant Conclusion," *Utilitas*, 7(2), 189–206.

Fenichel, E. P., and J. K. Abbott (2014), "Natural Capital: From Metaphor to Measurement," *Journal of the Association of Environmental and Resource Economics*, 1(1/2), 1–27.

Fenichell, E. P., J. K. Abbott, and S. Do Yun (2018), "The Nature of Nature Capital and Ecosystem Income," in P. Dasgupta, S. K. Pattanayak, and V. K. Smith, eds., *Handbook of Environmental Economics, Vol. 4* (Amsterdam: Elsevier).

Fortes, M. (1978), "Parenthood, Marriage and Fertility in West Africa," *Journal of Development Studies*, 14 (Special Issue on Population and Development), 121–149.

Freedom House (2017), *Freedom in the World 2017*, https://freedomhouse.org/report/freedom-world/freedom-world-2017.

Freeman, A. M., III (2002), *The Measurement of Environmental and Resource Values: Theory and Methods*, 2nd ed. (Washington, DC: Resources for the Future).

Galor, O. (2011), *Unified Growth Theory* (Princeton, NJ: Princeton University Press).

Ghate, R., N. S. Jodha, and P. Mukhopadhyay, eds. (2008), *Promise, Trust and Evolution: Managing the Commons of South Asia* (Oxford: Oxford University Press).

Goody, J. (1976), *Production and Reproduction* (Cambridge: Cambridge University Press).

Gordon, H. S. (1954), "The Economic Theory of a Common Property Resource: The Fishery," *Journal of Political Economy*, 62(2), 124–142.

Gosseries, A. (2010), "On Future Generations' Future Rights," in J. Fishkin and R. Goodin, eds., *Population and Political Theory—Philosophy, Politics and Society* (Chichester: Wiley-Blackwell).

Gottlieb, M. (1945), "The Theory of Optimum Population for a Closed Economy," *Journal of Political Economy*, 53(3), 289–316.

Griffin, J. (1986), *Well-Being: Its Meaning, Measurement, and Moral Importance* (Oxford: Oxford University Press).

Grootaert, C., and T. van Bastelaer, eds. (2002), *The Role of Social Capital in Development: An Empirical Assessment* (Cambridge: Cambridge University Press).

Guyer, J. L. (1994), "Lineal Identities and Lateral Networks: The Logic of Polyandrous Motherhood," in C. Bledoe and G. Pison, eds., *Nuptiality in Sub-Saharan Africa: Contemporary Anthropological and Demographic Perspectives* (Oxford: Clarendon Press).

Haberl, H., K.-H. Erb, F. Krasmann, V. Gaube, A. Bondeau, C. Plutzer, S. Gingrich, W. Lucht, and M. Fisher-Kowalski (2007), "Quantifying and Mapping the Human Appropriation of Net primary Production in Earth's Terrestrial Ecosystems," *Proceedings of the National Academy of Sciences*, 104(31), 12942–12947.

Hamilton, K., and M. Clemens (1999), "Genuine Saving Rates in Developing Countries," *World Bank Economic Review*, 13(2), 333–356.

Hammond, P. J. (1976), "Equity, Arrow's Conditions and Rawls' Difference Principle," *Econometrica*, 44(3), 793–804.

Haque, A. K. E., M. N. Murty, and P. Shyamsundar, eds. (2011), *Environmental Valuation in South Asia* (Cambridge: Cambridge University Press).

Hardin, G. (1968), "The Tragedy of the Commons," *Science*, 162(3859), 1243–1248.

Harford, J. D. (1997), "Stock Pollution, Child-Bearing Externalities, and the Social Rate of Discount," *Journal of Environmental Economics and Management*," 33(1), 95–105.

Harford, J. D. (1998), "The Ultimate Externality," *American Economic Review*, 88(1), 260–265.

Harrod, R. F. (1948), *Towards a Dynamic Economy* (London: McMillan).

Harsanyi, J. (1955), "Cardinal Welfare, Individualistic Ethics, and Interpersonal Comparisons of Welfare," *Journal of Political Economy*, 63(4), 309–321.

Hartwick, J. M. (1977), "Intergenerational Equity and the Investing of Rents from Exhaustible Resources," *American Economic Review*, 67(5), 972–974.

Haveman, R., and B. Wolf (1995), "The Determinants of Children's Attainments: A Review of Methods and Findings," *Journal of Economic Literature*, 33(4), 1829–1878.

Hector, A., B. Schmid, C. Beierkuhnlein, M. C. Cladeira, M. Diemer, P. G. Dimitrakopoulos, J. A. Finn, H. Freitas, P. S. Giller, J. Good, R. Harris, P. Högberg, K. Huss-Danell, J. Joshi, A. Jumpponen, C. Körner, P. W. Leadley, M. Loreau, A. Minns, C. P. H. Mulder, G.O'Donovan, S. J. Otway, J. S. Pereira, A. Prinz, D. J. Read, M. Scherer-Lorenzen, E.-D. Schultze, A.-S. D. Siamantziouras, E. M. Spehn, A. C. Terry, A. Y. Troumbis, F. I. Woodward,

S. Yachi, and J. H. Lawton (1999), "Plant Diversity and Productivity Experiments in European Grasslands," *Science*, 286(5442), 1123–1127.

Helliwell, J. F., R. Layard, and J. D. Sachs, eds. (2013), *World Happiness Report 2013* (New York: Earth Institute).

Henry, C. (1974), "Investment Decisions Under Uncertainty: The Irreversibility Effect," *American Economic Review*, 64, 1006–1012.

Heyd, D. (1992), *Genethics: The Morality of Procreation* (Berkeley: University of California Press).

Hooper, D. U., F. S. Chapin III, J. J. Ewel, A. Hector, P. Inchausti, S. Lavorel, J. H. Lawton, D. M. Lodge, M. Loreau, S. Naeem, B. Schmid, H. Setala, A. J. Symstad, J. Vandermeer, and D. A. Wardle (2005), "Effects of Biodiversity on Ecosystem Functioning: A Consensus on Current Knowledge," *Ecological Monographs*, 75(1), 3–35.

Huemer, M. (2008), "In Defense of Repugnance," *Mind*, 117(468), 899–933.

Hurka, T. (1983), "Value and Population Size," *Ethics*, 93(4), 497–507.

Irwin, E. G., S. Gopalakrishnan, and A. Randall (2016), "Welfare, Wealth, and Sustainability," *Annual Review of Resource Economics*, 8, 77–98.

Jodha, N. S. (1986), "Common Property Resources and the Rural Poor," *Economic and Political Weekly*, 21, 1169–81.

Jodha, N. S. (2001), *Living on the Edge: Sustaining Agriculture and Community Resources in Fragile Environments* (Delhi: Oxford University Press).

Jones, C. I., and P. M. Romer (2010), "The New Kaldor Facts: Ideas, Institutions, Population, and Human Capital," *American Economic Review: Macroeconomics*, 2(1), 224–245.

Kavka, G. S. (1982), "The Paradox of Future Generations," *Philosophy and Public Affairs*, 11(2), 93–112.

Kitzes, J., M. Wakernagel, J. Loh, A. Peller, S. Goldfinger, D. Cheung, and K. Tea (2008), "Shrink and Share: Humanity's Present and Future Ecological Footprint," *Philosophical Transactions of the Royal Society, B*, 363(25 July), 467–475.

Kolm, S.-C. (1969), "The Optimal Production of Social Justice," in J. Margolis and H. Guitton, eds., *Public Economics* (London: Macmillan).

Koopmans, T. C. (1960), "Stationary Ordinal Utility and Impatience," *Econometrica*, 28(2), 287–309.

Koopmans, T. C. (1965), "On the Concept of Optimal Economic Growth," *Pontificiae Academiae Scientiarum Scripta Varia*, 28. Reprinted in T. C. Koopmans, *The Econometric Approach to Development Planning* (Amsterdam: North Holland), 1966.

Koopmans, T. C. (1967), "Objectives, Constraints, and Outcomes in Optimal Growth Models," *Econometrica*, 35(1), 1–15.

Koopmans, T. C. (1972), "Representation of Preference Orderings over Time," in C. B. McGuire and R. Radner, eds., *Decision and Organization* (Amsterdam: North Holland).

Koopmans, T. C. (1977), "Concepts of Optimality and Their Uses," *American Economic Review*, 67(3), 261–274.

Kreps, D. (1979), "A Representation Theorem for Preference for Flexibility," *Econometrica*, 47(3), 565–577.

Kuznets, S. (1941), *National Income and Its Composition, 1919–1938* (New York: National Bureau of Economic Research).

Landes, D. (1998), *The Wealth and Poverty of Nations* (New York: W. W. Norton).

Laurance, W. F., A. A. Oliveira, S. G. Laurance, R. Condit, H. E. M. Nascimento, A. C. Sanchez-Thorin, T. E. Lovejoy, A. Andrade, S. D'Angelo, J. E. Ribeiro, and, C. W. Dick (2004), "Pervasive Alteration of Tree Communities in Undisturbed Amazonian Forests," *Nature*, 428, 171–175.

Laurance, W. F., J. Sayer, and K. G. Cassman (2013), "Agricultural Extension and Its Impact on Tropical Nature," *Trends in Ecology and Evolution*, 29(2), 107–116.

Lee, R. (2000), "A Cross-Cultural Perspective on Intergenerational Transfers and the Economic Life Cycle," in A. Mason and G. Tapines, eds., *Sharing the Wealth: Demographic Change and Economic Transfers Between Generations* (Oxford: Oxford University Press).

Lee, R. (2007), "Demographic Change, Welfare, and Intergenerational Transfers: A Global Overview," in J. Veron, S. Pennec, and J. Legare, eds., *Age, Generations and the Social Contract: The Demographic Challenge Facing the Welfare State* (Amsterdam: Springer).

Lewis, W. A. (1988), "The Roots of Development Theory," in H. Chenery and T. N. Srinivasan, eds., *Handbook of Development Economics, Vol. 1* (Amsterdam: North Holland).

Lind, R. ed. (1982), *Discounting for Time and Risk in Energy Policy* (Baltimore: Johns Hopkins University Press).

Little, I. M. D., and J. A. Mirrlees (1968), *Manual of Industrial Project Analysis in Developing Countries: Social Cost Benefit Analysis* (Paris: OECD).

Little, I. M. D., and J. A. Mirrlees (1974), *Project Appraisal and Planning for Developing Countries* (London: Heinemann).

Lomborg, B., ed. (2014), *How Much Have Global Problems Cost the World? A Scoreboard from 1900 to 2050* (Cambridge: Cambridge University Press).

Loreau, M., S. Naeem, P. Inchauti, J. Bengtsson, J. P. Grime, A. Hector, D. U. Hooper, M. A. Huston, D. Raffaelli, B. Schmid, D. Tilman, and D. A. Wardle (2001), "Biodiversity and Ecosystem Functioning: Current Knowledge and Future Challenges," *Science*, 294(5543), 804–808.

Lovejoy, T. E., and C. Nobre (2018), "Amazon Tipping Point," *Science Advances*, 4(2), eaat2340.

Luce, R. D., and H. Raiffa (1957), *Games and Decisions* (New York: John Wiley).

Maddison, A. (2001), *The World Economy: A Millennial Perspective* (Paris: OECD).

Managi, S., and P. Kumar (2018), *Inclusive Wealth Report 2018: Measuring Progress Toward Sustainability* (New York: Routledge).

Marothia, D. K., ed. (2002), *Institutionalizing Common Pool Resources* (New Delhi: Concept Publishing Company).

Maskin, E. S. (1978), "A Theorem on Utilitarianism," *Review of Economic Studies*, 45(1), 93–96.

McMahan, J. A. (1981), "Problems of Population Theory," *Ethics*, 92(1), 96–127.

Meade, J. E. (1955), *Trade and Welfare* (Oxford: Oxford University Press).

Micklethwait, J., and A. Wooldridge (2000), *A Future Perfect: The Challenge and Promise of Globalization* (New York: Random House).

Millennium Ecosystem Assessment, R. Hassan, R. Scholes, and N. Ash, eds. (2005a), *Ecosystems and Human Well-Being, I: Current State and Trends* (Washington, DC: Island Press).

Millennium Ecosystem Assessment, S. R. Carpenter, P. L. Pingali, E. M. Bennet, and M. B. Zurek, eds. (2005b), *Ecosystems and Human Well-Being, II: Scenarios* (Washington, DC: Island Press).

Millennium Ecosystem Assessment, K. Chopra, R. Leemans, P. Kumar, and H. Simmons, eds. (2005c), *Ecosystems and Human Well-Being, III: Policy Responses* (Washington, DC: Island Press).

Millennium Ecosystem Assessment, D. Capistrano, C. Samper K., M. J. Lee, and C. Randsepp-Hearne, eds. (2005d), *Ecosystems and Human Well-Being, IV: Multiscale Assessments* (Washington, DC: Island Press).

Mirrlees, J. A. (1967), "Optimum Growth When Technology Is Changing," *Review of Economic Studies*, 34(1), 95–124.

Mokyr, J. (2002), *The Gifts of Athena: Historical Origins of the Knowledge Economy* (Princeton, NJ: Princeton University Press).

Mokyr, J. (2016), *The Culture of Growth: The Origins of the Modern Economy* (Princeton, NJ: Princeton University Press).

Mukhopadhyay, P. (2008), "Heterogeneity, Commons, and Privatization: Agrarian Institutional Change in Goa," in R. Ghate, N. S. Jodha, and P. Mukhopadhyay, eds., *Promise, Trust and Evolution: Managing the Commons of South Asia* (Oxford: Oxford University Press).

Mulgan, T. (2002), "The Reverse Repugnant Conclusion," *Utilitas*, 14(3), 360–364.

Nagel, T. (1976), "Moral Luck," *Proceedings of the Aristotelian Society, Supplementary Volumes*, 50, 137–151. Republished in *Mortal Questions* (Cambridge: Cambridge University Press), 1979.

Nagel, T. (1979), "Death," in *Mortal Questions* (Cambridge: Cambridge University Press). Originally published in *Nous*, 1970, 4(1), 73–80.

Nagel, T. (1986), *The View from Nowhere* (New York: Oxford University Press). Chapter 9 republished as "Autonomy and Deontology," in S. Scheffler, ed. (1988), *Consequentialism and Its Critics* (Oxford: Oxford University Press).

Narveson, J. (1967), "Utilitarianism and New Generations," *Mind*, 76(1), 62–72.

Narveson, J. (1973), "Moral Problems of Population," *Monist*, 57(1), 62–86.

Norberg, J. (2016), *Progress: Ten Reasons to Look Forward to the Future* (London: One World).

Nordhaus, W. D. (1994), *Managing the Global Commons: The Economics of Climate Change* (Cambridge, MA: MIT Press).

Nordhaus, W. D. (2007), "A Review of the Stern Review on the Economics of Climate Change," *Journal of Economic Literature*, 45(3), 686–702.

Ostrom, E. (1990), *Governing the Commons: The Evolution of Institutions for Collective Action* (Cambridge: Cambridge University Press).

Ostrom, E., and T. K. Ahn, eds. (2003), *Foundations of Social Capital* (Cheltenham: Edward Elgar).

Ostrom, E., T. Dietz, N. Dolsak, P. C. Stern, S. Stonich, and E. U. Weber, eds. (2002), *The Drama of the Commons* (Washington, DC: National Academy Press).

Parfit, D. (1976), "On Doing the Best for Our Children," in M. Bayles, ed., *Ethics and Population* (Cambridge, MA: Schenkman). Reprinted in J. Fishkin and R. Goodin, eds., *Population and Political Theory—Philosophy, Politics and Society* (Chichester: Wiley-Blackwell), 2010.

Parfit, D. (1982), "Future Generations: Further Problems," *Philosophy and Public Affairs*, 11(2), 113–172.

Parfit, D. (1984), *Reasons and Persons* (Oxford: Oxford University Press).

Parfit, D. (2016), "Can We Avoid the Repugnant Conclusion?," *Theoria*, 82(2), 110–127.

Perrings, C. (2014), *Our Common Heritage: Biodiversity Change, Ecosystem Services, and Human Well-Being* (Cambridge: Cambridge University Press).

Phelps, E. S., and R. Pollak (1968), "Second-Best National Savings and Game Equilibrium Growth," *Review of Economic Studies*, 35(2), 185–199.

Pimm, S. L., C. N. Jenkins, R. Abell, T. M. Brooks, J. L. Gittleman, L. N. Joppa, P. H. Raven, C. M. Roberts, and J. O. Se (2014), "The Biodiversity of Species and Their Rates of Extinction, Distribution, and Protection," *Science*, 344(6187), 1246752.

Pinker, S. (2018), *Enlightenment Now: The Case for Reason, Science, Humanism, and Progress* (New York: Allen Lane).

Proceedings of the National Academy of Sciences (2012), "Special Feature: Critical Perspectives on Historical Collapse," *Proceedings of the National Academy of Sciences*, 109(10), 3632–3681.

Power, M. E., D. Tilman, J. A. Estes, B. A. Menge, W. J. Bond, L. S. Mills, G. Daily, J. C. Castilla, J. Lubchenco, and R. T. Paine (1996), "Challenges in the Quest for Keystones," *Bioscience*, 46(8), 609–620.

Pratt, J. A. (1964), "Risk Aversion in the Small and in the Large," *Econometrica*, 32(1–2), 122–136.

Prest, A. R., and R. Turvey (1965), "Cost-Benefit Analysis: A Survey," *Economic Journal*, 75(4), 683–735.

Putnam, R. D., with R. Leonardi and R. Y. Nanetti (1993), *Making Democracy Work: Civic Traditions in Modern Italy* (Princeton, NJ: Princeton University Press).

Raiffa, H. (1968), *Decision Analysis: Introductory Lectures on Choice Under Uncertainty* (Reading, MA: Addison-Wesley).

Räikkä, J. (2002), "The Repugnant Conclusion and the Welfare of Actual People," *Theoria*, 68(2), 162–169.

Ramsey, F. P. (1928), "A Mathematical Theory of Saving," *Economic Journal*, 38(4), 543–559.

Ramsey, F. P. (1931), "Epilogue," in R. B. Braithwaite, ed., *The Foundations of Mathematics and Other Logical Essays* (London: Routledge and Kegan Paul). Originally read at a meeting of the Apostles, University of Cambridge, on February 28, 1925, under the title "Is There Anything Left to Discuss?"

Rawls, J. (1972), *A Theory of Justice* (Oxford: Oxford University Press).

Rawls, J. (1993), *Political Liberalism* (New York: Columbia University Press).

Rees, M. J. (2003), *Our Final Century* (London: Random House).

Rees, W. E. (2006), "Ecological Footprints and Biocapacity: Essential Elements in Sustainability Assessment," in J. Dewulf and H. V. Langenhove, eds., *Renewable-Based Technology: Sustainability Assessment* (Chichester: John Wiley & Sons).

Rees, W. A., and M. Wackernagel (1994), "Ecological Footprints and Appropriated Carrying Capacity: Measuring the Natural Capital Requirements of the Human Economy," in A. M. Jansson et al., eds., *Investing in Natural Capital: The Ecological Economics Appropriate for Sustainability* (Washington, DC: Island Press).

Repetto, R., W. Magrath, M. Wells, C. Beer, and F. Rossini (1989), *Wasting Assets: Natural Resources and the National Income Accounts* (Washington DC: World Resources Institute).

Ricketts, T. H., G. C. Daily, P. R. Ehrlich, and C. D. Michener (2004), "Economic Value of Tropical Forest to Coffee Production," *Proceedings of the National Academy of Sciences*, 101(34), 12579–12582.

Ridley, M. (2010), *The Rational Optimist: How Prosperity Evolves* (London: Fourth Estate).

Rockström, J., W. Steffen, K. Noone, A. Persson, F. S. Chapin III, E. F. Lambin, T. M. Lenton, M. Scheffer, C. Folke, H. J. Schellnhuber, B. Nykvist, C. A. de Wit, T. Hughes, S. van der Leeuw, H. Rodhe, S. Sörlin, P. K. Snyder, R. Costanza, U. Svedin, M. Falkenmark, L. Karlberg, R. W. Corell, V. J.

Fabry, J. Hansen, B. Walker, D. Liverman, K. Richardson, P. Crutzen, and J. A. Foley. (2009), "A Safe Operating Space for Humanity," *Nature* 461: 472–475.

Sandel, M. J. (1982), *Liberalism and the Limits of Justice* (Cambridge: Cambridge University Press).

Scheffer, M. (2016), "Anticipating Societal Collapse: Hints from the Stone Age," *Proceedings of the National Academy of Sciences*, 113(35), 10733–10735.

Scheffer, M., S. R. Carpenter, T. M. Lenton, J. Bascompte, W. Brock, V. Dakos, J. Van d Koppel, I. A. van de Leemput, S. A. Levin, E. H. van Nes, M. Pascual, and J. Vandermeer (2012), "Anticipating Critical Transitions," *Science*, 338(6105), 344–348.

Scheffler, S. (1982), *The Rejection of Consequentialism* (Oxford: Clarendon Press).

Scheffler, S. (1985), "Agent-Centered Restrictions, Rationality, and the Virtues," *Mind*, 94(375), 409–419. Reprinted in S. Scheffler, ed., *Consequentialism and Its Critics* (Oxford: Oxford University Press), 1988.

Scheffler, S. (2013), *Death and the Afterlife* (Oxford: Oxford University Press).

Schell, J. (1982), *The Fate of the Earth* (New York: Avon).

Schultz, T. W. (1961), "Investment in Human Capital," *American Economic Review*, 51(1), 1–17.

Seabright, P. (1989), "Population Size and the Quality of Life, II: Creating Persons," *Proceedings of the Aristotelian Society, Supplementary Volumes*, 63, 41–54.

Sen, A. (1970), *Collective Choice and Social Welfare* (San Francisco: Holden Day).

Sen, A. (1985), *Commodities and Capabilities* (Amsterdam: North Holland).

Sen, A. (1992), *Inequality Reexamined* (Oxford: Clarendon Press).

Sen, A. (1999), *Development as Freedom* (Oxford: Oxford University Press).

Sen, A. (2009), *The Idea of Justice* (Cambridge, MA: Harvard University Press).

Sher, I. (2018), "Evaluating Allocations of Freedom," *Economic Journal*, 128(612), F65–F94.

Shyamsundar, P. (2008), "Decentralization, Devolution, and Collective Action," in R. Ghate, N. S. Jodha, and P. Mukhopadhyay, eds. (2008), *Promise, Trust and Evolution: Managing the Commons of South Asia* (Oxford: Oxford University Press).

Sidgwick, H. (1907), *The Methods of Ethics* (London: MacMillan), 7th Edition.

Sikora, R. I. (1978), "Is It Wrong to Prevent the Existence of Future Generations?," in R. I. Sikora and B. Barry, eds., *Obligations to Future Generations* (Philadelphia: Temple University Press).

Sikora, R. I. (1981), "Classical Utilitarianism and Parfit's Repugnant Conclusion: A Reply to McMahan," *Ethics*, 92(1), 128–133.

Sodhi, N. S., B. W. Brook, and C. J. A. Bradshaw (2009), "Causes and Consequences of Species Extinctions," in S. A. Levin et al., eds., *The Princeton Guide to Ecology* (Princeton, NJ: Princeton University Press).

Solorzano, R., R. de Camino, R. Woodward, J. Tosi, V. Watson, A. Vasquez, C. Villalobos, J. Jimenez, R. Repetto, and W. Cruz (1991), *Accounts Overdue: Natural Resource Depreciation in Costa Rica* (Washington, DC: World Resources Institute).

Solow, R. M. (1974a), "The Economics of Resources and the Resources of Economics," *American Economic Review*, 64, 1–21.

Solow, R. M. (1974b), "Intergenerational Equity and Exhaustible Resources," *Review of Economic Studies*, 41(Symposium Issue), 29–45.

Solow, R. M. (2000), "Notes on Social Capital and Economic Performance," in P. Dasgupta and I. Serageldin, eds., *Social Capital: A Multifaceted Perspective* (Washington, DC: World Bank).

Somanathan, E. (1991), "Deforestation, Property Rights and Incentives in Central Himalaya," *Economic and Political Weekly*, 26(Special Issue: January 26) PE37–PE46.

Steffen, W., J. Rockström, K. Richardson, T. M. Lenton, C. Folke, D. Liverman, C. P. Summerhayes, A. D. Barnosky, S. E. Cornell, M. Crucifix, J. F. Donges, I. Fetzer, S .J. Lade, M. Scheffer, R. Winklemann, and H. J. Schellnhuber (2018), "Trajectories of the Earth System in the Anthropocene," *Proceedings of the National Academy of Sciences*, 115(33), 8252–8259.

Sterba, J. P. (1987), "Explaining Asymmetry: A Problem for Parfit," *Philosophy and Public Affairs*, 16(2), 188–192.

Stern, N. H. (2006), *The Stern Review of the Economics of Climate Change* (Cambridge: Cambridge University Press).

Suppes, P. (1987), "Maximizing Freedom of Decision: An Axiomatic Analysis," in G. Feiwel, ed., *Arrow and the Foundation of the Theory of Economic Policy* (London: McMillan).

Tännsjö, T. (2002), "Why We Ought to Accept the Repugnant Conclusion," *Utilitas*, 14(3), 339–359.

Temkin, L. S. (1987), "Intransitivity and the Mere Addition Paradox," *Philosophy and Public Affairs*, 16(2), 138–187.

Thomson, J. T., D. H. Feeny, and R. J. Oakerson (1986), "Institutional Dynamics: The Evolution and Dissolution of Common Property Resource Management," in National Research Council, *Proceedings of Conference on Common Property Resource Management* (Washington, DC: National Academy of Sciences).

Tilman, D. (1982), *Resource Competition and Community Structure* (Princeton, NJ: Princeton University Press).

Tilman, D. (1997), "Biodiversity and Ecosystem Functioning," in G. Daily, ed., *Nature's Services: Societal Dependence on Natural Ecosystems* (Washington, DC: Island Press).

Tilman, D., and J. A. Downing (1994), "Biodiversity and Stability in Grasslands," *Nature*, 367, 363–367.

Tilman, D., and C. L. Lehman (1997), "Habitat Destruction and Species Extinctions," in D. Tilman and P. Kareiva, eds., *Spatial Ecology: The Role of Space in Population Dynamics and Interspecific Interactions* (Princeton, NJ: Princeton University Press).

Tomlinson, J. (2018), "Nigerian Briefing: How Engineers Can Help Steer a Sustainable Economy," *Proceedings of the Institution of Civil Engineers—Energy*, 171(3), 121–128.

Turner, B. L., and A. M. S. Ali (1996), "Induced Intensification: Agricultural Change in Bangladesh with Implications for Malthus and Boserup," *Proceedings of the National Academy of Sciences*, 93(25), 12984–14991.

UNDP (1990), *Human Development Report* (New York: United Nations).

UNFPA (1995), *Programme of Action of the International Conference on Population and Development* (New York: United Nations Population Fund).

UNPD (2015), *World Population Prospects: The 2015 Revision* (New York: United Nations Population Division).

UNU-IHDP/UNEP (prepared by A. Duraiappah et al.) (2012), *Inclusive Wealth Report 2012: Measuring Progress Toward Sustainability* (Cambridge: Cambridge University Press).

UNU-IHDP/UNEP (prepared by A. Duraiappah et al.) (2014), *Inclusive Wealth Report 2012: Measuring Progress Toward Sustainability* (Cambridge: Cambridge University Press).

Veblen, T. (1899). *The Theory of the Leisure Class: An Economic Study of Institutions.* Reprinted in 1925 (London: George Allen & Unwin).

Vincent, J. R., R. M. Ali, and Associates (1997), *Environment and Development in a Resource-Rich Economy: Malaysia Under the New Economic Policy* (Cambridge, MA: Harvard Institute for International Development).

Vosen, P. (2016), "Anthropocene Pinned Down to Post War Period," *Science*, 353(6302), 852–853.

Walker, B., A. Kinzig, and J. Langridge (1999), "Plant Attribute Diversity, Resilience, and Ecosystem Function: The Nature and Significance of Dominant and Minor Species," *Ecosystems*, 2(2), 95–113.

Waters, C. N., J. Zalasiewicz, C. Summerhayes, A. D. Barnosky, C. Poirier, A. Galuszka, A. Cerreta, M. Edgeworth, E. C. Ellis, C. Jeandel, R. Leinfelder, J. R. McNeill, W. Steffen, J. Syritski, D. Vidas, M. Wagreich, M. Williams, A. Zhisheng, J. Grineveld, E. Odada, N. Oreskes, and A. P. Wolfe (2016), "The Anthropocene Is Functionally and Stratigraphically Distinct from the Holocene," *Science*, 351(6269), aad2622.

Weisbrod, B. A. (1964), "Collective Consumption Services of Individual Consumption Goods," *Quarterly Journal of Economics*, 77(1), 71–77.

Williams, B. A. O. (1976), "Moral Luck," *Proceedings of the Aristotelian Society, Supplementary Volumes*, 50, 115–135.

Williams, B. A. O. (1985), *Ethics and the Limits of Philosophy* (London: Fontana).

Williams, B. A. O. (1993), *Shame and Necessity* (Berkeley: University of California Press).

Wilson, E. O. (1992), *The Diversity of Life* (Cambridge, MA: Harvard University Press).

Wilson, E. O. (2016), *Half-Earth: Our Planet's Fight for Life* (New York: Liveright).

World Bank (2016), *World Development Indicators* (Washington DC: World Bank).

Worm, B., E. B. Barbier, N. Beaumont, D. E. Duffy, C. Folke, B. S. Halpern, J. B. C. Jackson, H. K. Lotze, F. Micheli, S. R. Palumbi, E. Sala, K. A. Selkoe, J. J. Stachowicz, and R. Watson (2006), "Impacts of Biodiversity Loss on Ocean Ecosystem Services," *Science*, 314(5800), 787–790.

Wrigley, E. A. (2004), *Poverty, Progress, and Population* (Cambridge: Cambridge University Press).

World Wildlife Fund (2008), *Living Planet Report 2008* (Gland: WWF International).

Yaari, M. (1965), "Uncertain Lifetime, Life Insurance, and the Theory of Consumer," *Review of Economic Studies*, 32(2), 137–158.

Yamaguchi, R. (2018), "Wealth and Population Growth Under Dynamic Average Utilitarianism," *Environment and Development Economics*, 23(1), 1–18.

Yamaguchi, R., M. Sato, and K. Ueta (2016), "Measuring Regional Wealth and Assessing Sustainable Development: An Application to a Disaster-Torn Region of Japan," *Social Indicators Research*, 129(1), 365–389.

Commentary on Birth
and Death

SCOTT BARRETT

IN THIS book, Partha Dasgupta unites the issues that have been his lifelong professional passion: population, human well-being, and the environment.

Thomas Malthus wrote about the confluence of these same subjects in his book, *An Essay on the Principle of Population*. Malthus was concerned with the effects of population on "human happiness," and with humanity's "prospects respecting the future removal or mitigation of the evils which [population] occasions," those "evils" arising from Malthus's central assumption that "the power of population" necessarily overwhelms "the power of the earth to produce subsistence for man. . . . " Here, Dasgupta speaks of "well-being" rather than "happiness" and of the "biosphere" rather than the "earth," and he invokes no iron law of population growth, but at least to me the similarities in his and Malthus's concerns stand out more than the differences in their approaches.

Also like Malthus, Dasgupta is less sanguine than most of his contemporaries about humanity's prospects. Dasgupta's preferred measure of the biosphere's constraint is the "global ecological footprint," a ratio of humans' demands on the environment to Nature's supply. Based on estimates he cites (though with some hesitation), humanity has already pushed deep into unsustainable territory. How does one reconcile this view with evidence showing that, by many measures, including gross domestic product (GDP) per capita, humanity has never had it so good? One reason may be that lagging indicators in the natural system have yet to show the effects of current and past rates of exploitation, to suggest that the day of reckoning is just around the corner. Dasgupta, however, stresses a different reason, namely that GDP is largely blind to the effects of the biosphere's degradation and that, having been guided by the wrong measures, societies have made the wrong calculations. In the closing paragraph of Part II, he also questions whether people have given enough regard to the intrinsic value of Nature and to the ethics of our treatment of Nature, particularly when the consequences of our destructive tendencies are irreversible.

Normative Matters

Dasgupta's main concern is with the normative implications of human population in a world in which the "global ecological footprint" is a hard constraint. Starting from where we are now—a footprint in excess of the sustainable limit—something has to give: population times consumption per capita must be reduced. The question is, how much of the burden of sacrifice should fall on population and how much on consumption?

There is, of course, a related question: how much of the burden of sacrifice should be borne by the current generation and how much by future generations? Dasgupta's way of addressing intergenerational equity is to emphasize the moral obligation parents have to their existing children as opposed to the children they could potentially bring into the world, a view that gives rise to his preferred welfare criterion, Generation-Relative Utilitarianism. Unsurprisingly, this measure recommends a much lower optimal population (for a given subsistence level) than Total Utilitarianism. Dasgupta further argues that different generations can come to an understanding of the fertility decisions each generation should make, given its expectations of the decisions future generations will make, those expectations being confirmed by the decisions that future generations actually make. Toward the end of Part II, he offers some calculations, based on assumptions about the weight in the social well-being function that each generation places on the utility enjoyed by its potential descendants, and the consumption level that defines well-being subsistence. For both formulations of utilitarianism, a higher level of well-being subsistence implies a higher level of optimal consumption and a correspondingly lower level of optimal population. Of course, optimal population is higher and optimal consumption lower under Total Utilitarianism than under Generation-Relative

Utilitarianism, but what I found surprising is that we can't reject the hypothesis that today's population level is optimal under *either* criterion for seemingly plausible parameter values. The range in values revealed by his back-of-the-envelope calculations is enormous.

In these calculations, Dasgupta seeks to identify the combination of population and consumption that is optimal in a world in which humans respect Nature's constraint. But, as mentioned before, the evidence he cites says that humanity has already driven through this constraint. This suggests to me a parallel analysis. Why are we overusing the biosphere, and what are the implications of our doing that for consumption and population?

Positive Matters

Dasgupta's normative model imagines that a Decision-Maker (DM) chooses the balance between consumption and population. The DM is a fictional device, a stand-in for Government in a model that ignores politics. Because Dasgupta's interest lies in the welfare of "the world as a whole," his DM is a World Decision-Maker. (In his intergenerational model, each generation has its own World Decision-Maker.) Looking at the world from this fictional character's perspective is a legitimate— indeed, an essential—move for establishing a normative benchmark. But because there is no World Government, we should want also to know how things can be expected to play out in a world of n countries; that is, a world in which there isn't a single World Decision-Maker but n National Decision-Makers. What can we gain from a positive model of consumption–population choices?

It might be supposed that the national perspective also aggregates at too high a level in that it deprives individuals of agency. However, there is very strong evidence that public policies adopted at the national level are not only devised with the intention of influencing individual fertility choices but that they are *effective* in influencing those choices (de Silva and Tenreyro 2017). Ultimately, we should want to lay a foundation for Generation-Relative Utilitarianism by considering the decisions couples make about procreation in the privacy of their own bedrooms, and then ask why the state should intrude on these personal decisions (the obvious reason being that these personal choices have social consequences—in a word, that they involve "externalities"). Indeed, Dasgupta has done just that in his previous work (see especially Dasgupta 1993); see also Appendix 2 of this book. But because Dasgupta's concern in this book lies more with the global scale of impact than the local one, here I shall focus on the international aspects of population, well-being, and the environment.

Recognizing their collective interest in limiting population, member states of the United Nations convened a sequence of conferences on the subject. The first such conference was held in Rome in 1954. After that, the conference moved to a different host city, once per decade—to Belgrade in 1965, to Bucharest in 1974, to Mexico City in 1984, and, finally, to Cairo in 1994. After Cairo, population policy lost favor among policy elites, who turned their attention to "sustainable development." Most recently, UN members have embraced seventeen Sustainable Development Goals, none of which concerns population. Goal 3.7 comes closest to the mark, asking countries to provide, by 2030, "universal access to sexual and reproductive healthcare services, including for family planning . . . ." However, even this sub-category focuses on individuals and their capabilities and rights, not the social, let alone the global, consequences of individual fertility decisions. The central issue emphasized by Dasgupta—the unavoidable trade-off between population and consumption, and the ability of the biosphere to support the footprint associated with this aggregate of behavior—is not even hinted at in the global agenda to achieve sustainable development.

At the last world conference on population, the one held in Cairo, states adopted a Program of Action, which made recommendations "in a spirit of consensus and international cooperation, recognizing that the formulation and implementation of population-related policies is the responsibility of each country and should take into account [in addition to considerations of primarily national interest] *the shared but differentiated responsibilities of all the world's people for a common future* [emphasis added]." This comes close to the agenda Dasgupta champions when he says, "Globally, reductions in consumption and reproductive externalities cannot occur without international engagement."

What kind of "international engagement" is needed? To model decision-making by the ith of n countries, we can ask that country i's DM, DM_i, choose i's population, N_i. But how do we write the constraint imposed by the biosphere? Taking a first crack at the problem, we can imagine that countries are symmetric, that they have the same utility and production functions, and that Nature, K, is divided equally amongst all n countries; that is, $K_i = K/n$ for all i. In this case, all of Dasgupta's calculations will go through. Instead of a World DM calling the shots, there will be n National DMs doing so, and the outcome ultimately will be the same.

The obvious problem with this formulation is that K isn't divided in this way. The atmosphere and oceans are shared; persistent pollutants are dispersed far and wide by natural processes; species migrate long distances; regime shifts in local ecosystems like coral reefs are triggered by global forces, most especially acidification of the oceans and climate change, as well as local ones, like overfishing and nutrient and soil runoff.

This suggests that K_i, like N_i, is a variable for every DM_i to *choose*. Suppose, then, that every DM_i chooses K_i subject to $\sum_j K_j \leq K$. Here, K is a given, as it is in Dasgupta's formulation. Countries claim a share of the natural resource base, a zero-sum game. In this case, there exists a symmetric Nash equilibrium in which every country i chooses $K_i = K/n$, which is the same result as obtained above. Of course, there also exist many asymmetric equilibria, and in a world of unequals, international engagement may be needed to coordinate on an equilibrium that reflects countries' respective "differentiated responsibilities," as suggested by the Cairo declaration. However, this formulation also misses the mark because it gives countries no option but to limit their collective exploitation to K.

In keeping with Dasgupta's mention of regime shifts and societal collapse, imagine that the constraint $\sum_j K_j \leq K$ needn't be binding, but that there is a cost to be borne by all countries should any country cause the constraint to be exceeded. In a timeless model, one way to model this is as follows:[1]

$$V_i = N_i U\left(K_i F\left(N_i\right) / N_i\right) \text{ if } \sum_j K_j \leq K \quad \text{and}$$

$$V_i = N_i U\left(K_i G\left(N_i\right) / N_i\right) \text{ if } K < \sum_j K_j \leq \bar{K},$$

where $F\left(N_i\right) > G\left(N_i\right)$. Here, K isn't a hard constraint but a kind of threshold; you can think of it as the biosphere's "planetary boundary"

---

1. My approach here, little more than a sketch, is broadly consistent with the one developed formally in Barrett (2013).

(Rockström et al., 2009) or, to use Dasgupta's preferred concept, the "global ecological footprint" set equal to one. According to this formulation, the threshold may be breached—the "footprint" may exceed one—but only at a cost. Excessive use of the biosphere by all countries taken together shrinks the output that can be obtained for a given labor input, possibly to the point of triggering "societal collapse" (an outcome hardly distinguishable from Malthusian catastrophe).

Some imagination is needed in interpreting this move because the model is static and can't distinguish stocks from flows (for a dynamic model that addresses some of the same issues that concern me here, see Appendix 3 of this book). Normally we think of countries as choosing a flow (such as a rate of forest conversion), resulting in a reduction in a stock (the standing mass of primary forest, say). Here, we can think of K_i as a demand being placed on the biosphere (as more of the biosphere is used, output—and hence consumption—for a given population increases, so long as Nature's productive regime continues to hold), and K and $\bar{K}$ can be seen as representing different ecological regimes. If the world uses up no more than K, then production operates in a regime that supports F; if more than K is used up, then we shift to a regime that supports G.

Using less than K would clearly be wasteful (as it is in Dasgupta's analysis). Similarly, using more than K but less than $\bar{K}$ would be wasteful. Hence, in a symmetric equilibrium with n countries, each country's use of the biosphere will equal either $k = K/n$ or $\bar{k} = \bar{K}/n$. The solutions will then give

$$V_i^* = N_i^* U\left(kF\left(N_i^*\right)/N_i^*\right) \text{ and } V_i^{**} = N_i^{**}\left(\bar{k}G\left(N_i^{**}\right)/N_i^{**}\right).$$

Assuming $kF\left(N_i\right) > \bar{k}G\left(N_i\right) \forall N_i$, it should be clear that the World DM will behave the same way as in Dasgupta's analysis, choosing V^* over V^{**} and limiting harm to the biosphere. Indeed, if $kF(N_i)$ is large enough relative to $\bar{k}G(N_i)$, keeping on the safe side of the threshold will also be a Nash equilibrium. International engagement to coordinate use of the shared environment may be needed (as I noted above), but it should not be difficult to achieve.

The more interesting and realistic situation, I think, is to suppose that K, the threshold, is uncertain. Facing uncertainty about the threshold, the World DM will want to proceed cautiously so as to stay on the safe side of the threshold. Uncertainty about the threshold won't have much effect on the normative analysis. However, uncertainty about the threshold will tend to embolden the National DMs acting independently because each is likely to reason that, by increasing its use of the biosphere a bit more, taking as given the demands on the biosphere made by other countries, the chances that the biosphere will "tip" into the bad regime are very low. (Of course, as with the case of threshold certainty, each National DM will also ignore the consequences of its actions for others.) Thus, there will be a tendency for all countries to use the biosphere excessively, causing it to tip into a less productive regime, an outcome that no country would favor but that none can prevent from happening. Threshold uncertainty gives rise to a "tragedy of the commons."

The lesson is that the optimal population–consumption combination adjusts to the ecological regime we happen to be in; it doesn't cause us to be in one regime or the other. Dangerous regime shifts are caused more directly by the excessive demands we place on the biosphere.

Summary

To Malthus, humanity's ultimate need is to show restraint in reproduction. Facing Nature's hard constraint, the consequence of not doing so is painfully low consumption.

Partha Dasgupta's concerns in this book are similar, but his focus is different. He takes aim at the ethics of choosing the optimal consumption–population combination, assuming like Malthus that Nature's constraint is to be respected. A Total Utilitarian would choose a high population level and a low consumption level compared to a Generation-Relative Utilitarian, but the sensitivity of the results he provides is so enormous that disagreements about the appropriate parameter values would seem to matter almost as much as disagreements about the proper social objective.

If it is difficult to know whether the consumption–population combination humanity has chosen is far from the optimum, it is easier to know that our use of the biosphere has exceeded, or will soon exceed, the sustainable limit. Far from imposing a hard constraint, Nature exhibits thresholds that are tempting to overstep, easy to breach and, once crossed, difficult or impossible to return to. A problem for collective action is that these thresholds are also very uncertain. Population policy is a means for achieving well-being in a world in which Nature's thresholds are adhered to (as in Dasgupta's normative analysis) or run through (as suggested above), but other policies are needed to ensure that humanity's global footprint stays on the safe side of dangerous thresholds.

References

Barrett, S. (2013), "Climate Treaties and Approaching Catastrophes," *Journal of Environmental Economics and Management*, 66(2), 235–250.

Dasgupta, P. (1993), *An Inquiry into Well-Being and Destitution* (Oxford: Oxford University Press).

De Silva, T. and S. Tenreyro (2017), "Population Control Policies and Fertility Convergence," *Journal of Economic Perspectives* 31(4), 205–228.

Rockström, J., W. Steffen, K. Noone, A. Persson, F. S. Chapin 3rd, E. F. Lambin, T. M. Lenton, M. Scheffer, C. Folke, H. J. Schellnhuber, B. Nykvist, C. A. de Wit, T. Hughes, S. van der Leeuw, H. Rodhe, S. Sörlin, P. K. Snyder, R. Costanza, U. Svedin, M. Falkenmark, L. Karlberg, R. W. Corell, V. J. Fabry, J. Hansen, B. Walker, D. Liverman, K. Richardson, P. Crutzen, and J. A. Foley. (2009), "A Safe Operating Space for Humanity," *Nature* 461, 472–475.

Commentary on Birth and Death

ERIC MASKIN

NEARLY FIFTY years ago, Partha Dasgupta published a now-classic article on optimal population size, "On the Concept of Optimum Population" (Dasgupta, 1969). This was not a trendy subject in economics then (nor is it now), but something about it fascinated Dasgupta—perhaps it was the way it demands analysis of both an economic and a philosophical sort. And so he has returned to it from time to time over the years (e.g., in "Population Size and the Quality of Life"; Dasgupta, 1989).

Now, in *Birth and Death*, he has produced a profound and graceful essay that, besides economics and philosophy, brings in quite a bit of ecology, too. In fact, the ecological elements give *Birth and Death* a decidedly gloomy cast: Dasgupta argues persuasively that humans are living well beyond their environmentally sustainable means and that world population should be a good deal smaller than its current level, 7.4 billion, if humanity is to have a long and happy future.

At the heart of his analysis, Dasgupta proposes three formal models—one for a timeless world, one for a two-stage setting, and one for an indefinite succession of generations (the case of most relevance). In this brief commentary, I raise a few questions about the formulations and offer several alternative ways of looking at things.

Dasgupta begins the essay by reviewing how an outside observer of classical utilitarian inclination would choose the optimal population size in a timeless world. If total output available for consumption is $AF(K,N)$, where K is the stock of natural resources, N is population size, A is a scalar, and F is a linear homogeneous and concave production function, then the observer chooses N to solve

$$(*) \max_{N} \ NU(AF(K,N)/N),$$

where U is an individual's utility or "well-being" function (also presumed to be concave). Positive values of U correspond to a "good" life; negative values to a "not-good" life. Individuals are considered to be identical so that formula $(*)$ corresponds to maximizing the sum of individuals' utilities (i.e., maximizing *total* utility).

This optimization entails a trade-off between population and utility: as N rises, U must fall (and vice versa). In particular, Dasgupta shows that if U is sufficiently concave, then the solution implies a large value of N (a big population) and a positive value U near 0 (individuals are leading good lives, but barely). The conclusion follows because for a highly concave U, increasing individuals' consumption more than a little above the zero-utility level doesn't improve their utilities much, but it *does* entail reducing the population considerably. So from the standpoint of *total* utility, it is better to keep utilities low and population high.

Derek Parfit has called this the "repugnant conclusion"—the idea that individuals' utilities could be nearly zero in what purports to be an optimum—and accordingly he rejects Utilitarianism. Dasgupta counters Parfit by suggesting that once the point of zero utility has been established, we "should acknowledge that life for a person is good at *any* [emphasis added] standard of living exceeding it" (p. 54). Dasgupta's logic is unassailable here. But even so, I think there may be one (narrow) setting in which Parfit has a valid point.

Suppose that we think of the outside observer as a parent rather than an observer. The population he is choosing are his children. This interpretation seems consistent with the "Genesis Problem" label that Dasgupta gives to optimization $(*)$; think of God the Father doing the choosing. Like parents everywhere, this parent doesn't want life to be merely good for his progeny—he wants is to be *really* good. Thus, he chooses to bring children into the world only if their utilities exceed some critical level U^c. Dasgupta discusses Critical-Level Utilitarianism in Section 5.6 of the essay and doesn't regard it favorably (for good reason). But perhaps under the parent–child interpretation that I am suggesting, it makes some (though limited) sense.

A couple more comments on the Genesis Problem $(*)$. First, let me quibble with the assumption that the function U is concave (this grumble is not with Dasgupta's own essay, but with the previous literature).

The standard justifications of concavity are inequality aversion and risk aversion. But I think both rationales are somewhat problematic here.

Inequality aversion is a matter that, in my view, arises when individuals' utilities are combined to produce *social* welfare; if $W(U_1,..., U_n)$ is the social welfare function (where the U_is are individuals' utilities), then we say that society (or the observer) is averse to differences across individuals, provided that W is concave. That is, inequality aversion is a property of W, not of the individual U_is. In Problem (*), however, W is linear; utilities are simply added together, so there is no room for inequality aversion.

As for risk aversion, I'm not sure that it has much to do with Problem (*). Yes, an individual's von Neumann–Morgenstern utility function will be concave if he is risk-averse, but this von Neumann–Morgenstern utility function need not correspond to his *well-being*. Indeed, in Problem (*) there is no uncertainty at all, and so it is not clear to me why an individual's attitudes toward risk should even be ethically relevant here.

Of course, U may turn out, in reality, to be concave for other reasons. I'm merely suggesting that the two conventional rationales for concavity are questionable.

Second, let me suggest that the assumption that, holding K fixed, the production function F is concave—although also standard—may be doubtful on a macro level. As the population grows, we typically expect there to be more goods available and, as Adam Smith explained vividly, more specialization of labor. But this implies that F should not be concave in N, but rather *convex* up to the point where natural resource constraints kick in. Now, because F will *eventually* be concave, none of Dasgupta's conclusions will be affected by allowing for a region of convexity. Nevertheless, once such a region is introduced, it becomes interesting to explore *Average Utilitarianism* à la John Stuart Mill—in which U, rather than NU, is the maximand—as an alternative to Dasgupta's Total Utilitarianism. Average Utilitarianism in such a setting implies a finite and positive population size, but one considerably smaller than that under Total Utilitarianism (Dasgupta rightly dismisses Average Utilitarianism as unworthy of analysis when F is concave throughout, because it then produces the absurd result that $N = 0$).

When Dasgupta moves from the static setting of the Genesis Problem to a world with multiple generations of individuals, he reasons—convincingly—that the ethically relevant frame of reference is no longer that of an outside observer but rather that of those currently alive. Adapting the agent-centered prerogative advocated by Samuel Scheffler, furthermore, he makes a strong case that the current generation should give less weight to people not yet alive than to themselves.

Actually, it might be interesting to go even *farther* than Dasgupta in exploring Scheffler's principle that individuals should favor themselves over others. In the Dasgupta formulation, all existing people in an individual's cohort get the same weight as she does, and other (potential) individuals get less. But an alternative—and perhaps more purely "Schefflerian"—approach would be for a single (existing) individual (rather than the entire current generation) to perform the population optimization. This individual would put less weight on *all* other people, existing and potential. In the population 0/population 1 model of Section 8.1, an individual in the existing population 0 of size N_0 would choose N_1 (the number of additional people to create) to solve

$$(**) \quad \max_{N_1} \ (1 + \mu(N_0 - 1 + N_1)) U(AF(K, N_0 + N_1) / (N_0 + N_1)),$$

where μ is the weight placed on other people (notice that because all individuals in population 0 are identical, the solution is the same for all of them). This contrasts with formula (20) in Dasgupta's text, in which population 0 chooses N_1 to solve

$$(20) \quad \max_{N_1} \ N_0 U(AF(K, N_0 + N_1)/(N_0 + N_1))$$
$$+ \mu N_1 U(AF(K, N_0 + N_1)/(N_0 + N_1)).$$

I'm not necessarily in favor of replacing (20) with (**), but a comparison of the two formulations may warrant some attention.

Dasgupta's final—and most important—model is one with a potentially infinite sequence of generations. I have two thoughts about it.

First, Dasgupta is utterly cogent on the point that the current generation should not seek to choose population sizes for generations beyond the next one; that is for future people to do. He views intertemporal population choices to be the *equilibrium outcome* of a game played among the generations. I agree completely with this perspective. However, rather than adopting the concept of a *Nash* equilibrium here (as Dasgupta proposes on p. 93), I recommend a *subgame perfect* equilibrium. To be more specific, Dasgupta has the current generation taking future generations' choices *as given* in equilibrium. Yet, if the current decision about population were to change, those later choices would likely change, too. In other words, later choices should be thought of as *functions* of the current generation's decision. And it is this functionality that subgame perfect equilibrium delivers (and that Nash equilibrium doesn't).

Second, let's consider what happens if we adopt a fully individual-centered Schefflerian reformulation of the third model (analogous to my reformulation (∗∗) of the second model). Notice that each individual in the current generation will put more weight on his own children than on those of others. So, if the choice of how many children to have is made family by family (rather than collectively), then the reformulated model will result in *higher* population levels than in the original model. This is because the modified model implies that a family will give less weight to the negative externality that more children imposes on others. This externality may be worth exploring further.

Even if we disregard other aspects of the essay (for example, its highly original ecological arguments), the models developed in *Birth and Death* already mark it as a major contribution to the ethics of population. If any of my remarks on modeling are worthwhile, my hope is that they can help enrich the lively discussion that will surely follow the essay's publication.

References

Dasgupta, P. (1969), "On the Concept of Optimum Population," *Review of Economic Studies*, 36(3), 295–318.

Dasgupta, P. (1989), "Population Size and the Quality of Life," *Proceedings of the Aristotelian Society*, 63, 23–54.

Commentary on Birth and Death

JOSEPH STIGLITZ

IN THIS beautiful lecture on optimum population policy, Partha Dasgupta returns to some of the path-breaking themes he touched upon in his Cambridge doctoral dissertation (the central chapter of which was published in 1969), enlightened by his own thinking over the ensuing decades and that of others. It is unfortunate that these topics have not received the attention they deserve, especially as we have become increasingly aware of our planetary boundaries, limitations that standard economists, with their love of constant returns to scale technologies and exponential growth, have consistently ignored.

No question could be of greater economic or philosophical importance than that addressed here, especially now that we have the easy means of controlling our population. Dasgupta devotes much of his attention to some deep philosophical questions about how we should think about an increase in population size, questions that were discussed early on by the utilitarians. A Benthamite, for whom the social welfare function is simply the sum of utilities (and what Dasgupta refers to as Total Utilitarianism), would presumably seek simply to maximize that sum. The resulting calculus is simple: compare the utility of an added individual to the decrement in utility of those previously existing. This requires not only an assessment of marginal utilities, but also of "absolute" utility levels, both of which the New Welfare Economics that came into fashion in the middle of the twentieth century strongly eschewed. Dasgupta provides a persuasive argument against such welfare nihilism.

In these brief remarks, I do not want to comment further on the many philosophical issues that Dasgupta exposits better than I possibly could. Rather, I want to highlight some intuitions and complexities associated with even the simplest utilitarian frameworks. Still, I should emphasize that Dasgupta approaches the problem somewhat differently, from a more philosophical/ethical set of concerns, and accordingly his analysis does not necessarily fit squarely with that presented in these comments.

It is clear that population is an arena where individual rationality cannot be relied upon to generate socially optimum outcomes. Each individual, in making his own decision, presumably focuses on his own well-being, appropriately framed to include his evaluation of the well-being of his descendants and the weight that he gives to their well-being. Even if we assumed a high degree of rationality in that decision-making process, each individual presumably takes prices and the state of congestion of the world as given, taking no account of the fact that, when other like-minded people similarly make decisions, it does affect prices and the state of congestion. In short, what are now referred to as macroeconomic externalities are pervasive.[1]

Wearing another hat, the individual (as a citizen), wishing to maximize some notion of social welfare, might have views that differ from those of the (same) individual, making his own private decisions. That there can be such discrepancies is familiar: in paying my taxes, I may minimize my tax obligations, *given the law*. At the same time, I may vote for laws that result in higher taxes for myself (and other similarly situated individuals). When I don the hat as a voter, I think of what kind of society I want to live in. In this role, I may well put more or less weight on the desirability of having a larger population.

Dasgupta's discussion adds further to the analysis by calling attention to a critical distinction between developing and developed countries and the consequences of the limitations of our biosphere. In developing countries, there are market failures, and children are both

---

1. Macroeconomic externalities are the extension to macroeconomics of the important microeconomic pecuniary externalities uncovered by B. Greenwald and J. E. Stiglitz (1986), "Externalities in Economies with Imperfect Information and Incomplete Markets," *Quarterly Journal of Economics*, 101(2), 229–264. See the discussion below for a further elaboration on these externalities.

productive assets and a means of reducing the risks associated with old age. In developed countries, children often represent a financial liability, and whatever pleasure they generate for the parents, they surely reduce the levels of "own-consumption" available to the parents. And while children often bear some of the risks associated with old age, much of the burden has shifted to the public. Thus, there is a change in the calculus of child-bearing, reflected in most advanced countries: the demographic transition, resulting in smaller families—indeed, in many advanced countries, below the self-sustaining level.

There is one more important element in the demographic transition: the reduction in uncertainties associated with early death. With a risk-averse utility function, families may target a larger family size to offset the risk that large numbers may die in infancy or childhood. Dasgupta's formal analysis abstracts from these elements of uncertainty.

The greater awareness of the limitations of our biosphere should also lead to a smaller optimum population—smaller than would be individually rational. It acts much like a congestion externality. Assume that individuals do not like being on crowded beaches. Then an increase in the size of the population lowers the well-being of each individual, an effect which each family does not take into account in making its reproductive decisions (unless it is acting perfectly altruistically). Similarly, if we were all engaged in agrarian activities, and there were a fixed amount of land, increased population would be reflected in a decrease in output per hour worked, and a decrease in standards of living as population increases. Each family (with rational expectations) takes wages and land rents as given, and thus ignores the macroeconomic externality generated as increased population pressure drives down wages (with consequent implications for labor supply).

One more change in our societies that amplifies the effects just discussed is urbanization, the result of the change in the structure of production. We no longer live in an agrarian economy, so the effects just described on wages and agrarian land rents are of less importance, but there are many other aspects of the population pressure on our biosphere. But setting those aside, with urbanization there is now an "artificial" scarcity created by the desire to be, say, near the city center or other locations where economic and social activities occur.

As population increases, these urban land rents increase, and especially so in contexts where there is not an optimum spatial distribution of population and/or there are natural geographical limitations (e.g., those posed by the island of Manhattan). Again, each family, in making its decisions, ignores these macroeconomic consequences.

The factors just discussed, by themselves, would presumably lead to too large a population (even in developed countries, where not taking into account congestion effects would lead to too large a family). Yet, there are some counteracting forces. A somewhat nationalistic example illustrates: Consider a country worried about conflict with its neighbors, in a world (largely gone by) where victory depends on the (relative) size of the population. As a voter, I would like others to have more children, so much so that I would be willing to vote for a child subsidy. It is clearly possible that in this situation, the optimum population is greater than that which is individually rational. Dasgupta naturally abstracts from such situations in his lecture: he focuses on the problem of the world as a whole.

But there are still other factors that might lead to a too small population, most importantly related to one more aspect of changes in the structure of production: the importance of technological change, whether the result of research and development, learning by doing, or investing (which were discussed by Arrow in his classic 1962 papers[2]). These give rise to a natural non-convexity, increasing returns to scale. The larger the population, the higher the output per capita and/or the rates of increase in output per capita. Think of this most simply: the real advances in standards of living are a result of innovations, breakthroughs in science.[3] Assume that those capable of making such breakthroughs occur at the extreme tails of the distribution; then the larger the population, the larger the number of these "innovation" individuals and the faster the pace of innovation—from which all benefit.

In this perspective in the absence of the constraints imposed by the biosphere or of congestion effects, the larger the population, the

---

2. K. Arrow (1962), "Economic Welfare and the Allocation of Resources for Invention," in *The Rate and Direction of Inventive Activity: Economic and Social Factors*, ed. R. Nelson (Princeton, NJ: Princeton University Press), 609–626; K. Arrow (1962), "The Economic Implications of Learning by Doing," *Review of Economic Studies* 29(3), 155–173.

3. See, e.g., J. E. Stiglitz and B. Greenwald (2014), *Creating a Learning Society: A New Approach to Growth, Development, and Social Progress* (New York: Columbia University Press). Reader's Edition published in 2015 (originally presented as the first Arrow lecture).

higher the average utility, and so long as, on average, the marginal individual has a positive utility, the greater the population, the higher social welfare. But we cannot abstract away from those effects, and the implication is that there is a population that maximizes average utility (i.e., there is an inverted U-shaped curve of utility as a function of population size; note the contrast between our analysis, balancing the constraints of space and the biosphere and returns to scale in innovation, with the conventional analyses, which simply assume constant returns to scale). Denote the level of population at which average utility is maximized by N^*. So long as the social welfare population assigns some weight to the size of the population (i.e., so long as the utility level of the marginal individual at the optimum is positive), then the optimum population size is greater than that which maximizes (average) utility. Because individuals in their own reproductive decision-making ignore both the congestion and scale effects (negative and positive externalities), the equilibrium population will be at $N = N^*$ (i.e., it is less than the social optimum).

There are still other complexities. Dasgupta rightly, in my judgment, emphasizes the importance of sustainability, using a more general social welfare criterion focusing on relative well-being. If individuals, in making their own reproductive decisions, focus less on the well-being of future generations than society as a whole would and should, then individuals will pay insufficient attention to how decisions today decrease future well-being; but this is even true if individuals and societies use the same criterion, simply because individuals fail to take into account the macroeconomic externalities associated with their decisions. This restores the presumption that there will be excessive population.

The discrepancy will be especially large if there are large non-linearities in the stresses population imposes on the biosphere, in the absence of adequate regulatory and pricing systems. Individuals at time t may decide to have a population at time $t + 1$ that is greater than the tipping point, at which there is systemic collapse, described so vividly by Jared Diamond (2005). If that is the case, the approximations provided by Dasgupta on the extent of overpopulation may not be valid. And this may be especially so if there are stochastic fluctuations in reproduction (given any set of reproductive decisions) or the biosphere's carrying capacity.

An important question that follows from any analysis suggesting that the population is likely to be too large is whether there are policy interventions that could correct the market distortion. The answer is probably yes, especially given recent evidence that, in advanced countries, family decision-making is resulting in reduced populations. Making families bear more of the costs of children and imposing charges to reflect macroeconomic externalities can help align private and social costs. However, especially the former can have large implications for societal equity. Regulatory measures, such as softer versions of China's one-child policy, may be more equitable, but in democratic societies they are socially distasteful.

One of the hardest issues raised by population ethics concerns equity: when families bear some of the costs of child-rearing (and children are not productive assets), then richer families have an opportunity set that may "allow" them to have more children than poor families; for instance, if parents have to pay for the education of their children, and basic decency requires them to provide a minimum level of education to each child, then a poor family might be able to afford at most one child, while a rich family is unconstrained. Specific egalitarianism (Tobin, 1970) argues that there are certain goods to which access should be given regardless of income. The constitutions of many countries recognize this principle in terms of basic rights (e.g., the right to access to health care). The right to have at least two children may be viewed by some to fall within this rubric. Thus, measures to discourage excessive populations must be progressive. This can be achieved by combining per-child transfers to families for up to, say, two children, with the charges described in the previous paragraph. But this puts some of the burden of population policy on the children of lower-income parents who decide to have larger families. It may well be argued that it is unethical to make these children pay for the "sins" of their parents.

The use of the utilitarian calculus, even the subtle and important variants explored by Dasgupta, raises difficult issues once we depart from models in which all individuals in all generations are assumed to be the same, or sufficiently similar, to represent their well-being (at least from the perspective of Dasgupta's Decision-Maker) by the same utility function. For just as we can ask how do we weigh the current generation against the future, we need to ask how do we weigh the well-being of some within the current generation against others. And then we need to combine the two. Upon first reading Edgeworth's (1881) discussion of optimum population decades ago, I was deeply disturbed, and upon rereading it in preparing for these comments, I remain so. Edgeworth notes differences in productive and consumption capacities of different individuals, and that there is intergenerational transmission of these capacities. He asks, "*not* assuming that all sections multiply equally, [how do we] . . . find the average issue for each section, so that the happiness of the next generation may be the greatest possible?" After showing that, in the presence of resource constraints (i.e., the limited biosphere), population should be limited, he concludes with an extreme eugenic/Spencerian solution: "the average issue shall be as large as possible for all sections above a determinate degree of capacity, but zero for all sections below that degree."

In short, the implementation of optimum population policies raises a hard set of philosophical and ethical issues, perhaps as complex as those posed by the analysis of optimum population itself. That these questions are difficult is not a justification for not facing up to them; whether we like it or not, there will be profound implications for our society today and the future if we neglect to confront them head on.

For all the niceties I have raised in these comments on Dasgupta's Arrow Lecture, the central message, I believe, is correct: Societies, on their own, are likely to arrive at a population that is greater than the social optimum.

References

Arrow, K. (1962), "The Economic Implications of Learning by Doing," *Review of Economic Studies*, 29(3), 155–173.

Arrow, K. (1962), "Economic Welfare and the Allocation of Resources for Invention," in R. Nelson, ed., *The Rate and Direction of Inventive Activity: Economic and Social Factors* (Princeton, NJ: Princeton University Press), 609–626.

Dasgupta, P. (1969), "On the Concept of Optimum Population," *Review of Economic Studies*, 36(3), 295–318.

Diamond, J. (2005), *Collapse: How Societies Choose to Fail or Survive* (London: Allen Lane).

Edgeworth, F. Y. (1881), *Mathematic Psychics: An Essay on the Application of Mathematics to the Moral Sciences* (London: C. Kegan Paul), 70.

Greenwald, B., and J. E. Stiglitz (1986), "Externalities in Economies with Imperfect Information and Incomplete Markets," *Quarterly Journal of Economics*, 101(2), 229–264.

Stiglitz, J. E., and B. Greenwald (2014), *Creating a Learning Society: A New Approach to Growth, Development, and Social Progress* (New York: Columbia University Press).

Tobin, J. (1970), "On Limiting the Domain of Inequality," *Journal of Law and Economics*, 13(2), 263–277.

Response to Commentaries

PARTHA DASGUPTA

POPULATION ETHICS involves five overlapping areas of concern. At its core is population axiology, which searches for principles on which to base population ethics. Second, there needs to be a socio-ecological model where the principles are to be put to work. Third, there are tactical moves to be made in the model so as to prepare the way for translating principles into policy. Fourth, the model has to be calibrated so that we can uncover quantitatively the social objectives that are implied by the principles. Finally, we have to identify policies that would help to further those objectives. By "policy" I don't simply mean a tax on this or a subsidy on that or a regulation on something else. Encouraging people to alter their behavior with respect to such delicate matters as biodiversity loss in distant parts of the world is not a common objective in economic reasoning; it is novel territory. It is also a delicate territory when that loss can be expected to be felt only in the future and be traceable to activities elsewhere. In my Arrow Lecture, I studied the first four areas of concerns but resisted the fifth because of a lack of expertise. In Part I of "Socially Embedded Preferences, Environmental Externalities, and Reproductive Rights," which is reprinted in this volume, my coauthor Aisha Dasgupta and I broached population policy, but only tentatively and only by study-ing a few aspects of family planning programs.

Robert Solow in his Foreword to my Arrow Lecture, and Scott Barrett, Eric Maskin, and Joseph Stiglitz in their Comments, together discuss all four areas of concern I covered in the Lecture, and I am most grateful to them for raising searching questions of my treatment of every one of them. The subject is hard and there is a long way to go.

Generation-Relative Utilitarianism

In the formal model I used to develop Generation-Relative Utilitarianism (Sect. 9), people are taken to be identical, they are assumed to live for two periods, time is identified with generations, generations overlap for one period (the latter three assumptions can be easily relaxed), and the horizon is conditionally infinite. In the notation of Section 9.6 (eq. (32)), the social valuation function of someone of generation-t is

$$V(t) = N(t)U(C(t)) + \mu N(t+1)U(C(t)) + \mu\{_{u=t+1}\Sigma^\infty\{\theta^{(u-t)}[(N(u)$$

$$+ N(u+1))U(C(u))]\}\}, 0 < \mu, \theta < 1; t = 0,1, \ldots \qquad (1)$$

Because the model assumes people of each generation to be fully synchronized, it is possible to pretend that, using her ethical motivation, any member of generation-t can serve as a representative of generation-t. That enabled me to replace each person by her generation and interpret agent-centered prerogatives as generation-centered prerogatives. That's where the inequality $0 < \mu < 1$ enters the formulation. In contrast, Total Utilitarianism insists $\mu = 1$.

Both Kenneth Arrow (letter #3) and Robert Solow ask who the decision-maker, charged with maximizing $V(t)$, could be. Solow is of course right when he says it is Us. But it is central to the Arrow Lecture that we distinguish Us from the Decision-Maker (DM) at Genesis. For a number of decades now, at least since 1974, I have felt it would place an unwarranted burden on anyone, even when the person is Us, to expect of her to award the same ethical concern for potential lives as for the lives of living people and actual-future people. Which is why I thought (and still think) Total Utilitarianism can only be the valuation function of DM at Genesis. Eric Maskin cuts to the chase and identifies DM as "God the Father." I have been more reticent in my writings.

The valuation function in equation (1) can also be interpreted as the informed, dynastic point of view of a member of generation-t. I haven't followed that route in the Arrow Lecture because I wanted to stay close to the literature on population axiology. In stating his principle of just saving, however, John Rawls used the motivation of a dynastic head (Appendix 3 of my Arrow Lecture). In an early attempt at developing Generation-Relative Utilitarianism (Dasgupta, 1974),

I followed what I thought was Rawls' motivation assumption and took, but only as an example, the valuation function of someone of generation-t to be

$$V(t) = \log C(t) + \mu[n(t)\log C(t+1) + an(t) - bn^2(t)] + B \quad (2)$$

In equation (2), $0 < \mu < 1$; $a, b > 0$; B is a constant; and $n(t)$ is the number of children the person considers having.

The quadratic term, $an(t) - bn^2(t)$, in equation (2) was taken to represent the externalities associated with isolation and crowding.[1] Previously, in Dasgupta (1969), I had introduced crowding externalities in the individual well-being function U, but I had relegated it to a brief section (Sect. 6). I have ignored it in the Arrow Lecture because of the two reasons Solow offers: In population axiology nothing specific can be said about ways of including isolation and crowding in personal experiences; moreover, when considering the world as a whole, there is in all probability a large range of population numbers where neither of the two experiences bites, at least not systematically.

In a later work, Becker, Murphy, and Tamura (1990) introduced a dynastic model, which in the notation here reads as

$$V(t) = U(C(t)) + \mu(n(t))n(t)V(t+1) \quad (3)$$

In equation (3), $dU/dC > 0$, $d^2U/dC^2 < 0$, $d\mu/dn < 0$, and $n(t)$ is the number of children.

Because theirs was an explanatory model of fertility behavior, the authors didn't probe the normative foundations of their formulation. But even if we were to assume that $d\mu/dn(t) = 0$, the formulations in equations (2) and (3) differ. Parents whose valuation function can be represented by equation (2) care about their children's personal well-beings. In contrast, parents whose valuation function can be represented by equation (3) care about their children's valuation of *dynastic*

---

1. (p. 121): "One may . . . have views on the size of the next generation—the feeling that one would not want the human race to die out. . . . By the same token, one may have views on the size of the present population— the feeling of isolation if there are too few of one's contemporaries, or indeed the feeling of congestion in many other circumstances."

well-being. The valuation function in equation (1) differs from both: DM awards agent-centered prerogatives on her own well-being over potential well-beings irrespective of the generation being considered.

I developed Generation-Relative Utilitarianism as an alternative to Total Utilitarianism for people who are not persuaded by Total Utilitarianism but want closely related ethical guidance for reproductive decisions. As Solow reminds us, an earlier literature advocated Average Utilitarianism for that end. In place of equation (31) in the text of the Arrow Lecture, a dynamic version of Average Utilitarianism (AU), evaluated at t, would read as

$$AU_{(t)} = {}_{u=t}\Sigma^{\infty}[(N(u) + N(u+1))U(C(u))]\theta^{(u-t)}/{}_{u=t}\Sigma^{\infty}[(N(u)$$
$$+ N(u+1))]\theta^{(u-t)} \qquad (4)$$

In his comments, Eric Maskin suggests it is worth considering Average Utilitarianism in worlds where average well-being increases with population when population is small but declines with population when population is large. That's the world studied by a previous generation of economists (Gottlieb, 1949) and which Solow exposits with great probity. There is an immediate problem with Average Utilitarianism, even the Dynamic Average Utilitarianism of equation (4). Suppose maximum average utility is a large positive figure. It is hard to explain why DM should not favor the creation of another person whose utility, other things equal, would be only a bit smaller.

Maskin suggests also that Critical-Level Utilitarianism may be a valid ethical framework for potential parents, who could be expected to want life for their progeny to be *really* good, not *merely* good. The problem with Critical-Level Utilitarianism is one it shares with all absolutist theories. Suppose a potential parent learns that the well-being of any child she has will be just below the critical level. It is hard to imagine her choosing to remain childless on that count. Nor would anyone advise her to do so. Trade-offs matter to us. Generation-Relative Utilitarianism is designed to meet Actual Problems, that is, it is a normative theory for potential parents. It admits trade-offs. The parameter μ captures agent-centered prerogatives and accommodates the desire that one's children will have lives well in excess of zero well-being. The exercises in Section 11 in the Arrow Lecture were designed to illustrate that. I return to this point below.

The Socio-Ecological Model

In a wide-ranging set of remarks, Joseph Stiglitz identifies not only reasons we have to think that population in the contemporary world is too large (population "overshoot"), but also reasons we have to think that population in the contemporary world is too small (population "undershoot"). Taken together, they determine the sign of the demographic distortion we should be led to believe characterizes today's world. Among the latter reasons, Stiglitz points to increasing returns-to-scale in production accompanying advances in technology. In recent centuries, scale economies have played a significant role in raising the global standard of living. If I have understated the role technological advances are likely to play in directing the contemporary world toward sustainable development, it's because I combined the two tendencies Stiglitz points to by studying the adverse externalities those scale economies bring with them when they are deployed on common property resources. In any event, much of Part II (Sects. 10 and 12) of the Arrow Lecture was designed to remind us that the scale economies of new technologies we believe we enjoy are measured in terms of market prices, not accounting prices. That practice may not have mattered decades ago, but it matters today. The current state and future prospects of the biosphere, which I have reported all too briefly in the Lecture, tell us that the scale economies we estimate with conventional economic tools come with a hidden bite. They are significant over-estimates.

Scott Barrett explores the system of property rights to goods and services that should be embedded in population ethics. He observes that a necessary condition for arriving at globally optimum states of affairs is the parceling of the biosphere into pieces of national property; say, by a use of national quotas. The proposal requires that the quotas be independent of nations' future population sizes and is the one he studies. But if the quotas are designed to respond positively to changes in population size, as is often the case even for local common property resources, then (other things equal) the outcome is a population overshoot (Appendix 2). Of enormous significance to population ethics is Barrett's own work and the work he is doing jointly with Astrid Dannenberg, on the prospects for reaching international agreements over the use of the global commons. The thoughts he sketches here—for example, the influence on international negotiations of our lack of knowledge of the biosphere's tipping points—are far-reaching (see especially Barrett and Dannenberg, 2012; Barrett, 2013).

Both Solow and Stiglitz point to a glaring limitation of the socio-ecological model I (and also Aisha Dasgupta) have used for developing population ethics. The model assumes an absence of inequality among contemporaries (I am referring to Parts I and II of the Arrow Lecture and Part II of the paper with Aisha Dasgupta reprinted in this volume). We did it for the reason Solow identifies: population axiology is hard enough even without inequality. In the Arrow Lecture I was also concerned with exploring, with the data that are currently available, what economists call *full optima*, which in an economy of identical individuals would not countenance inequality in the distribution of inclusive wealth. But that's not a reason for not taking a shot here at studying population ethics in a world where the government is unable, for one reason or another, to bring about equality in the distribution of (inclusive) wealth.

Begin by defining inequality as wealth inequality among households. As was noted in Section 5.5 (see also Kenneth Arrow's letter #3), among Utilitarian households those that are wealthier will have greater numbers of children. There is a sizeable literature explaining why the evidence (Table 1) goes so counter to that prediction. I collated those arguments in Section 1, but it pays to search for simple explanations that override the direct Utilitarian motivation.

A now-traditional explanation among economists is based on the (market) value of time (Becker, 1960; Becker, Murphy, and Tamura, 1990). Wealthier households are wealthier because, or so the argument goes, their wages are higher. And their wages are higher because they have acquired more human capital than less wealthy households. So, the value of time is higher for wealthier households. If you now acknowledge that bearing and rearing children, taken together, is very time consuming, you have an explanation. But the explanation is restricted to market economies. Understanding fertility behavior in poor societies requires help from anthropologists. In Section 1 of the Arrow Lecture, I moved away from the Beckerian framework because it does not work there. In poor countries, rural women are required to do a huge amount of work each day.

An explanation equally as simple as Becker's can be constructed if we acknowledge that household preferences for goods and services are socially embedded. Table 1 and the reasoning we deployed in Section 1 to understand it using socially embedded preferences suggest that μ is large and C^S is small in poor societies relative to their respective values in rich societies, other things equal. In work under preparation, Simon Beard, Aisha Dasgupta, and I are developing this line of thinking so as to include inequality and poverty in population ethics.

Tactical Moves Within the Socio-Ecological Model

Maskin makes the entirely valid point that because well-being isn't the same as utility when the latter is based on revealed preference, it is illegitimate to borrow evidence on the degree of risk aversion people are thought to display and use it in the numerical exercises in Section 11. He also makes the more general point that I haven't provided any defense of the assumption that the *U*-function in the exercises is concave.

Beggars can't be choosers. As we have little quantitative feel for even the most general features of informed desires as they bear on the consumption of goods and services, I had next to nothing to go on. Recent work in behavioral psychology suggests that estimates of risk aversion built on expected utility theory are suspect.[2] So there are problems on all sides with the traditional literature on attitudes to risk. One can argue though that the axioms leading to "expected utility" are more likely to be satisfied by informed desire. Leonard Savage, who had given choice under uncertainty much thought, argued that the axioms of choice leading to expected utility are ones an informed person would subscribe to. However, the empirical estimates of risk aversion that economists studying consumer demand have arrived at by using a questionable theory of human behavior as we go about our daily lives are pretty much all we have got on offer. And even though no direct mention was made in the model in Section 9 of risk, I did give the discount factor θ in the social valuation function (eq. (32) in the Arrow Lecture and eq. (1) above) the interpretation of *extinction risk*, meaning that risk was not absent from the model. I appealed

---

2. O'Donohue and Somerville (2018) is a fine review of problems with the existing literature on risk aversion.

to data on risk aversion to inform Generation-Relative Utilitarianism; but only as a first cut into a complex matter. In any event, we have no reason to think degrees of risk aversion among those who maximize expected well-being are wildly different from those that have been estimated from behavior, even when the behavior has been modeled somewhat wrongly. Which is why my move is far from the one the proverbial drunk makes when looking for his keys at night under the lamp post when he knows they aren't there.

Maskin is right to explore alternative formulations of agent-centered prerogatives. I chose my formulation of Generation Relative Utilitarianism deliberately. I wanted to introduce the mildest form of agent-centered prerogatives so as to make comparison of the theory's implications with those of Total Utilitarianism transparent. The exercises in Section 11 display the differences sharply.

What of concavity of the U-function when U represents a quantitative measure of informed desires? Concavity of multi-variate well-being functions reflects a desire for a balanced life, not one of extremes (unless extremes are forced upon one by contingencies). We may not have much information on the structure of informed desires in the contemporary literature on decision-making, but the ancients had a lot to say on the matter. Sages in the distant past in many cultures advised us that, if we are to flourish, we should seek balance in our lives. (The Buddha stressed the virtue of moderation, which is a style of life that would be required by the desire for balance because of budgetary constraints.) So, concavity is not to be dismissed without hard evidence to the contrary. Nevertheless, suppose as a research strategy we were to abandon concavity. We would then have to postulate a non-concave U-function, but with little guidance on the kind of non-concavity we should entertain. We could of course proceed to build a taxonomy of cases, but that could be unending. Moreover, some would have weird implications, which would make us question whether we are taking a sensible route.

Consider a simple case in which the U-function is sigmoid (i.e., it is an increasing function of C, and is convex at small Cs but concave at large Cs). Assume people are identical. Under a wide range of circumstances, Generation-Relative Utilitarianism (or, for that matter, Total Utilitarianism) would recommend the establishment of a two-class society in which one group enjoys less consumption than the other.[3] It is hard to reconcile that implication with most people's considered ethical judgments. I continue to think it pays to work with well-understood formulations when exploring unchartered problems.

Maskin is right to question my use of the Nash equilibrium in identifying optimum population profiles under Generation-Relative Utilitarianism (Sects. 9 and 11). I wanted to nail the idea of a population optimum across the generations with the littlest of fuss. As a route from abstract reasoning to concrete numbers, the Nash equilibrium worked well for me. The refinement of the Nash equilibrium that Maskin recommends, namely sub-game perfection, takes a little more doing. If you follow its logic and impose stationarity on the resulting recursive function, you arrive at a refined version of equations (34a–b)–(35). The ratio of optimum living standard to well-being subsistence remains independent of K^* and, if the parameter values are the same, the ratio is larger.

Model Calibration

The decision to study stationary optima in Section 11 was forced on me because of a lack of data. Appendix 4 identifies the minimum set of data that would be needed to characterize optimum consumption, population, and resource-use policies in a dynamic economy. We know that the biosphere can be thought of as a gigantic renewable natural resource, but we know next to nothing about the parameters that define its dynamics. So I took the desperate steps of stopping the biosphere and all other capital goods in their tracks and calibrating the model by using estimates of our global ecological footprint. The idea that society can stop so complex an object as the Earth system on its tracks is wholly beyond belief, but it's the only move I had available to me for finding my way through a fogbound maze. The numbers I reached on the basis of the calibration are not attainable, nor are they to be taken literally; I have nevertheless presented them here to show how far off humanity is from where we should probably now be.

---

3. The reasoning is that DM, other things equal, can make use of the convex range of the *U*-function to raise average well-being via a two-class society.

Joseph Stiglitz worries that my approximations of optimum stationary profiles of consumption, output, and population may not be valid because of the existence of tipping points in the Earth system's dynamics. He notes too that stochasticity of the dynamics would further reduce its validity.

The features of the biosphere Stiglitz points to are of enormous significance (I discussed them, even if all too briefly, in Sections 10 and 12 and Appendix 4); but the idea of a stationary optimum doesn't suffer from contradiction on those counts. It will be recalled that I took the global ecological footprint to be 1.5 when estimating the aggregate demand today's biosphere could support indefinitely. There is, of course, a risk that the biosphere would be unable to oblige, that it would cross a tipping point and move into a different stability regime. That's Stiglitz's point. We should imagine, however, that by reducing our demands on the biosphere we could lower the risk that it crosses a tipping point. So, for example, it would be a simple matter to re-compute the estimates in Section 11 by using a larger figure with which to shrink the global demand, say 2 rather than the 1.5 I used. Such a move would suffice for a deterministic world. But Stiglitz rightly points to the uncertainty we harbor about the location of the biosphere's tipping points. The probability distribution in this case is defined on the space of the biosphere's various possible states. The trick is to use that probability distribution to construct the corresponding probability distribution over the (future) date at which the economy first reaches a tipping point. The latter distribution is, of course, endogenous to the analysis, because it depends on the economic path that is being followed. For example, the risk of being at a tipping point would be small if the demands that are made of the biosphere were small relative to the biosphere's ability to supply us with goods and services. Dasgupta, Heal, and Majumdar (1977) proved that in such a model the following is true: In the face of the risk of a catastrophic event (there may even be a cascade of catastrophic events in store), the optimum policy is to pretend the event will never occur, but to then replace the expression under summation at time t by the expected value of U at t plus the expected value at t of an assessment of the biosphere's productivity following the event. The hazard rate for the occurrence of the catastrophe is of course endogenous to the analysis. The theorem speaks to a form of "certainty equivalence," and it legitimizes the stationarity assumption in Section 11.[4] Of course, the assumption that DM is able to formulate her understanding of the socio-ecological system she is studying in terms of a probability distribution over the system's states could be wrong. Some of the evidence that she draws on would be ambiguous, meaning that she may not be able to arrive at even a subjective probability distribution over the system's states. In the Arrow Lecture I have bypassed these problems because there is as yet no settled theory of decision under ambiguity.

Robert Solow shares my disappointment and frustration at the paucity of data that are crucially needed in population ethics. He notes especially the parameter μ, on which Generation-Relative Utilitarianism is built, and feels the figures I worked with to illustrate the theory (0.01, 0.05, and 0.1) are shockingly low. He suspects that I worked backward (he doesn't say so outright—he is far too generous to do that—but I can tell!); that is, he suspects that I chose values of μ that, in conjunction with figures for well-being subsistence, yielded living standards that I felt one could subscribe to in the first place.

Solow is, of course, quite right; that's exactly what I did. Like him, I have no intuitive feel for values of μ that one could directly justify. That's one reason we should not feel the figures I chose to work with are overly low.[5] The other, far more important reason is that μ applies only to *potential* well-beings, not to the well-beings of one's children.

---

4. The theorem I am alluding to generalizes the one which says that if there is a risk of human *extinction*, a Total Utilitarian could well pretend there is no such risk but raise the time discount rate by the hazard rate of extinction. Yaari (1965) used that insight to build a theory of optimum annuities. I used that same argument in Section 9.1 when developing the idea of discounting for risk. There we did not need to augment the U-function under summation because humanity would cease to exist after the catastrophe, at least in any recognizable form. The exercises in Section 11 are best thought of as being based on that assumption.

5. There is no place for μ in the accompanying paper with Aisha Dasgupta because the analysis there is based on a stipulated living standard. The task before the social evaluator there was to estimate the size of the global population that could be supported at that standard over an indefinite future.

The hallmark of Generation-Relative Utilitarianism is backward induction. Once a child is born, she receives the same considerations as everyone else for the allocation of resources. Potential parents know in advance that this is how they will treat the children they eventually have. And it is on this understanding that they choose how many children *to* have. That is why I believe one way to get a feel for μ is to infer its value from reproductive stopping rules that couples have been known to follow. The attenuated version of agent-centered prerogatives that underlies Generation-Relative Utilitarianism *curbs* births; it doesn't discriminate against other people, and it most certainly doesn't discriminate against one's own children.

All of this explains to me why I found it surprising that Scott Barrett expresses surprise that the estimates of optimum population (and correspondingly, the optimum living standard) that I arrived at in Section 11 vary widely, depending on the figures that are chosen for well-being subsistence C^S and for the weight μ for generation-centered prerogatives. Suppose you had asked even fifteen years ago for an estimate of the social cost of a ton of carbon. You would have been informed that the figures that were then on offer by experts on the economics of climate change ranged from 5 to 500 U.S. dollars, depending on, among other things, the model that was used to estimate damages and the rates that were chosen for discounting time and the generations. I imagine you would then have said that a range of 5 to 500 U.S. dollars is pretty wide.

Today, however, you would be quoted a narrower range, largely because experts have developed better intuition for the parameters that determine the social cost of carbon. For example, Tol (2011) found that values near the extremities in the 5 to 500 U.S. dollar range are improbable. The accepted range is now a lot narrower. In 2016, for example, the U.S. Environmental Protection Agency suggested a range of 11 to 56 U.S. dollars per ton of carbon.

In contrast, well-being subsistence and generation-relative prerogatives remain alien concepts in economics. We could, as I have suggested, estimate them from behavior; which would be a start. But as of now, there is nothing in the literature on the values of parameters of crucial importance for population ethics. The estimates in Section 11 illustrate how the population-consumption-environment nexus can be studied, they tell us how far we are today from where we probably should be, but they don't tell us much more.

References

Arrow, K. J., P. Dasgupta, L. H. Goulder, G. Daily, P. R. Ehrlich, G. M. Heal, S. A. Levin, K.-G. Mäler, S. Schneider, D. A. Starrett, and B. Walker (2004), "Are We Consuming Too Much?" *Journal of Economic Perspectives*, 18(3), 147–172.

Barrett, S. (2013), "Climate Treaties and Approaching Catastrophes," *Journal of Environmental Economics and Management*, 66(2), 235–250.

Barrett, S., and A. Dannenberg (2012), "Climate Negotiations Under Scientific Uncertainty," *Proceedings of the National Academy of Sciences*, 109(43), 17372–17376.

Becker, G. S. (1960), "An Economic Analysis of Fertility," in *Demographic and Economic Change in Developed Countries*, NBER Publication (New York: Columbia University Press).

Becker, G. S., K. M. Murphy, and R. Tamura (1990), "Human Capital, Fertility, and Economic Growth," *Journal of Political Economy*, 98(5), S12–S37.

Dasgupta, P. (1969), "On the Concept of Optimum Population," *Review of Economic Studies*, 36(3), 295–318.

Dasgupta, P. (1974), "On Optimum Population Size," in A. Mitra, ed., *Economic Theory and Planning: Essays in Honour of A. K. Dasgupta* (Delhi: Oxford University Press).

Dasgupta, P., and K.-G. Mäler (2000), "Net National Product, Wealth, and Social Well-Being," *Environment and Development Economics*, 5(1), 69–93.

Dasgupta, P., G. Heal, and M. Majumdar (1977), "Resource Depletion and Research and Development," in M. Intriligator, ed., *Frontiers of Quantitative Economics, Vol. 3B* (Amsterdam: North Holland).

Gottlieb, M. (1945), "The Theory of Optimum Population for a Closed Economy," *Journal of Political Economy*, 53(3), 289–316.

O'Donohue, T., and J. Somerville (2018), "Modeling Risk Aversion in Economics," *Journal of Economic Perspectives*, 32(2), 91–114.

Tol, R. S. J. (2011), "The Social Cost of Carbon," *Annual Review of Resource Economics*, 3, 419–443.

World Wildlife Fund (in collaboration with the London Zoological Society) (2018), *Living Planet Report 2018* (Gland: WWF International).

Yaari, M. (1965), "Uncertain Lifetime, Life Insurance, and the Theory of Consumer," *Review of Economic Studies*, 32(2), 137–158.

Epilogue

PREPARING A monograph on a largely unchartered subject is, I imagine, rather like the routines we read of the hard-boiled detective at work in an unfamiliar terrain. Each piece of evidence that presents itself, be it analytical or empirical, offers an unexpected lead. The problem is, it isn't always clear what amounts to evidence and which leads are worth chasing. When, in August 2014, I began composing the book that became the Arrow Lecture, I thought it would be an easy exercise. I was wrong. The more I worked on the book, the more interconnected the bits and pieces at the population-consumption-environment nexus appeared to me (and I had been studying the nexus for years). Moreover, such evidence that I studied had been collected by scientists in several disciplines, over many years. Pulling them together and translating them into my language took time and required help from colleagues in those other disciplines.

My native tongue is modern economics, so my translation will be unfamiliar to many. In the Arrow Lecture I have tried to construct a reasoning that offers more than just a glimpse of the socio-ecological processes at work in our engagement with our descendants. That reasoning has uncovered an extensive body of unaccounted for consequences that our activities have given rise to. Those consequences are "externalities," which are rather like dendrites: they branch out over time and across space. Their presence and growth help to explain how even reasoned decisions at the individual level can have led us to a situation where our collective demands for the biosphere's goods and services exceed by a lot more than a margin its ability to supply them. To infer from our collective profligacy that at the personal level we don't care about our descendants would be wrong. Each of us extracts more of the biosphere's supply of goods and services than we would ideally like to, because the biosphere is largely an open-access resource. For the same reason, the discount rates that are inferred from our market transactions are very likely to be a lot higher than the rates we would use to discount future generations if we assumed the role of DM. Our weakness is not necessarily myopia, it is rather our inability (even perhaps unwillingness) to alter our engagements so as to meet our collective needs.

In his comments Eric Maskin writes that he is persuaded by the reasoning but finds it gloomy. I had not intended to convey that impression. I have a cheerful disposition (even my children would attest to that) and feel that if we social scientists were to uncover and publicize the really problematic features of the socio-ecological processes humanity has unleashed, we would all take heed, if for no other reason than that our descendants appear in the reckoning. As I type this, there is for example an increasing recognition that our use of plastic materials is causing untold damage to marine life and to other parts of the biota. Many people are doing something about it, through changes in their practices and persuading the powers that be to regulate our use of those materials. For most people, I would imagine, the unaccounted-for consequences of our use of plastics came as a surprise. But it was believed because scientists and broadcasters produced visible evidence. Fortunately also, or so it can be argued, biodegradable alternatives to plastics are available, and that possibility encourages us to seek technological solutions. The problem is that those alternatives also require material to be drawn from the biosphere, and as demand for them grows, so will our ecological footprint grow. There is no getting away from the scale of the contemporary human enterprise. The World Wildlife Fund (2018) notes that over the past 40 years there has been on average a 60 percent decline in the populations of mammals, birds, fish, reptiles, and amphibians, mostly centered in the tropics. The publication points to the growth in palm oil and soya plantations, and to the construction of dams, mines, and roads as proximate causes.

As with animals, so with plant life. The biological extinctions the Anthropocene has unleashed include the disappearance of plants species. It is an obvious corollary of economic reasoning that the international community ought now to pay nations to protect the biodiversity that is harbored in their territories. Our ecological footprint exceeds

1 and is growing. That's our diminishing planet. But I know of no reasoned projection of humanity's demands over the coming decades that doesn't involve further deforestation and transformation of grasslands so as to create more plantations, farms, and grazing fields. And I don't know of any plausible scenario where technology comes to our rescue by enabling us to avoid those extensive demands. Even the background papers for the United Nations' Sustainable Development Goals didn't enquire whether the biosphere has the capacity to serve those of our enlarged needs that would arise if the goals were met in a world with a far larger population than our current number. That is why in Part II of the Arrow Lecture I focused on the exceptional growth that has taken place in our use of land and the seas since the middle of the 20th century. The pace at which we accomplished our over-reach on the biosphere came as a surprise to me when I first read the biogeochemical evidence. So I undertook the crude calculations of global GDP growth over the past 70 years (Sect. 10) in order to make sense of what Earth scientists had uncovered. Seventy years is a brief moment in economic history, which is a reason we should not feel reassured on being told that technology will come to our aid to solve the biospheric problems we have created.

The optimum stationary states we studied in Sections 9 and 11 are at odds with today's sensibilities. They read as a throwback to John Stuart Mill, who, as Robert Solow remarks, should have known better by the time he came to write his treatise on political economy. The Industrial Revolution was under way, and progress was in the air. Today we take it as axiomatic that tomorrow should be better than now, at least on average. But progress is nearly always seen in terms of measures (e.g., GDP) that demand even more of the biosphere's goods and services than they do currently. And that's a demand that can't be met indefinitely. Which is why I have worked backward in the Arrow Lecture, by first freezing the biosphere in its track and then determining the implications of Generation-Relative Utilitarianism. The move ensured that the limits imposed by the biosphere would not be violated; but it doesn't necessarily take us all the way to the study of stationary states. If by progress we mean, as I believe we should mean, a rise in social well-being over time (Dasgupta and Mäler, 2000, and Arrow et al., 2004, called that rise "sustainable development"), then, as the wealth/well-being equivalence theorem says, it would be accompanied by a corresponding rise in inclusive wealth. To bring that about would require devising institutions and habits and practices (i.e., styles of life) that improve life's quality without further encroaching on the biosphere. The models I constructed in the Arrow Lecture eschew those possibilities, because as of now we can but see only a glimmer of what those styles of life would be, let alone how they could be adopted. What we *can* say is that those innovations would be embodied in human capital (its quality, and habits and practices) and what we have called "enabling capital." Inclusive wealth would increase over time, and it would involve the accumulation of produced capital, human capital, and enabling capital, with no concomitant decumulation of natural capital. In modeling that, I could of course have introduced a term in the factors determining personal well-being that increases exogenously over time; but that would have been cheating. Social scientists have given these matters so very little thought that we have nothing to go on. In any case, to try to anticipate the character of those innovations is not the right way to proceed. We should instead expect such habits and practices, and the institutions that encourage them, to evolve if people are given half a chance. And that chance requires measures that encourage us to discipline our demands on the Earth system.

Until that happens, there are in all probability more alarming surprises in store for us. It seems to me the problem isn't so much that citizens don't care about the future as that the treatment we have been meting out to the Earth system since we ushered in the Anthropocene is not generally appreciated. And if citizens don't appreciate that, they can hardly be expected to be curious about the socio-ecological mechanisms that have encouraged us to so extend our demands of it. In great measure that gap in our appreciation persists because official statistics suppress the costs our habits and practices are storing up for our descendants. That's not necessarily evidence of conspiracy at work, but rather of the fact that modern economics hasn't recognized the transformation we have brought about over the past decades in our relationship with the natural world. Our collective sense can be expected to prevail only if we are reliably informed of where we are, and where we are likely to be heading unless we act to curb our over-reach.

Socially Embedded Preferences, Environmental Externalities, and Reproductive Rights

AISHA DASGUPTA *AND* PARTHA DASGUPTA

AMONG ECONOMISTS and demographers, the dominant view of the effect of growing human numbers on the natural environment has alternated between concern and dismissal. If in the years immediately following World War II scholars were anxious that population growth would retard economic development in poor countries, they have not worried in recent decades. A series of influential reviews of the modern growth experience (National Research Council 1986; Birdsall 1988; Kelley 1988; Temple 1999; Helpman 2004) studied cross-country data and saw a negligible link—possibly even a small positive link—between population growth and growth in per capita gross domestic product. These analyses were convincing, but the underlying assumption that economic betterment is best seen in terms of growth in GDP per capita should be questioned. The presence of the qualifier "gross" in gross domestic product signals that the measure does not record

Reprinted from Dasgupta, Aisha, and Partha Dasgupta. "Socially Embedded Preferences, Environmental Externalities, and Reproductive Rights." *Population and Development Review* 43, no. 3 (2017): 405–441. https://www.doi.org/10.1111/padr.12090.

The views expressed in this essay are entirely those of the authors and do not necessarily reflect the views of the United Nations. For their helpful comments on a previous draft, we are grateful to John Cleland, Rachel Friedman, and Robert Solow.

the depreciation of natural capital that can accompany the production of goods and services.[1] Other things equal, depreciation of natural capital reduces a nation's productive capacity, the correct measure of which is an inclusive notion of wealth. And normative economics tells us that the index we should deploy for assessing the sustainability of human development is the wealth of nations (Arrow et al. 2012), not the GDP of nations, nor the Human Development Index of nations.[2]

A rich demographic literature has offered insights into fertility behavior in the contemporary world. Those insights have been used by the United Nations to frame family planning programs (UNFPA 1995). More recently they have influenced the way family planning has been placed within the UN's Sustainable Development Goals. We apply those insights to argue that the basis on which women's expressed desired for children is elicited misestimates their desire. More importantly, it underestimates women's true need for family planning.

Parental desires and wants constitute one set of factors in population ethics. Another set of factors is the effect on others of a household's reproductive behavior. Ehrlich and Holdren (1971) coined the metaphor $I = PAT$ to trace humanity's *i*mpact on the biosphere (more generally, the Earth system) to *p*opulation size, *a*ffluence (income per capita), and "*t*echnology"-in-use (including knowledge, institutions, social capital). The authors observed that Nature responds to the demands we make of it, not to rates of change in those demands nor to rates of change in the rates of change in those demands. Their observation has had little influence on either economics or demography. That the growth rate of global population has been declining in recent years is seen by development experts as a hopeful sign of a transition to sustainable development (World Bank 2016); in fact the decline does not say much about the prospect of realizing sustainable development.

---

1. The term natural capital is now in routine use among ecologists and economists to remind us that Nature is a capital asset with both intrinsic and use value. In what follows we use the terms nature, natural capital, and the natural environment synonymously. The influence of human numbers on the natural environment is again being noted in demographic writings. See, for example, Birdsall, Kelley, and Sinding (2001), Bryant et al. (2009), and Jiang and Hardee (2011).

2. The latter index was proposed by UNDP (1990) and has been revised and updated by the organization ever since.

Under foreseeable technological developments, a long-run population of 10–11 billion can be expected to make far greater demands on the biosphere than one of, say, 3 billion. Recent books that have drawn attention to the remarkable gains in the standard of living during the past century have focused on advances in scientific knowledge and the accumulation of manufactured and human capital; the state of the biosphere and its trends accompanying that progress have for the most part gone unnoted (Micklethwait and Wooldridge 2000; Ridley 2010; Deaton 2013; Lomborg 2014; Norberg 2016). But humanity's future will be shaped by the portfolio of assets we choose to hold and the balance we strike between them and the size of our population. It should be a concern that the enormous economic success we have enjoyed in recent decades may be a down payment for future failure.

Among the visible products of the biosphere are food, fibers, fuel, and fresh water, but many of the services it provides are hidden from view. Ecosystems maintain a genetic library, preserve and regenerate soil, fix nitrogen and carbon, recycle nutrients, control floods, mitigate droughts, filter pollutants, assimilate and decompose waste, pollinate crops, operate the hydrological cycles, and maintain the gaseous composition of the atmosphere. Since most of these services are not visible, they are easy to overlook. Some environmental stresses are global, many are spatially localized; some occur slowly and may therefore miss detection until it is too late, while others are noticeable and a cause of persistent societal stresses. The wide divergence of environmental problems may explain why people differ in the perceived urgency that they express about carbon emissions and loss of biodiversity that extend beyond nations, regions, and continents; about degradation of oceanic life arising from the energy and materials we release into them; about the hardship communities face when grasslands transform into shrub-lands; and about declines in firewood, water sources, and soil productivity that are specific to the needs and concerns of the poor in village communities.[3] Environmental problems differ in their location and in their spatial and temporal scales, which is why it is possible to be optimistic about humanity's collective ability to overcome environmental problems if one studies small-scale environmental successes

---

3. For extended discussions on the place of Nature in the lives of the world's poor, see Dasgupta (1993, 2007, 2010).

(Balmford and Knowlton 2017) but to be deeply worried if one looks at continued failure to stem global biodiversity loss. Contemporary data at the global level tell us that environmental successes to date have been few and far between.

Environmental scientists have compiled data on the state of the biosphere and its changing character over past decades (MEA 2005a–d). Corresponding data at local levels are scattered and range from the detailed to nothing. But global happenings are an aggregate of large numbers of local happenings. Below we develop an analytical framework for studying fertility behavior and humanity's impact on the natural environment at local levels (Part I) and use aggregate data to obtain a quantitative assessment of the impact at the global level (Part II). We find that humanity's demand for Nature's goods and services in the aggregate exceeds by a considerable margin Nature's ability to supply them. Our hope is that the framework we construct will point to the way the balance between population size and the portfolio of our assets could be struck.

Externalities

Processes driving the balance between population size and the assets we hold give rise to externalities, which are the unaccounted-for consequences for others of actions taken by one or more persons. The qualifier "unaccounted for" means that the consequences in question follow without prior engagement with those who are affected.

The way we have formulated the notion of externalities could appear ineffective, on grounds that our actions inevitably have consequences for future generations, who by the nature of things cannot engage with us. In fact future people engage with us constantly, albeit indirectly. Parents care about their children and know that they in turn will care about their children. By recursion, thoughtful parents take the well-being of their descendants into account when choosing the rates at which they save for their children and invest in them. Intergenerational engagement would be imperfect if parents choose without adequate concern for their children (e.g. if they discount the future well-being of their children at overly high rates). Externalities across the generations would be rampant in that case. We ignore that line of analysis here. Our aim is to study systematic reasons why choices made even by thoughtful parents do not reflect adequate engagement with *others'* descendants. Since they are symptoms of institutional failure, externalities cannot be eliminated without considered and tenacious collective action. That is why reasoned reproductive decisions at the individual level can nevertheless result in collective failure.

Two broad categories of externalities are studied here. One consists of the consequences of household consumption and reproduction that work through open-access resources ("the commons"). That is the familiar variety of externalities, much noted and studied by environmental economists (e.g. Baumol and Oates 1975). Institutional failures in this class of externalities arise from an absence of appropriate property rights to Nature's goods and services. By property rights we mean not only private rights, but also communitarian and public rights. One reason rights to natural capital are difficult to define, let alone enforce, is that Nature is constantly on the move (the wind blows, particulates diffuse, rivers flow, fish swim, birds and insects fly). No one can contain the environmental asset they damage. As a result, the price paid by someone for environmental services (the private cost) is less than the cost borne by all (the social cost). In cases involving the global environment, such as the atmosphere as a sink for carbon emissions, the damage an individual suffers from his own emissions is negligible even though the damage to all from the climate change that arises from everyone's emissions is large and positive. From the collective point of view there is excessive use of the atmosphere as a carbon sink. The environmental externalities to which our use of open-access resources gives rise are adverse.

The other category of externalities we uncover here has been less studied in the literature. It arises because our desire to have children is in part influenced by the number of children others have. No doubt a single household cannot much influence others, but the aggregate effect of all households on one another is not negligible. The social embeddedness of household preferences—we call the resulting behavior "conformist"—can lead to high fertility even when those same preference structures can sustain the low fertility that perhaps all households would prefer. Either situation—high fertility (allied to low educational attainment of children) or low fertility (allied to high educational attainment)—can be self-sustaining. Fertility transitions can be interpreted as moves from one equilibrium to the other.

The two classes of externalities have very different internal structures. The problem of choice in the use of open-access resources resembles the well-known prisoner's dilemma. In contrast, socially embedded preferences give rise to coordination games. Communities can turn the latter class of externalities to their advantage by coordinating behavior (e.g. through an appeal to social norms), whereas the former requires, at least over the global commons, more traditional policy measures such as environmental regulations.

Outline of the essay

In Part I (Sections 1–5) we study the clash of rights among contemporaries and between present and future people. We then study the implications of those clashes for the design of family planning programs. In attributing rights to future people, we are appealing to a widely shared view that no matter who and how many our descendants happen to be, they will have a justifiable claim to a reasonably abundant resource base. Future people's personal identities do not matter in this context. The question arises whether the environmental externalities we identify here are quantitatively significant. To explore that question, we make use of global estimates of humanity's demand for the biosphere's products and services relative to their supply. That exercise is conducted in Part II (Sections 6–10).

In Section 1 we review the proposed distinction by the legal philosopher Charles Fried between positive and negative rights. We apply the distinction to study the clash between the moral directives flowing from adverse environmental externalities and the exercise of personal rights. That step acts as a backdrop for Section 2, where we recall that some prominent social scientists have insisted that there are no environmental externalities arising from procreation.

In Section 3 we explore the interplay of parental motivations and socio-ecological constraints that help to explain differences in reproductive behavior across regions and across socioeconomic groups within regions. We look briefly also at what has been called "African exceptionalism" in reproductive behavior and identify a class of inter-household externalities that may have contributed to high fertility rates in that region. Socially embedded preferences are identified in Section 4 as a source of inter-household externalities, sustaining high fertility rates. We note possible mechanisms by which behavior stemming from such preferences can be redirected toward lower fertility rates. None of the mechanisms involves taxation or coercion.

A central plank of family planning programs is the idea of reducing unmet need. In Section 5 we argue that the methods currently deployed for measuring unmet need for family planning underestimate it. We also show that the UN's Sustainable Development Goals include a measure for judging the success of family planning programs that potentially creates wrong incentives for officials overseeing the programs. Our analysis reveals that family planning programs are undervalued by national governments and international agencies.

By how much? To determine that, we go beyond measuring unmet need and try to quantify environmental externalities. Estimates of the environmental externalities traceable to procreation are sparse. Customary methods for measuring externalities infer people's willingness to pay for Nature's products and services from their behavior or from their expressed preferences. Those methods are unavailable for reaching global estimates, nor are they appropriate for the purpose at hand. We circumvent those problems by studying global statistics on natural capital and identify key processes that drive the biosphere (Sections 6–7). Such information is not sufficient for quantifying the benefits of family planning programs, but it offers a way to estimate the annual global demand we make of the biosphere and compare it to the annual global supply. That is done in Section 8, where we report that demand has for some time exceeded supply. The finding says we are drawing down natural capital and therefore that environmental externalities are substantial.

In Section 9 we provide crude estimates of the size of the global population that the biosphere can support at a comfortable standard of living under contemporary technologies and institutions. The gap between the figure we reach and the current size of the world's population is substantial. Our estimate of the gap could be viewed as being an overestimate of what lies in the future, inasmuch as sustainable population at a comfortable living standard would be higher if future technological advances economize on the use of natural capital. On the other hand, our estimate could be viewed as an underestimate, inasmuch as global population has been projected to rise to 11.2 billion by the end of the present century and the UN's Sustainable Development Goals are simultaneously aimed at significantly increasing per capita incomes. Whether resource-saving technological advances are likely to blunt humanity's demand for Nature's products and services even as economic activities increase is, of course, a matter of speculation. We therefore identify reasons why technological changes in the past and the evolution of our consumption patterns have been rapacious in the use of natural capital. Those reasons point to policies that would be expected to encourage technological innovations and lifestyles that place lighter demand on Nature's products and services.

The analysis in Sections 8–9 is based on figures using global averages. Central to the Sustainable Development Goals, however, is poverty alleviation. In Section 10 we study the impact of poverty alleviation measures on the global demand for Nature's goods and services. Our analysis uncovers yet another clash of rights among contemporaries and between present and future people.

Although the externalities we classify here arise in all contemporary societies, there is a difference between rich (high-consuming) societies with low desired family size and poor (low-consuming) societies with high desired family size. Environmental externalities arising from the activities of people in rich countries are included in our analysis (they are due to the high consumption enjoyed by new births over their lifetime). Simple calculations show that contemporary global environmental problems cannot be traced to high fertility in today's poorest parts of the world. Nevertheless, we focus on reproductive behavior in the world's poorest region, sub-Saharan Africa, because desired family size there is strikingly large in comparison to standards elsewhere and because the costs of the correspondingly high population growth rate can be expected to be borne in great measure by future Africans themselves. The benefits of family planning programs have been routinely underestimated by the international community, but perhaps most conspicuously by governments in sub-Saharan Africa (Section 11).[4]

---

4. By providing access to subsidized contraceptive commodities and services, family planning programs were successful in accelerating fertility declines in Asia and Latin America in the 1960s–1980s. One rationale for vigorously expanding the content and reach of such programs today lies in the 189 million married/in-union women of reproductive age in the developing world (41 million in sub-Saharan Africa) who have an unmet need for modern methods of contraception (UNPD 2016). In addition to reducing unintended births, contraceptive use among women enhances their own health and that of their children by spacing births. And yet family planning remains a neglected feature of public policy. Currently less than 1 percent of overseas development assistance is awarded to it. Moreover, developing countries relegate family planning expenditures to minor government departments. Despite evidence that family planning reduces poverty, the World Bank does not have family planning at its core.

Part I

1. Rights

The legal philosopher Charles Fried distinguished positive rights from negative rights (Fried 1978). We are to think of positive rights as a claim *to* something, a share of material goods or some commodity such as education and medical attention. A negative right is a right that something *not* be done to one, that some particular imposition be withheld. Fried observed that positive rights are asserted to scarce goods and that scarcity implies a limit to their claim. He also suggested that negative rights, for example the right not to be interfered with in forbidden ways, do not appear to have such natural limitations. ("If I am let alone, the commodity I obtain does not appear of its nature to be a scarce or limited one. How can we run out of people not harming each other, not lying to each other, leaving each other alone?" (p. 110).)[5]

Fried's dichotomy is useful for studying the place of rights in family planning programs, but his suggestion that the exercise of negative rights does not involve costs is questionable. The claim that one's proximity should not be contaminated by cigarette smoke is a negative right, which is violated when someone smokes in that proximity. To protect that right, governments in many countries prohibit people from choosing at will where they smoke. That represents a cost to smokers. In contrast, a right to exercise one's agency would appear to be a positive right (e.g. freedom of speech), but it does not inevitably demand resources from others. It is not so much that negative rights do not suffer from resource limitations whereas positive rights do, it is more that the two sets of rights have separate frames of reference. The contrasting phrases, right to self-determination and right to have an imposition withheld, point in different directions.

The 1994 International Conference on Population and Development reaffirmed the language of rights in the sphere of family planning and reproductive health. The Conference's conclusions stated:

---

5. The binary classification of rights corresponds to Isaiah Berlin's classification of freedom into positive and negative categories (Berlin 1959).

"Reproductive rights . . . rest on the recognition of the basic right of all couples and individuals to decide freely and responsibly the number, spacing, and timing of their children, and to have information and means to do so, and the right to attain the highest standards of sexual and reproductive health" (UNFPA 1995: Ch. 7, Sect. 3).

The qualifier "responsibly" could be read as requiring couples to take into account the adverse environmental externalities their reproductive decisions may give rise to; but that probably would be a stretched construction. Certainly, writings affirming the UN declaration have interpreted the passage and its intent more narrowly. For example, the fundamental right of individuals "to decide freely and for themselves whether, when, and how many children to have" is central to the vision and goals of Family Planning 2020 (FP2020). It is also pivotal in the reproductive health indicators of the Sustainable Development Goals. Both positive and negative rights are in play here. Rights to information and other services pertaining to family planning and reproductive health are positive rights. The right to choose one's family size, on the other hand, would appear to be a negative right.[6]

Even though Fried's classification is not without problems, it is useful for studying the relationship between externalities and rights. First, to insist that the rights of individuals and couples to decide freely the number of children they produce trump all competing interests is to minimize the rights of all those (most especially, perhaps, future people) who suffer from the environmental externalities that accompany additions to the population. Second, UNFPA's statement ignores the latent need among those who do not want family planning now but

---

6. Kumar and Hardee (2015) offer a useful manual for family planning programs based on the protection and promotion of reproductive rights. Rights had been deployed as an ethical category in discussions on family planning and reproductive health prior to the 1994 International Conference on Population and Development. Hardee et al. (2014) provide an account of that history as well as a framework for achieving the goals of FP2020. Cottingham, Germaine, and Hunt (2012) offer an account of the power of the language of rights in encouraging governments and international agencies to provide the resources needed to meet women's unmet need for family planning and reproductive health facilities (see Section 5).

would want it if others among their peer group were using modern contraceptives. We study the two in turn.[7]

2. Ours vs. Theirs

That reproductive decisions may involve a clash of rights is not self-evident. In a powerful essay that dismissed concerns on over-population, Bauer (1981, pp. 61–64) wrote: "The comparatively high fertility and large families in many ldcs (less developed countries) should not be regarded as irrational, abnormal, incomprehensible or unexpected. They accord with the tradition of most cultures and with the precepts of religious and political leaders. . . . Allegations or apprehensions of adverse or even disastrous results of population growth are unfounded. They rest on seriously defective analysis of the determinants of economic performance; they misconceive the conduct of the peoples of ldcs; and they employ criteria of welfare so inappropriate that they register as deterioration changes which are in fact improvements in the conditions of people."

One problem with Bauer's critique is that it gives the impression that societies in past eras were characterized by large families. But if fertility rates were high then, so were mortality rates; and high fertility rates are a rational response to high mortality rates. The contemporary demographic problem in the world's poorest regions is that fertility rates remain high even though mortality rates have fallen considerably. The main problem with Bauer's critique, however, is that even when men and women at the household level prefer large numbers of children to small numbers, it does not follow there is no resource-allocation failure they themselves would acknowledge if only they were asked. As in every other field of personal choice, we should ask whether a collection of reasoned decisions at the individual level may harbor

---

7. Brock (2010) contains an interesting discussion of possible clashes between parental rights and societal interests and how societies variously resolve them. But he was not concerned with the clash that is embodied in environmental externalities. The tension between reproductive rights and sustainable development has been commented upon recently (e.g. Hardee 2014; Newman et al. 2014), but it would appear not to have influenced development thinking.

collective failure. This is the central question raised by externalities, and it is particularly apposite in the case of adverse externalities and socially embedded preferences.

That family planning services bring many benefits (health, education, income, women's empowerment) to those who make use of them has been documented repeatedly in recent years (Koenig et al. 1992; Debpuur et al. 2002; Cleland et al. 2006; Cleland et al. 2012; Tsui, McDonald-Mosley, and Burke 2010; Canning and Schultz 2012; Sonfield et al. 2013; Bongaarts 2016; Miller and Babiarz 2016). Our focus on externalities points to the fact that they bring benefits to others as well. Those additional benefits should be included in the design of social policies.

Policies for curbing adverse reproductive externalities can take several forms. Education, especially female education, is one route; some argue it is the most effective route (Lutz, Butz, and KC 2014). But that can take time, and female education is not the only factor driving fertility.[8] Another tool involves demonstrative persuasion, which can be attempted through community discussions on the need for behavioral change. The agent of persuasion could be the community, NGOs, or the state.[9] A further tool is taxation, which permits people to choose as they wish, but at a price. Although taxation as a device for curbing environmental externalities is familiar in wealthy countries, it is not available for reducing the demand for children in poor countries, where the poorest households (who do not pay taxes) are most often the ones that have the highest demand. A further policy tool is a quota, such as China's previous directive of the one-child family, or the Chinese government's recently revised two-children-per-couple directive.

Quotas are an extreme form of non-linear tax schedule: zero tax up to the quota, followed by a severe tax beyond it. (The tax need not

---

8. World Bank (2012) reported that in 2010 the proportion of people who completed primary education was 96 percent in India, 67 percent in Pakistan, and 65 percent in Bangladesh. Total fertility rates (TFRs) in those countries were 2.6, 3.4, and 2.2. It should also be noted that in Bangladesh nongovernmental organizations at work on social matters have a far more extensive reach than in India and Pakistan. Reproductive behavior is not mono-causal.

9. Nudge theory advocates a weak version of that idea. See Thaler and Sunstein (2008).

be monetary; it could be strong collective disapproval.) An alternative to taxing people if they exceed their quota is to reward them if they stay within it. We are thinking of quota here in the same way as people think of quotas when they are imposed as food rations in periods of extreme shortage, compulsory vaccination against communicable diseases, and prohibition on smoking in public spaces. The first example ensures equality in the distribution of a positive right; the second and third examples protect and promote negative rights.

The classification of externalities suggests a variety of policy tools for reducing fertility rates. The tools differ in the extent to which the right to self-determination is compromised. None is likely to prove uncontroversial. The issues remain unsettled.[10]

3. The Demand for Children and African Exceptionalism

Social anthropologists have shown that children are valuable to us not only because of our innate desire to bear and rear them, but also because they represent the fulfillment of tradition and religious dictates and are the clearest avenue to self-transcendence. One such injunction emanates from the cult of the ancestor, which, taking religion to be the act of reproducing the lineage, requires women to bear many children.[11] This motivation was used by Caldwell and Caldwell (1990) to explain why sub-Saharan Africa has for the most part proved so resistant to fertility decline.

---

10. Sen (1982) likens the emission of persistent pollutants to torturing future people. The clash between reproductive rights and adverse environmental externalities allied to new births is at its most striking under his reading.

11. Writing about West Africa, Fortes (1978, pp. 125–6) said "a person does not feel he has fulfilled his destiny until he or she not only becomes a parent but has grandchildren. . . . [Parenthood] is also a fulfilment of fundamental kinship, religious and political obligations, and represents a commitment by parents to transmit the cultural heritage of the community. . . . Ancestry, as juridically rather than biologically defined, is the primary criterion . . . for the allocation of economic, political, and religious status."

A weakness of the argument is that, although it explains why fertility rates in Africa are high (the total fertility rate is 5.1 today, in contrast to 2.5 in India, 1.6 in China, and the global TFR of 2.5), it does not explain why the rates have not responded to declines in infant mortality to the extent one might have thought on the basis of experience elsewhere.[12] Even in sub-Saharan Africa fertility rates have been lower than the maximum possible. Below we study possible reasons why the response has been slower than expected. We should expect the reasons to vary across regions within the sub-continent. Under increasing urbanization some will have also weakened over time (e.g. the cult of the ancestor). But because quantitative evidence on their relative significance across regions is patchy, we only identify them here.

In places where formal institutions are underdeveloped, children also substitute for other assets and are thus also valuable for the many benefits they bring to their parents. This is most apparent in the poorest regions of the world. Children serve as security in old age in places that have neither pension schemes nor adequate land markets. They are also a source of labor in households possessing few labor-saving devices. Children mind their siblings, tend to domestic animals, pick berries and herbs, collect firewood, draw water, and help with food preparation. The need for additional hands is especially strong among rural communities in dry and semi-arid regions. Children in poor countries are valued by their parents also as capital and producer goods.

Caldwell (1981, 1982) proposed that the inter-generational transfer of resources is from children to parents in poor societies, and from parents to children in rich societies. The suggestion has been easier to confirm in rich countries, where the rate of investment in children's education has been found to be as high as 6–7 percent of GDP (Haveman and Wolfe 1995). Confirming the reverse flow in poor countries has been a lot harder, in part because data are sparse but in part also because even within poor regions there are significant differences in attitudes toward reproduction. Those differences are traceable to kinship structures, marriage practices, and rules of inheritance. The implied line of thinking says that over the long run it is differences in institutions and social norms—originating perhaps in some measure

---

12. Between 1965 and 2015 the infant mortality rate in sub-Saharan Africa declined from about 150 deaths per 1,000 live births to around 60 per 1,000.

in geography—that lie behind differences in reproductive behavior among groups. Theoretical models have been built on the premise that institutional failure, broadly defined, is the deep cause of pronatalism. Causality is not traced to differences in income or wealth. It is not that fertility and mortality rates are high and health status and education attainments are low in poor regions because people there are poor, it is that very low incomes go hand in hand with those other features of life. Each variable influences the others over time; in the long run they are mutually determined.[13]

A potential source of reproductive externality is the wedge between the private and social costs of childrearing. The costs borne by parents are lower when childrearing is shared among kin than when households are nuclear. In sub-Saharan Africa fosterage within the kinship is a commonplace. Children are not raised solely by their parents; the responsibility is more diffuse within the kinship group (Caldwell 1991; Bledsoe 1990, 1994). In parts of West Africa up to half the children have been found to be living with their kin at any given time. Nephews and nieces have the same rights of accommodation and support as do biological offspring. There is a sense in which children are seen as a common responsibility, which makes it important that in surveys that seek to identify desired numbers of children it is made clear that the questionnaire refers to biological children. However, fosterage creates a free-rider problem if the parents' share of the benefits from having children exceeds their share of the costs. The corresponding externalities are confined to the kinship. Other things equal, reduction in those externalities would be accompanied by a fall in the demand for children and all households would benefit.[14]

---

13. For theoretical models that speak to the mutual determination, see Dasgupta (1993, 2000), Brander and Taylor (1998), Harford (1998), Dasgupta and Ehrlich (2013), and Bohn and Stuart (2015). The mutual determination does not necessitate a demographic trap, but it may lead to one. See in particular Dasgupta (2000, Appendix).

14. To see that there are no externalities if the shares were the same, suppose c is the cost of rearing a child and N is the number of couples within a kinship. Assume that each child makes available y units of output to the entire kinship, which is then shared equally among all couples in their old age. Suppose also that the cost of rearing each child is shared equally by

Related to this is a phenomenon observed by Guyer (1994) in a Yoruba area of Nigeria. In the face of deteriorating economic circumstances, some women bear children by different men so as to create immediate lateral links with them. Polyandrous motherhood enables women to have access to more than one resource network. Children are a further form of wealth for their mothers; desired fertility is consequently higher.

The idea of wealth-in-people has been developed by anthropologists to reflect the additional status and other social advantages that are conferred on women (more generally, households) in African societies by having children (Guyer and Eno Belinga 1995). There is formal resemblance here to Veblen's account of status in an entirely different context, namely, conspicuous consumption in the Gilded Age in America. In the present context, desired fertility is higher because of the competition generated by the desire for status, and it leads to a collective loss in well-being.

Communal land tenure of the lineage social structure in sub-Saharan Africa has offered an inducement for men to procreate: a larger family can claim a greater amount of land. In addition, conjugal bonds are frequently weak, so fathers often do not bear their fair share of the costs of siring a child. Anthropologists have observed that the unit of African society is a woman and her children, rather than parents and their children. Frequently, there is no common budget for the man and woman. Descent in sub-Saharan Africa is, for the most part, patrilineal and residence is patrilocal. That suppresses women's

---

all couples. Let n^* be the number of children each couple other than the one under study chooses to have. If n is the number of children this couple produces, they would incur the resource cost $C = [nc + (N-1)n^*c]/N$, and eventually the couple would receive an income from the next generation equaling $\Upsilon = [ny + (N-1)n^*y]/N$. Denote the couple's aggregate utility function by the form $U(\Upsilon)-K(C)$, where both $U(.)$ and $K(.)$ are increasing and strictly concave functions. Letting n be a continuous variable for simplicity, it is easy to confirm that the couple in question will choose the value of n at which $y\,dU(\Upsilon)/d\Upsilon = c\,dK(C)/dC$. The choice sustains a social equilibrium when $n = n^*$. It is easy to check that this is also the condition that is met in a society where there is no reproductive free-riding. It follows that there is free-riding if the parents' share of the benefits from having children exceeds their share of the costs.

voice; and because women bear a disproportionate share of the costs of reproduction, it raises the fertility rate. Taken together, patrilineality, weak conjugal bonds, communal land tenure, and a strong kinship child support system have been broad characteristics of the region. They provide a powerful stimulus to fertility. Admittedly, patrilineality and patrilocality are features of the northern parts of the Indian sub-continent also. But conjugal bonds there are substantially greater. Moreover, since agricultural land is not communally held, large family sizes lead to fragmentation of landholdings. In contrast, large families in sub-Saharan Africa are (or, at least were, until recently) rewarded by a greater share of land belonging to the lineage or clan.[15]

4. Socially Embedded Preference Structures and Conformism

That children are a parental end (and not just a means toward other parental goals) provides a potentially powerful mechanism by which reasoned fertility decisions at the level of every household could lead to an unsatisfactory outcome from the perspectives of all households. The mechanism arises from the possibility that traditional practice is

---

15. In an early review of fertility intentions, Cochrane and Farid (1989) noted that both the urban and rural and the educated and uneducated in sub-Saharan Africa have more, and want more, children than their counterparts in other less-developed regions. Even young women expressed a desire for an average of 2.6 more children than women in the Middle East, 2.8 more than women in North Africa, and 3.6 to 3.7 more than women in Latin America and Asia. Updated versions of these figures are available, but we are presenting data from the mid-1980s because the income gap between Africa and the rest of the developing world was smaller at that time than it is now.

African society's exceptionalism has been much written about. See in addition Goody (1976), Bledsoe and Pison (1994), Bongaarts (2011), and Bongaarts and Casterline (2013). But changes have been observed, at least in East Africa. Fostering is declining, land registration is increasing, and urbanization is eroding pronatal institutions. Whether those changes will markedly influence fertility rates in the near future is unclear. And delay matters to Africa's future prospects (Section 11). We are grateful to John Cleland for helpful discussions on this.

perpetuated by conformity. Reproductive decisions are not only a private matter; they are subject to social mores, which in turn are influenced by family experiences and the cultural milieu. But social mores are shaped by the behavior of all. There is circularity in this, which we can unravel by supposing that household preference structures are socially embedded. Behavior is conformist when the family size that each household desires is positively related to the average family size in the community (Dasgupta 1993: Ch. 12).

Douglas and Ney (1998) regard consumption as an expression of social engagement. Taken literally that would appear odd, but what the authors were pointing to is that a meal taken alone is different from a meal enjoyed in the company of others. Fads and fashion may be short-run expressions of social engagement (we refer to such expressions as conformism); what Douglas and Ney showed us is that our need to belong is deep and enduring. We rely on one another for safety, consolation, information, companionship, and governance. Many of our actions are undertaken in a social setting, and all of our actions are influenced in part by attention to others.

Whatever the basis of conformism, there would be practices encouraging high fertility that no household would unilaterally desire to break. Such practices could have had a rationale in the past, when mortality rates were high, population densities were low, natural resources were plentiful, the threat of extermination from outside attack was large, and mobility was restricted. But practices can survive even when their original purposes have disappeared. One reason they can survive is that if all other households continue to follow the practice and aim at large family sizes, no conformist household would on its own wish to deviate from the practice; however, if all other households were to restrict their fertility, every household would wish to restrict its fertility as well. Conformism can thus be a reason for the existence of multiple social equilibria. A society could get embedded in a self-sustaining mode of behavior characterized by high fertility and low educational attainment, even when there is another potentially self-sustaining mode of behavior characterized by low fertility and high educational attainment and which is preferred by all. Economists think of an economy becoming stuck in a low-level equilibrium for lack of a "big push," which, if only it would happen, would move them to a higher-level equilibrium. Big push is not to be identified with government fiat. Below we see that societies can experience big pushes from unexpected sources.

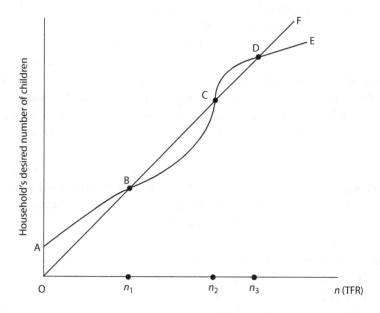

Figure 1 Socially Embedded Preferences for Children

Socially embedded preferences for children are shown in Figure 1. The curve ABCDE is the representative household's desired number of children, plotted against the average number of children per household (the horizontal axis). The curve is upward sloping and intersects the 45° line OF at three points: B, C, D. Each is a social equilibrium, at TFRs n_1, n_2, and n_3 respectively. To interpret ABCDE with concrete numbers, imagine that each household regards 5 to be the ideal number of children if all other households have 5 children (n_3 on the horizontal axis)); 4 to be the ideal number if all others have 4 (n_2); and 2 to be the ideal number if all others have 2 (n_1). Imagine now that each household prefers the outcome where all households have 2 children. It can nevertheless be that their society is stuck in a situation where each household has 5 children. It can get stuck because no household would have a reason to deviate from 5 if all other households have 5; which is another way of saying that 5 is a self-enforcing choice. It is easy to confirm that both 2 and 5 are stable equilibria, in that a small deviation from 2 (or from 5) would in time return to a situation where each household chooses 2 (or 5). It follows that 5 would be just as tenacious a TFR as 2.[16]

That does not mean society would be stuck at 5 forever. As always, people differ in the extent of their absorption of traditional practice. There would inevitably be those who experiment, take risks, and refrain from joining the crowd. They are the tradition-breakers, and they often lead the way. Educated women are among the first to make the move toward smaller families.[17] A possibly even stronger pathway is the influence that newspapers, radio, television, and now the internet play in transmitting information about other lifestyles (Freedman 1995 was one of the first to detect that pathway). The media could be a vehicle by which conformism increasingly becomes based on the behavior of a wider population than the local community (the peer group widens). And that disrupts behavior.[18]

A number of studies on fertility point to choices that are guided in part by attention to others. In her highly original work on demographic change in Western Europe over the period 1870–1960, Watkins (1990) showed that differences in fertility and nuptiality within each country declined. She also found that in 1870, before the large-scale declines in marital fertility had begun in most areas of Western Europe, demographic behavior differed considerably within countries. Differences among provinces within a country were high even while differences within provinces were low. Spatial behavioral clumps suggest the important influence of local communities on behavior. In 1960 differences within each country were considerably less than in 1870. Watkins explained this by increases in the geographical reach

---

16. Formally, we are studying Nash equilibria in a coordination game (see Dasgupta 1993, 2000; Kohler 2000). It can be shown that the social equilibrium in which each household has 4 children (n_2) is unstable. It would take us far afield to explain why, but see Dasgupta (2002) for the reason.

17. Farooq, Ekanem, and Ojelade (1987) is an early study of the phenomenon in West Africa. Lutz, Butz, and KC (2014) is a collection of essays on the effect of education on fertility behavior. Interactions between the elite and the general public can be a vehicle by which fertility behavior among the poor changes.

18. The media are increasingly used to such an end. For example, Development Media International runs media campaigns aimed at changing behavior.

national governments achieved over the 90 years in question. The growth of national languages could have been the medium through which reproductive behavior was able to spread.

Watkins's study was historical, as were the studies Montgomery and Casterline (1998) used to distinguish pathways by which reproductive practices diffuse within a society. In a commentary on West Bengal, where fertility rates declined in the early 1970s ahead of the northern states of India and neighboring Bangladesh, Basu and Amin (2000) attributed the West Bengal experience to historical and cultural factors there that combined to promote interaction between the elite and the general public. Jensen and Oster (2009) in contrast have studied a natural experiment. They found that state-level fertility rates declined in step following the staggered introduction of cable TV in Indian states.[19]

A feature of historical studies of the diffusion of behavior across space and time is that they do not necessarily identify the behavioral fundamentals (or "drivers") on which the diffusion process is built. They also differ from one another in terms of the transmission mechanism. The drivers could be knowledge acquisition, or they could be pure mimicry, or what Cleland and Wilson (1987) called "ideation," or the advent of modernity, or the desire to belong to one's (possibly expanding) group, or the force of celebrity culture, and so on. These fundamentals are not unrelated, but they are not the same. Regarding transmission mechanisms, it could be that people observe successful behavior and copy it, or that the language in which newspapers are read spreads, or that people discuss and debate among themselves, and so forth.[20]

The model in Figure 1 is built on the common structure of all such diffusion processes. Studying the common structure offers the advantage that we are able to analyze the resting (i.e., equilibrium) points

---

19. For a wide-ranging discussion of the role of societal norms in fertility behavior, see Bongaarts and Watkins (1996).
20. Diffusion processes had been studied long before, in connection with technology adoption. In a classic paper, Griliches (1957) conducted an empirical study of the spread of hybrid corn in the US. In his model, farmers observed the successful adoption of new varieties before adopting them themselves. The process gave rise to the now-familiar logistic pattern of adoption. On the effect on reproductive behavior of the diffusion of ideas brought about by family planning programs, see Babalola, Folda, and Babayora (2008) and Krenn et al. (2014).

of a wide variety of diffusion processes without having to identify the processes themselves. Our model assumes that fertility preferences are socially embedded, but it does not specify the reasons households are influenced by the behavior of others. Being analytical, the model is able to entertain counterfactuals. It allows us to ask how a household's behavior would differ if the social parameters underlying the curve ABCDE were to be otherwise. This is a necessary exercise in policy analysis, because policies can be used to shift the curve ABCDE (and therefore the equilibrium points n_1, n_2, and n_3) as well as to influence the beliefs on the basis of which households act. The common structure also tells us that fertility transitions can be interpreted as disequilibrium phenomena (Dasgupta 2002), where practices change slowly in response to gradual changes in the social environment, until a tipping point is reached from which society shifts rapidly to a new stable equilibrium, say from high fertility to low fertility.

The common structure of diffusion processes that we are studying proves useful also for interpreting statistical regularities between actual fertility (TFR) and wanted fertility (WTFR). Pritchett (1994), for example, regressed TFR on WTFR in 43 countries in Asia, Africa, and Latin America and found that about 90 percent of cross-country differences in TFR are associated with differences in WTFR. He also found that excess fertility (TFR—WTFR) was not systematically related to actual TFR, nor an important determinant of it.

Pritchett concluded that high fertility is due entirely to the strong desire for children. Our model draws a different conclusion. That fertility preferences are socially embedded tells us we should expect the correlation Pritchett obtained, but it also warns us not to attribute causality to the relationship. It would be as true to say fertility rates in those countries where they are high are high because people have a strong desire for children as it would be to say that people there have a strong desire to have children because fertility rates are high.

5. Unmet Need, Desired Family size, and the UN's Sustainable Development Goals

UNFPA (1995) took it that family planning and reproductive health policies should address unmet need, meaning that they should be made to serve women aged 15–49 who are seeking to stop or delay childbearing but are not using modern forms of contraception (Bradley et al. 2012; Alkema et al. 2013). Although the idea of unmet need could appear straightforward, it has in practice been interpreted in different ways over the years. It is currently measured using more than 15 survey questions, including questions on contraceptive use, fertility intentions, pregnancies, postpartum amenorrhea, sexual activity, birth history, and menstruation. Women's reported fertility intentions are inferred from such questions as: "Now, I have some questions about the future. Would you like to have a(nother) child or would you prefer not to have (any more) children?" This is followed by a question about how long the woman wants to wait if she responded to the previous question that she does want a(nother) child.[21]

There are deep problems here. Unmet need as calculated is based on the respondent's expressed wants for children, and—taken together with responses to other questions—this response is used to infer unmet need for family planning. But in matters of life and death, resource needs assume an independent status; they even serve as the basis on which commodity rights are founded. The philosopher David Wiggins has argued that a statement of the form "person A needs commodity X" is tantamount to a challenge to imagine an alternative future in which A escapes harm without X (Wiggins 1987, p. 22). Expressed wants or desires for children—used to calculate unmet need for family planning—may not adequately convey her true need for family planning, that is, for her own best interests. A poor woman, suffering from iron deficiency and living in a setting where she is compelled to have sex and bear children, has a need for contraception for her own benefit that could remain undetected in her responses to questions regarding her desire for children. To infer needs solely from wants is therefore to undervalue the significance of family planning. Moreover, none of the survey questions is conditioned on the behavior of others.

Closely related to wants and desires is the notion of desired family size, which is obtained from answers to the following question: "If you could go back to the time when you did not have any children and could choose exactly the number of children to have in your whole life, how many would that be?" The wanted total fertility rate

---

21. Casterline and Sinding (2000) discuss ways in which the measure of unmet need can be used to inform family planning policies.

is calculated by first dividing the number of observed births into those that occurred before and after the desired family size is reached (the former are considered as wanted, the latter unwanted). WTFR is then obtained with the same procedure as the one used in calculating TFR (that is, from age-specific fertility rates), but only wanted births are included in the numerator of these rates.

There are dangers of biases in responses to the question at the basis of desired family size, but the need for family planning programs to have quantitative estimates of it is clear enough. Notice, though, that the questionnaire does not ask a woman what her desire would be if the prevailing fertility practices of others were different. In fact there is no mention of the prevailing fertility rate. Since respondents are not invited to disclose their conditional desires, it is most likely they disclose their desired family size on the assumption that fertility will remain at its prevailing rate. A direct way to discover socially embedded preferences would be to reconstruct the questionnaires by asking a series of conditional questions, which we collapse here for convenience into one: "If you could go back to the time when you did not have any children and could choose exactly the number of children to have in your whole life, how many would that be, assuming everyone else in your community had n children over their whole life?"

The survey could pose the conditional question in an ascending order of n, say from 0 to 10. The example in Figure 1 imagines that the answers to $n = 2, 4,$ and 5 are, respectively, 2, 4, and 5. It also imagines that answers to the questions in which $n = 0, 1, 3, 6–10,$ respectively, differ from 0, 1, 3, 6–10; which is why the latter numbers are not social equilibria. No doubt responding to a string of conditional questions would tax respondents, but not to ask them is to misread fertility desires.[22]

Fabic et al. (2015) defined total demand for modern contraception to be the number of women who want to delay or limit childbearing (i.e., the sum of contraceptive users and women with unmet need). The role of family planning, the authors argued, is to supply that demand. The suggestion is that the success of family planning should

---

22. Because people's preferences differ, we should expect the responses to differ but discover that each individual's preferred number of children is an increasing function of n. That finding would reveal socially embedded preferences.

be measured by the ratio of family planning users to the total demand. The United Nations has adopted this measure in its Sustainable Development Goal 3.7.1. It is known as "demand for family planning met with modern contraceptive methods," or "demand satisfied" for short. Formally, if X is the number of women aged 15–49 who are users of modern contraceptives, Y is the number of women with unmet need, and Z is total demand for modern contraception, then $Z = X+Y$ and the UN's "demand satisfied" is $X/Z = X/(X+Y)$.

Reproductive rights are at the heart of X/Z, which is its attraction. The indicator reflects voluntarism, rights and equity, informed choice, and the imperative of satisfying individuals' and couples' own choices with regard to the timing and number of children. But there are problems. The use of demand satisfied as the measure of success could create perverse incentives among programs managers. A program's performance would improve if more women were to declare that they want to get pregnant. As long as women want many children, Y (unmet need) remains small, and therefore Z (total demand) is only marginally greater than X (the number of modern contraceptive users). The country scores well on the indicator demand satisfied and appears not to need further family planning program effort. The success could mask a situation where contraceptive use is low and stagnant and high fertility rates persist. Moreover, as we saw in Section 4, fertility preferences, which contribute to the measurement of Y, are themselves influenced by the behavior of others. Y could therefore be small in a society that harbors another equilibrium in which Y is large.

The concept of reproductive rights, as currently framed, undervalues family planning. There are collective benefits to be enjoyed if members of a community are enabled to alter their fertility desires in a coordinated manner. Family planning can help to bring about changes in such social norms. Our analysis does not run against rights as a plank for family planning; it expands the sphere in which rights are acknowledged, protected, and promoted.[23]

---

23. Moral philosophers would argue that the evaluation of family planning programs should include the quality of lives that will not be lived on account of the programs. We avoid those further considerations by assuming that thoughtful parents reach their fertility desires by taking into account the potential well-being of their offspring and, by recursion, the well-being of their dynasty.

Part II

6. The Biosphere as an Open-Access Resource

To the best of our knowledge there are no national estimates of the environmental benefits of family planning. So we make a direct approach to estimating the benefits by reviewing humanity's demand for ecological services at the global level. For that purpose it proves useful to regard the biosphere as a single renewable natural resource. This requires a heroic aggregation exercise, in which billions of assets are aggregated into a single measure. If that seems an absurd undertaking, we should recall that global fisheries and forest biomes are routinely measured in units of biomass, which also involves giant aggregation exercises. No doubt problems of aggregation are magnified when we study the biosphere as a whole, but they are not magnified that much in complexity.

One reason the biosphere is hard to aggregate is that the biogeochemical processes that shape natural capital differ widely in both speed and spatial reach. Since most global environmental resources have no prices attached to them (there is an absence of property rights to open-access resources), indirect methods have to be found in order to obtain notional prices that reflect their scarcity value (what economists call shadow prices) for them. Nevertheless, there is no escaping the need for imagining the biosphere as a gigantic piece of natural capital if we are to discuss the adverse environmental externalities accompanying births. We denote the aggregate stock of the biosphere by K. K may alternatively be called the global stock of natural capital.

A concrete way to imagine the biosphere is to focus on its biomass. In that case K, measured in units of biomass, is the state variable of the biosphere. The composition of biomass (grasslands differ from agricultural fields) is reflected in the aggregate measure K. Let $K(t)$ be the biomass at time t, and let $F(K(t))$ be the net output of biomass over a brief interval of time (say, a year), starting at t. $F(K)$ is a flow or flux (so many units of biomass per year), whereas K is a stock (so many units of biomass). Ecologists call F "net primary production." When the occasion demands, we will refer to F as "ecosystem services."

To imagine the biosphere as a renewable natural resource requires facing a further problem. Even 2,000 years ago, when global population was under 250 million and per capita income a bit over a dollar a day (Maddison 2001), a reasonable approximation would have been to treat humanity as a separate entity from the biosphere. Today it is no longer possible to do so. We are much engaged in transforming the biosphere, by both creating biomass and destroying it. So we have to imagine humanity as being at the same time a constituent of the biosphere and an entity separate from it. No doubt that is a stretch, but it is possible to do it without running into contradictions. We avoid contradiction by noting that a portion of $F(K)$, say α, is needed for the maintenance of the biosphere. So if, over a period of time, $F(K)$ was usurped entirely by humanity, K would shrink and biodiversity would be reduced. If during an interval of time, humanity was to consume even more than $F(K)$, K would shrink even more, further drawing down biodiversity. Humanity is consuming at that level now, which is what has led Wilson (2016) to propose that we should leave half the biosphere alone. $(1-\alpha)F(K)$ should therefore be interpreted as the *usable* flow of biomass; usable, that is, by humanity.[24]

One might think that $F(K)$ must be an increasing function of K for all values of K, but that would be to overlook that Earth is finite in extent. F should therefore be taken to be an increasing function of K for small values of K, but a declining function of K for large values of K. Earth's carrying capacity for the prevailing life forms (a formidable notion in itself, but one that cannot be avoided) is that positive value of K at which $F(K)$ is zero.[25]

---

24. α is not a constant and is most likely a decreasing function of K.

25. A tractable form of $F(K)$, in wide use among ecologists for a variety of ecosystems, is quadratic:

$$F(K) = rK(1-K/K^*),$$

where r and K^* are positive constants. In this equation r is the intrinsic growth rate of K (because r at small values of K is the percentage rate of growth of K) and K^* is Earth's carrying capacity (because $F(K^*) = 0$).

The view that the biosphere is a renewable natural resource covers pollution as well (e.g., contemporary carbon emissions into the atmosphere). Pollutants are the reverse of natural resources. One way to conceptualize pollution is to view it as the depreciation of capital assets. Acid rains damage forests; carbon emissions into the atmosphere trap heat; industrial seepage and discharge reduce water quality in streams and underground reservoirs; fibers and plastics damage life in the oceans; sulfur emissions corrode structures and harm human health; and so on.

7. Ecosystem Losses in the Anthropocene

Humanity's success in raising the standard of living over the past 250 years has involved creating and then using ideas and accumulating reproducible (or manufactured) capital and human capital, while mining and degrading K. The socioeconomic processes that drive the production, dissemination, and use of ideas and the accumulation of reproducible and human capital are at the heart of modern growth and development economics, but the decumulation of natural capital has remained unrecognized (e.g., Helpman 2004). The decumulation is also unrecorded in official economic statistics.

This bias is not a reflection of an indifference to the natural world; it is more a disconnect between the social and environmental sciences. It is widely known, for example, that even while industrial output increased by a multiple of 40 during the twentieth century, the use of energy increased by a multiple of 16 (contributing to climate change and degrading the oceans), the methane-producing cattle population grew in pace with human population (contributing to climate change and degrading the oceans), and fish catch increased by a multiple of 35 (reducing stocks in the open seas).[26] Environmental scientists have found that the application of nitrogen to the terrestrial environment from the use of fertilizers, fossil fuels, and leguminous crops is now at least as great as that from all natural sources combined. They have also found that soil nitrogen and phosphorus inventories have

---

The damage inflicted on each type of asset (buildings, forests, the atmosphere, ocean fisheries, human health) should be interpreted as depreciation. For natural resources, depreciation amounts to the difference between the aggregate rate at which they are harvested and their natural regenerative rate; for pollutants the depreciation they inflict on natural resources is the difference between the rate at which pollutants are discharged into the resource base and the rate at which the resource base is able to degrade it. The task in either case is to estimate those depreciations. It follows that there is no reason to distinguish the analytical structure of resource management problems from pollution management problems. Roughly speaking, "resources" are "goods," while "pollutants" (the degrader of resources) are "bads." Pollution is the reverse of conservation.

26. Carbon and sulfur dioxide emissions rose by a factor of more than 10.

doubled over the past century (nitrate levels in Greenland ice today are higher than at any time in the previous 100,000 years) and that 25–30 percent of some 130 billion metric tons of carbon harnessed annually by terrestrial photosynthesis is now appropriated for human use (Vitousek et al. 1986; Vitousek et al. 1997; Haberl et al. 2007). That signals the stupendous presence of a single species and helps to explain why extinction rates of species since the early modern era have been far above background rates and have increased much further since the nineteenth century (RSPB et al. 2013). These figures all point to rates of biomass transformation in excess of the usable flux, $(1-\alpha)F(K)$. Consequently, they point to reductions in K.

The Millennium Ecosystem Assessment (MEA 2005a–d) reported that 15 of the 24 ecosystems the authors had investigated worldwide are either degraded or are being exploited at unsustainable rates. Population pressure on land and the habitat destruction that accompanies human encroachment are the proximate causes. The figures put the scale of humanity's presence on the planet in perspective and record that we are now Earth's dominant species (Ehrlich and Ehrlich 2008). The statistics also explain why our epoch has now been named the Anthropocene.[27]

8. Net Demand on the Biosphere

Studying biogeochemical signatures of the past 11,000 years, Waters et al. (2016) have provided a sketch of the human-induced evolution of, among other signatures on the biosphere, soil nitrogen and phosphorus inventories in sediments and ice. The authors reported a sharp increase in their inventories in the middle of the twentieth century. Their work shows that the now-famous figure of the "hockey stick" that character-izes time series of carbon concentration in the atmosphere also char-acterizes a broad class of geochemical signatures and signals a sharp increase in the rate of deterioration of Earth's life-support system. Biological extinctions, rises in greenhouse gas concentrations, contam-ination of marine species with persistent pollutants, nutrient overload

---

27. The term Anthropocene was popularized by Crutzen and Stoermer (2000) to mark a new epoch that began with the Industrial Revolution some 250 years ago.

in soil and water, and oceanic dead zones are but five signatures of those stresses. Waters et al. proposed that mid-twentieth century should be regarded as the time we entered the Anthropocene.[28]

Their reading is consistent with macroeconomic statistics. World population in 1950 was 2.5 billion, global GDP a bit over 7.5 trillion international dollars (at 2015 prices). The average person in the world was poor, with an annual income of a bit over 3,000 international dollars. Since then, the world has prospered materially beyond recognition. Population has increased to 7.4 billion and world output of final goods and services today is about 110 trillion international dollars, meaning that world income per capita now is about 15,000 international dollars. A 15-fold increase in global output over a 65-year period not only helps to explain the stresses to the Earth system that we have just reviewed, but also hints at the possibility that humanity's extraction of biomass has for some time exceeded sustainable levels. So, in addition to the direct benefits of family planning programs, which are currently assessed according to the extent to which reproductive rights are met, we should estimate the decline in reductions in K owing to a prevented birth and place a value on that reduction. If the reduction is estimated to be ΔK per prevented birth and the social value of a unit of natural capital is Q, then the environmental benefits from a family planning program would be the product of $Q \Delta K$ and the number of births the program is expected to prevent.[29]

In the field of family planning nothing is simple. Addressing one problem simply leads to several more. If Q remains largely unestimated by economists, determining ΔK from a prevented birth poses

---

28. The "hockey stick" graph refers to time series of carbon concentration in the atmosphere over the past 500 years. The variable grew gently from the late eighteenth century until the twentieth century, when it displayed a sharp increase. The Anthropocene Working Group has recently proposed that the immediate postwar years should be regarded as the start of the Anthropocene. See Vosen (2016).

29. Q is also called the notional price and, more often, shadow price. The literature on valuing natural capital is vast (see for example, Freeman 2003; Haque, Murty, and Shyamsundar 2011). A number of studies have estimated shadow prices of specific types of natural capital at the local level (water, air quality, woodlands, mangroves, coral reefs), but economic demographers estimating the value of family planning programs at the local level have not made use of them.

problems for the demographer. Some family planning on the part of women involves delaying births, not limiting numbers. Better spacing is a good in itself, but if numbers are not affected, the environmental consequences would be slight (ΔK would be negligible).

In a review of the state of the Earth's life-support system, WWF (2012) reported that in the early years of this century, humanity's demand for ecological services exceeded by 50 percent the rate at which the biosphere is able to supply those services. The figure is based on the idea of a "global ecological footprint," which is the surface area of biologically productive land and sea needed to supply the resources a human population consumes (food, fibers, wood, water) and to assimilate the waste it produces (materials, gases). The Global Footprint Network (GFN) regularly updates its estimates of the global ecological footprint.[30] A footprint in excess of 1 means demand for

---

In recent years estimating costs of carbon emissions for the global climate has been a major research topic. The basic idea is to estimate the net present value of the impact over the next 100 years (or more) on, for example, agriculture from changes to the global climate that are traceable to carbon emissions. That is Q when restricted to the stock of carbon in the atmosphere. The net present value has been found to be negative (meaning that global climate change is expected to hurt the world economy; that is, the notional price of carbon is negative) and has been estimated using a range of plausible figures for the rates at which future costs and benefits are to be discounted. See Moore and Diaz (2015), who arrive at a figure of 220 US dollars per ton of carbon emitted into the atmosphere. In contrast, the US government uses a figure of 37 dollars per ton. The wide difference in the estimates reflects differences in assumptions regarding the effect of carbon emissions on the global climate and in turn the effect of changes in the global climate on the fruits of human activities.

Bohn and Stuart (2015) offer estimates of the social cost of carbon emissions owing to a new birth (that is $Q\Delta K$, but where K is restricted to carbon concentration and Q is the shadow price of carbon in the atmosphere). In contrast, the literature contains next to nothing on the valuation of changes that humanity is inflicting on the oceans and the biomass they harbor. We do not know Q for the biosphere.

30. For pioneering work on the idea of ecological footprints, see Rees and Wackernagel (1994) and Rees (2001, 2006). See also Kitzes et al. (2008). Wakernagel, who founded the Global Footprint Network (www .footprintnetwork.org/public), was a lead author of WWF (2008).

ecological services exceeds their supply. GFN's most recent estimate is a footprint of a bit over 1.6, which in our terminology means humanity has in recent years been consuming ecological services at the rate $1.6(1-\alpha)F(K)$. Humanity's demand for ecological services can exceed supply for a period, but not indefinitely. Our model would interpret a footprint in excess of 1 as a decline in K (i.e., $\Delta K < 0$). Sustainable development would require that the footprint over time must on average equal 1. To be sure, the entire function $F(K)$ can be made to increase by measures that reduce the footprint to less than 1. Advances in biotechnology, for example, are designed to increase $F(K)$. But the advances would be successful only if they do not have large unintended adverse consequences for the biosphere. Moreover, irreversible losses, arising say from biological extinctions (declines in K), would act as constraints on the biosphere's ability to recover. Moves toward consumption and production practices that make smaller demands on the biosphere would be a more direct approach to reducing our impact on the Earth system. We return to those possibilities in Section 11.

The greatest contributors to the ecological-footprint overshoot are the OECD countries. Estimating national footprints poses enormous conceptual and practical difficulties; and without notional shadow prices to guide us, it is impossible to estimate the value of environmental externalities associated with an average new birth. But for the global economy the matter is less opaque because errors in measuring national footprints that arise on account of trade in goods and services would cancel in the aggregate.

Assuming that the global ecological footprint is 1.6, we may conclude that to maintain the current global average living standard at the prevailing distribution of income, we would need 1.6 Earths. It is against this background that we offer a quantitative account of the adverse environmental externalities humanity is inflicting on itself by allowing a substantial portion of Nature's goods and services to be free. No doubt estimates of global ecological footprint are very crude. Moreover, in contrast to estimates of such development indicators as GDP, population size, life expectancy, and literacy, which are made by a multitude of national and global institutions, we are obliged here to rely on the estimates of a solitary research group (albeit aided by a wide network of ecologists and environmental scientists). Nevertheless, that there is an overshoot (an ecological footprint in excess of 1) is entirely consistent with a wide range of evidence on the state of the biosphere, some of which we have reviewed here. Since the figures are the only ones on offer, we make use of them.

9. How Many People can Earth Support in Comfort?

Ecologists estimating sustainable world populations have sought to calculate the human numbers Earth can support at a reasonable standard of living. Daily, Ehrlich, and Ehrlich (1994) quantified the stresses to the biosphere that are being caused by humanity's use of energy. In the early 1990s world population was 5.5 billion and global energy consumption was an annual 13 terawatts (13 trillion watts). The authors assumed that an annual consumption of 13 terawatts of energy is unsustainable (it would play havoc with K). As we now know from the work of climate scientists, their presumption was right. The authors noted the vast differences in energy use between the world's rich and poor, but on assuming an equitable distribution of energy use, they estimated that a population of 2 billion (world population in the early 1930s) could enjoy a comfortable life based on an annual 3 terawatts of energy consumption; and that a population of 1.5 billion (world population at the start of the twentieth century) could enjoy an even more comfortable life based on an annual 4.5 terawatts of energy consumption.[31] Those estimates were a first cut on a neglected problem. An alternative procedure is to identify a standard of living that can be justified on grounds that it supports a high quality of life— we identify one from surveys on "reported happiness"—and ask how many people can be supported at that quality of life.[32]

---

31. The Daily–Ehrlich–Ehrlich study was based on the assumption that the sources of energy will continue to be fossil fuels. Today there is hope that energy in due course will altogether be obtained from renewable resources. Meanwhile K will have been further depleted. And climate change is not the only source of stress to the Earth system. Cohen (1995) collated a wide range of estimates that had been published in the past century of Earth's capacity to support human numbers and their demands.

32. The literature on reported happiness is huge. See Helliwell, Layard, and Sachs (2013) for a fine review of the large-scale surveys that ask people to report their feelings and emotions and collate their responses.

An analysis of one set of global surveys on happiness and their relationship with household incomes has revealed that in countries where per capita income exceeds 20,000 international dollars, additional income is not statistically related to greater reported happiness.[33] We work with that figure, even though we are not at all sanguine we understand the finding; 20,000 international dollars is the per capita income in Panama, Mauritius, and Uruguay today, and it is hard to imagine that happiness hits a roadblock at that level. On the other hand, 20,000 international dollars (at 2015 prices) was the per capita income in the early 1980s in today's high-income countries. Were people there on average less happy then than they are now? The matter remains unclear. So, for want of price estimates of natural capital (Q), we follow the lead of studies on reported happiness.

World income (or global GDP) today is about 110 trillion international dollars. Using 1.6 as the figure for the global ecological footprint today and assuming that the demand on ecological products and services is proportional to GDP, we conclude that sustainable world GDP is an annual 110 trillion/1.6 international dollars; that is, 70 trillion international dollars. That level of global economic activity would be sustainable because K would not decline. If we now regard 20,000 international dollars as the desired standard of living for the average person, maximum sustainable population comes to 3.5 billion.

This estimate is close to the ones obtained by Daily, Ehrlich, and Ehrlich. Both estimates arrive at a global population under half of

---

33. Layard (2011, pp. 32–35) reports the finding and commends it. A number of explanations can be given for the finding, one being that what matters most to a household beyond a certain level of income is its income relative to the average income in its peer group. Veblen (1899 [1925]) based his theory of the leisure class on this particular psychology of consumption. Veblen's observation on human psychology found a telling expression in a remark attributed to a Garry Feldman of Stamford, Connecticut, one of the wealthiest towns in the US: "I might be in the top 1 percent, but I feel that I am in the bottom third of the people I know" (*The Guardian*, 16 February 2013).

Another explanation for happiness saturation bases itself on the idea that people are conformists on styles of living. The problem is not that either explanation is implausible (they are both all too believable), but that either dominates all other factors affecting the demand for goods and services beyond 20,000 international dollars. We use the figure only for illustration.

what it is today. This suggests that under current technologies and institutions, the Earth system offers tight bounds on global population if a comfortable living standard is to be sustained. World population was about 3 billion in the 1960s, so we are not talking of unfamiliar figures. But suppose our goal was less demanding; suppose humanity would be content with an average income of 10,000 international dollars, which is below today's global per capita income.[34] Sustainable global population would then be 7 billion. As noted earlier, we are now 7.4 billion in numbers, moving toward a possible figure of 11.2 billion in the year 2100. And we have not built into the analysis deep inequalities in living standards and the human migrations that are often a response to the distress to which they give rise. We turn to that topic now.

10. Poverty and the Distribution of Global Income

By the Global Footprint Network's reckoning, the world's ecological footprint in 1960 was about 0.6. The figure suggests that humanity's reliance on the biosphere in 1960 was sustainable and that the biosphere's composition was much different then from what it is now. World population in 1960 was about 3 billion and per capita income approximately 4,500 international dollars. These statistics are consistent with the finding that the Anthropocene is only a couple of generations old.

Central to the UN's Sustainable Development Goals is the elimination of deep poverty and reductions in global wealth inequality. How does the balance of rights change when we cease talking exclusively in terms of global averages? Most economists believe that success in reducing the proportion of the world's population in absolute poverty from 37 percent in 1990 to just over 10 percent today can be traced to strong growth in GDP that prominent developing countries (China and India in particular) have enjoyed since then and the investment in health and education that such growth made possible.[35] It is

---

34. 10,000 international dollars is the per capita income in contemporary Albania and Indonesia.

35. See for example the regular commentaries in *The Economist*. The absolute poverty line is currently taken by the World Bank to be 1.90 international dollars a day. It is an adjustment to the dollar-a-day figure that was introduced by the Bank in the 1980s.

today almost universally taken as given (e.g., Jamison et al. 2013) that eliminating absolute poverty and narrowing health disparities require robust growth in GDP. But based as it is on market prices, GDP is insensitive to consumption and production externalities; nor does it record the depreciation of natural capital that accompanies economic activity. As the currency in which to measure the sustainability of development programs, GDP should be abandoned.

Related to poverty and inequalities in living standards is the question whether the global ecological footprint is proportional to world GDP. In our previous calculation we assumed the answer is yes. The assumption requires that household footprint is proportional to household income; that is, the composition of household expenditure does not matter to the biosphere. That assumption is in all probability incorrect (Liu et al. 2003). Consider by way of example the case where the ecological footprint increases less than proportionately with income. If the distribution of income remains the same, growth in global GDP by g percent would be accompanied by a less than g percent growth in the demand for ecological services. And that is a good outcome.[36]

But what if absolute poverty were to be eliminated by a redistribution of incomes toward greater equality? Such a policy has strong appeal to egalitarian convictions. But policymakers would be faced with a cruel dilemma: even if average income were to remain the same, the demand for ecological services would increase. That means improving the distribution of income among today's contemporaries,

---

36. To confirm this, suppose population size is N; people are indexed by i ($= 1, 2, \ldots, N$); and y_i is person i's income. Let e_i be i's demand for ecological services. A simple way to formulate the assumed relationship between income and biomass consumption is

$$e_i = Ay_i^{\pi},$$

where $0 < \pi < 1$ and $A > 0$ are constants. Global demand for ecological services is then

$$E = \sum_i e_i = A \sum_i y_i^{\pi},$$

where $\sum_i$ denotes summation over i.

Suppose there is an increase in all incomes by g, expressed in percentages. Then the global demand for ecological services (E^*) would be

$$E^* = (1+g)^{\pi} E < (1+g)E.$$

a good thing in itself, would worsen the economic prospects of future generations. There is a clash here between present and future rights.[37]

If the ecological footprint increases more than proportionately with income, our conclusions are reversed. Equalizing incomes among contemporaries would improve the economic prospects of future generations, but a *g* percent growth in global GDP would be accompanied by a more than *g* percent growth in the demand for ecological services.[38] Either way, the environmental consequences of growth and distribution point in opposite directions. That is another problem for the hapless policymaker.

11. Dilemmas

The clash of rights we have identified in this essay arises from the fact that much of the biosphere is treated as a free good. Imagine it were possible to establish international agreements on policies under which the private costs of using Nature's goods and services are something like their social scarcity values. If that were to come about, environmental externalities associated with consumption and reproduction would be eliminated, and policies that address socially embedded preferences could be used to further reduce the demands we make on Nature, perhaps even to the point where our demands are sustainable.

An additional route to sustainable dependence on the biosphere is technological progress. Economic historians of the Industrial Revolution point to the role institutions have played in providing incentives to create the technological innovations that have been responsible for reducing natural resource constraints.[39] Looking into the future, though, the rate of resource-saving technological progress has to be large enough to substitute for rising consumption levels. Otherwise

---

37. To see why, we use the notation introduced in the previous endnote and consider the extreme case where there is complete equality of incomes following the redistribution. For vividness, label people so that $y_1 < \ldots < y_i < \ldots < y_N$. Write the mean global income as y^*. Then $y^* = \Sigma_i \, y_i/N$. Suppose $g = 0$ (global GDP does not change). By assumption $0 < \pi < 1$. That means $NA(y^*)^\pi > A \Sigma_i \, y_i^\pi$. But $NA(y^*)^\pi$ is the global demand for ecological services under complete equality.
38. To confirm, one could use the model in endnote 37, but assume $\pi > 1$.
39. Landes (1998) is a classic on the subject.

our ecological footprint will not decline to 1 (a prerequisite for sustainable development). But we can be optimistic about the character of technological advances and the consumption patterns we correspondingly adopt only if natural capital is priced appropriately. Understandably, entrepreneurs economize on the expensive factors of production, not the cheap ones. As long as Nature's goods and services remain underpriced, technological advances and our lifestyles can be expected to be biased toward their use. Moreover, technological advances that are patently good can have side effects that are not benign. The ability to use fossil-based energy at large scales has transformed lives for the better, but it has created the unintended consequence of global climate change. Bulldozers and chain saws enable people to deforest land at rates that would have been unimaginable 250 years ago, and modern fishing technology to devastate large swathes of sea beds in a manner unthinkable in the past. If technological progress is our hope, it has to come allied with elimination of environmental externalities.

The World Bank in its 2016 World Development Indicators reports that the 1.4 billion people living in high-income countries enjoy a per capita income of 40,700 international dollars. Thus the richest 19 percent of the world's population consume about 51 percent of world income (57 trillion/110 trillion). Assuming humanity's impact on the biosphere is proportional to incomes, 51 percent of that impact can be attributed to 19 percent of world population. If the UN's Sustainable Development Goals are to be met, resource-intensive consumption patterns in these countries have to decline substantially. Our calculations in the previous section suggest that, otherwise, efforts to shrink global income inequalities will be unsustainable. Consumption behavior is influenced both by our urge to compete with others (Veblen's "conspicuous consumption") and by our innate desire to conform. Each is a reflection of socially embedded consumption preferences. Since both drivers give rise to consumption externalities, the psychological cost to a person of a collective reduction in consumption is likely to be far less than it would be if he were to reduce consumption unilaterally. The aggregate cost could even be negative, especially if the working poor were less poor relative to the working rich, as the former are far greater in number.

To see the numbers involved, recall that in Section 9 we noted that one set of global surveys on stated happiness and their relationship with household incomes revealed that in countries where per capita income exceeds 20,000 international dollars, additional income is not statistically related to greater reported happiness. Imagine that the

1.4 billion people in today's high-income countries were to reduce their average consumption (or income) to 20,000. The drop of 20,700 (viz. 40,700 – 20,000) international dollars per person in a population of 1.4 billion adds up to a total of 31 trillion international dollars. Other things equal, world income would then be 79 (viz. 110 – 31) trillion international dollars, a figure not far above the 70 trillion international dollars we obtained (Section 9) as a crude estimate of sustainable global income under present-day technologies and social institutions.

But problems abound. According to the projections in UNPD (2017), world population will increase from the current 7.4 billion to 11.2 billion in 2100. More than three-quarters of that increase is projected to be in sub-Saharan Africa, from today's approximately 1 billion to 4 billion. (Figure 2 presents the UN's latest projections for

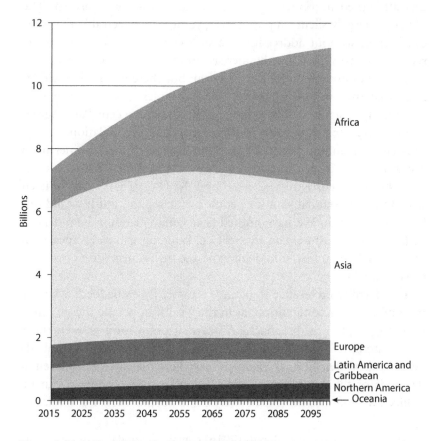

Figure 2 Total Population by Region, 2015–2100

Source: UNPD 2017.

regional populations up to the year 2100.) Per capita income in sub-Saharan Africa is currently 3,500 international dollars. Comprising a little over 13 percent of the world's population, the region represents a bit in excess of 3 percent of the world economy. So, sub-Saharan Africa cannot remotely be held responsible for the global environmental problems we face today. But to raise incomes there even to the current global average income (15,000 international dollars) in the face of a 3-billion rise in numbers would require an increase in the region's annual output from 3.5 trillion dollars to 60 trillion dollars. That rise, assuming it is possible, would have severe consequences for the region's ecology, contributing to further societal conflicts there and to greater attempts by people to move both within the region and out of it. It is not difficult to imagine the international tensions that attempted movements on such a scale would give rise to. The SDGs are largely silent on population, yet it is inconceivable that they can be met without addressing the subject.[40] Goal 13, for example, recognizes that restricting the increase in mean global temperature to 2°C will require urgent collective action; but there is no acknowledgment that the target is unlikely to be met unless population growth is reduced substantially (O'Neill et al. 2010). The recent Paris Agreement on climate change also made no mention of population.

If family planning programs were intensified to meet unmet need everywhere in Africa, population there would be some 1 billion smaller in 2100 than is currently projected by UNPD (2015).[41] That in itself would be a substantial gain for people in the region, but it would not be nearly enough. We have argued that family planning is undervalued. Greater investment in the service, bringing it into alliance with other social programs, could be expected to reduce the population projections further.

That fertility preference structures are socially embedded (whether by conformity or competition, as in the wealth-in-people thesis) offers hope to people in sub-Saharan Africa that population growth there can be stemmed without much personal cost to them. That embeddedness also offers hope to people everywhere that the environmental demands of the 1.4 billion people in high-income countries can be reduced without too much personal cost to people there. For if relative

---

40. Starbird, Norton, and Marcus (2016) contains a good discussion of this.
41. We are grateful to John Bongaarts for correspondence on this.

consumption matters, a uniform reduction in consumption among all should be expected to prove not too costly to people. The population–consumption–environment nexus is one area of the human experience where the cost of necessary social change is probably much less than is feared by social scientists.

References

Alkema, L., V. Kantorava, C. Menozzi, and A. Biddlecom. 2013. "National, regional, and global rates and trends in contraceptive prevalence and unmet need for family planning between 1990 and 2015: A systematic and comprehensive analysis," *Lancet* 381: 1642–1652.

Arrow, K.J., P. Dasgupta, L.H. Goulder, K.J. Mumford, and K. Oleson. 2012. "Sustainability and the measurement of wealth," *Environment and Development Economics* 17(3): 317–355.

Babalola, S., L. Folda, and H. Babayaro. 2008. "The effects of a communication program on contraceptive ideation and use among young women in Northern Nigeria," *Studies in Family Planning* 39(3): 211–220.

Balmford, A. and N. Knowlton. 2017. "Why Earth optimism?," *Science* 356(6335): 225. Editorial.

Basu, A.M. and S. Amin. 2000. "Conditioning factors for fertility decline in Bengal: History, language identity, and openness to innovations," *Population and Development Review* 26(4): 761–794.

Bauer, P.T. 1981. *Equality, the Third World and Economic Delusion*. London: Weidenfeld and Nicolson.

Baumol, W.M. and W.E. Oates. 1975. *The Theory of Environmental Policy*. Englewood Cliffs, NJ: Prentice-Hall.

Berlin, I. 1959. *Two Concepts of Liberty*. Oxford: Oxford University Press.

Birdsall, N. 1988. "Economic approaches to population growth," in H. Chenery and T.N. Srinivasan (eds.), *Handbook of Development Economics, Vol. 1*. Amsterdam: North Holland.

Birdsall, N., A.C. Kelley, and S.W. Sinding (eds.). 2001. *Population Matters: Demographic Change, Economic Growth, and Poverty in the Developing World*. Oxford: Oxford University Press.

Bledsoe, C. 1990. "The politics of children: Fosterage and the social management of fertility among the Mende of Sierra Leone," in W.P. Handwerker (ed.), *Births and Power: Social Change and the Politics of Reproduction*. Boulder: Westview Press.

——. 1994. " 'Children are like young bamboo trees': Potentiality and reproduction in sub-Saharan Africa," in K. Lindahl-Kiessling and H. Landberg (eds.), *Population, Economic Development and the Environment*. Oxford: Oxford University Press.

Bledsoe, C. and G. Pison (ed.). 1994. *Nupitality in Sub-Saharan Africa: Contemporary Anthropological and Demographic Perspectives*. Oxford: Clarendon Press.

Bohn, H. and C. Stuart. 2015. "Calculation of a population externality," *American Economic Journal: Economic Policy* 7(2): 61–87.

Bongaarts, J. 2011. "Can family planning programs reduce high desired family size in sub-Saharan Africa?," *International Perspectives in Sexual and Reproductive Health* 37(4): 209–216.

———. 2016. "Slow down population growth," *Nature* 530: 409–412.

Bongaarts, J. and J.B. Casterline. 2013. "Fertility transition: Is sub-Saharan Africa different?," *Population and Development Review* 38(1): 153–168.

Bongaarts, J. and S.C. Watkins. 1996. "Social interactions and contemporary transitions," *Population and Development Review* 22(4): 639–682.

Bradley, S.E.K., T.N. Croft, J.D. Fishel, and C.F. Westoff. 2012. "Revising unmet need for family planning," *DHS Analytical Studies No. 25*. Calverton. MD: ICE International.

Brander, J.A. and M.S. Taylor. 1998. "The simple economics of Easter Island: A Ricardo-Malthus model of renewable resource use," *American Economic Review* 88(1): 119–138.

Brock, D. 2010. "Shaping future children: Parental rights and societal interests," in J. Fishkin and R. Goodin (eds.), Population and Political Theory—Philosophy, Politics and Society 8. Chichester: Wiley-Blackwell.

Bryant, L., L. Carver, C.D. Butler, and A. Anage. 2009. "Climate change and family planning: Least developed countries define the agenda," *Bulletin of the World Health Organization* 87(11): 852–857.

Caldwell, J.C. 1981. "The mechanisms of demographic change in historical perspective," *Population Studies* 35(1): 5–27.

———. 1982. *Theory of Fertility Decline*. New York: Academic Press.

———. 1991. "The soft underbelly of development: Demographic transition in conditions of limited economic change," *Proceedings of the World Bank Annual Conference on Development Economics 1990*. Supplement to the World Bank Economic Review, pp. 207–254.

Caldwell, J.C. and P. Caldwell. 1990. "High fertility in sub-Saharan Africa," *Scientific American* 262(5): 82–89.

Canning, D. and T.P. Schultz. 2012. "The economic consequences of reproductive health and family planning," *Lancet* 380: 165–171.

Casterline, J.B. and S.W. Sinding. 2000. "Unmet need for family planning in developing countries and implications for population policy," *Population and Development Review* 26(4): 691–723.

Cleland, J., A. Conde-Agudelo, H. Peterson, J. Ross, and A. Tsui. 2012. "Contraception and health," *Lancet* 380(9837): 149–156.

Cleland, J. and C. Wilson. 1987. "Demand theories of the fertility transition: An iconoclastic view," *Population Studies* 44(1): 5–30.

Cleland, J. et al. 2006. "Family planning: The unfinished agenda," *Lancet* 368(9549): 1810–1827.

Cochrane, S. and S. Farid. 1989. "Fertility in sub-Saharan Africa: Analysis and explanation," World Bank Discussion Paper No. 43. Washington, DC: World Bank.

Cohen, J. 1995. How Many People Can the Earth Support? New York: W.W. Norton.

Cottingham, J., A. Germaine, and P. Hunt. 2012. "Use of human rights to meet the unmet need for family planning," *Lancet* 380: 172–180.

Crutzen, P.J. and E.F. Stoermer. 2000. "The Anthropocene," *Global Change Newsletter* 41: 17–18.

Daily, G.C., A.H. Ehrlich, and P.R. Ehrlich. 1994. "Optimum population size," *Population and Environment* 15(6): 469–475.

Dasgupta, P. 1993. *An Inquiry into Well-Being and Destitution*. Oxford: Clarendon Press.

———. 2000. "Reproductive externalities and fertility behaviour," *European Economic Review* 44(4–6): 619–644. Presidential Address to the European Economic Association Annual Conference 1999.

———. 2002. "A model of fertility transition," in B. Kristrom, P. Dasgupta, and K.-G. Lofgren (eds.), *Economic Theory for the Environment: Essays in Honour of Karl-Goran Maler*. Cheltenham: Edward Elgar.

———. 2007. *Economics: A Very Short Introduction*. Oxford: Oxford University Press.

———. 2010. "The place of nature in economic development," in D. Rodrik and M. Rosenzweig (eds.), *Handbook of Development Economics, Vol. 5*. Amsterdam: North Holland.

Dasgupta, P. and P. Ehrlich. 2013. "Pervasive externalities at the population, consumption, and environment nexus," *Science* 340: 324–328. https://doi.org/10.1126/science.1224664.

Deaton, A. 2013. *The Great Escape: Health, Wealth, and the Origins of Inequality*. Princeton University Press.

Debpuur, C. et al. 2002. "The impact of the Navrongo Project on contraceptive knowledge and use, reproductive preferences, and fertility," *Studies in Family Planning*, 33(2): 141–164.

Douglas, M. and S. Ney. 1998. *Missing Persons: A Critique of Personhood in the Social Sciences*. Berkeley: University of California Press.

Ehrlich, P.R. and A.H. Ehrlich. 2008. *The Dominant Animal: Human Evolution and the Environment*. Washington, DC: Island Press.

Ehrlich, P.R. and J.P. Holdren. 1971. "Impact of population growth," *Science* 171(3977): 1212–1217.

Fabic, M.I. et al. 2015. "Meeting demand for family planning within a generation," *Lancet* 385(9981): 1928–1931.

Farooq, G., I. Ekanem, and S. Ojelade. 1987. "Family size preferences and fertility in south-western Nigeria," in C. Oppong (ed.), *Sex Roles, Population and Development in West Africa*. London: James Currey.

Fortes, M. 1978. "Parenthood, marriage and fertility in West Africa," *Journal of Development Studies* 14 (Special Issue on Population and Development): 121–49.

Freedman, R. 1995. "Asia's recent fertility decline and prospects for future demographic change," Asia-Pacific Population Research Report No. 1, East-West Center, Honolulu.

Freeman III, A.M. 2003. *The Measurement of Environmental and Resource Values: Theory and Methods*. Washington, DC: Resources for the Future.

Fried, C. 1978. *Right and Wrong*. Cambridge, MA: Harvard University Press.

Goody, J. 1976. *Production and Reproduction*. Cambridge: Cambridge University Press.

Griliches, Z. 1957. "Hybrid corn: Explorations in the economics of technological change," *Econometrica* 25(4): 501–522.

Guyer, J.L. 1994. "Lineal identities and lateral networks: The logic of polyandrous motherhood," in C. Bledsoe and G. Pison (eds.), *Nuptiality in Sub-Saharan Africa: Contemporary Anthropological and Demographic Perspectives*. Oxford: Clarendon Press.

Guyer, J.L. and S.M. Eno Belinga. 1995. "Wealth in people as wealth in knowledge: Accumulation and composition in Equatorial Africa," *Journal of African History* 36(1): 91–110.

Haberl, H. et al. 2007. "Quantifying and mapping the human appropriation of net primary production in Earth's terrestrial ecosystems," *Proceedings of the National Academy of Sciences* 104(31): 12942–12947.

Haque, A.K.E., M.N. Murty, and P. Shyamsundar (eds.). 2011. *Environmental Valuation in South Asia*. New York: Cambridge University Press.

Hardee, K. 2014. "Climate change: What does population and reproductive health have to do with it?," in A. Kulczycki (ed.), *Critical Issues in Reproductive Health*. Amsterdam: Springer.

Hardee, K. et al. 2014. "Voluntary, human rights–based family planning: A conceptual framework," *Studies in Family Planning* 45(1): 1–18.

Harford, J.D. 1998. "The ultimate externality," *American Economic Review* 88(1): 260–265.

Haveman, R. and B. Wolfe. 1995. "The determinants of children's attainments: A review of methods and findings," *Journal of Economic Literature* 33(4): 1829–1878.

Helliwell, J.F., R. Layard, and J.D. Sachs (eds.). 2013. *World Happiness Report 2013*. New York: Earth Institute.

Helpman, E. 2004. *The Mystery of Economic Growth*. Cambridge, MA: Belknap Press.

Jamison, D.T. et al. 2013. "Global health 2035: A world converging within a generation," *Lancet* 382(December 7): 1898–1955.

Jensen, R. and E. Oster. 2009. "The power of TV: Cable television and women's status in India," *Quarterly Journal of Economics* 124(3): 1057–1094.

Jiang, L. and K. Hardee. 2011. "How do recent population trends matter to climate change?," *Population Research and Policy Review* 30(2): 287–312.

Kelley, A.C. 1988. "Economic consequences of population change in the third world," *Journal of Economic Literature* 26(4): 1685–1728.

Kitzes, J. et al. 2008. "Shrink and share: Humanity's present and future ecological footprint," *Philosophical Transactions of the Royal Society, B* 363(25): 467–475.

Koenig, M.A., U. Rob, M.A. Khan, J. Chakraborty, and V. Fauveau. 1992. "Contraceptive use in Matlab, Bangladesh in 1990: Levels, trends, and explanations," *Studies in Family Planning* 23(6): 352–364.

Kohler, H.-P. 2000. "Fertility decline as a coordination problem," *Journal of Development Economics* 63: 231–263.

Krenn, S., L. Cobb, S. Bababola, M. Odeku, and B. Kusemiju. 2014. "Using behaviour change communication to lead a comprehensive family planning program: The Nigerian Urban Reproductive Health Initiative," *Global Health Science and Practice* 2(4): 427–443.

Kumar, J. and K. Hardee. 2015. "Rights-based family planning: 10 resources to guide programming," in *Resource Guide: The Evidence Project*. Washington, DC: Population Council.

Landes, D.S. 1998. *The Wealth and Poverty of Nations: Why Some Are So Rich and Some So Poor*. New York: W.W. Norton.

Layard, R. 2011. *Happiness: Lessons from a New Science*. London: Penguin.

Liu, J., G.C. Daily, P.R. Ehrlich, and G.W. Luck. 2003. "Effects of household dynamics on resource consumption and biodiversity," *Nature* 421: 530–533.

Lomborg, B. (ed.). 2014. *How Much Have Global Problems Cost the World? A Scorecard from 1900 to 2050*. Cambridge: Cambridge University Press.

Lutz, W., W.P. Butz, and Samir KC (eds.). 2014. *World Population and Human Capital in the Twenty-First Century*. Oxford: Oxford University Press.

Maddison, A. 2001. *The World Economy: A Millennial Perspective*. Paris: OECD.

MEA (Millennium Ecosystem Assessment). R. Hassan, R. Scholes, and N. Ash (eds.). 2005a. *Ecosystems and Human Well-Being, I: Current State and Trends*. Washington, DC: Island Press.

——. S.R. Carpenter, P.L. Pingali, E.M. Bennet, and M.B. Zurek (eds.). 2005b. *Ecosystems and Human Well-Being, II: Scenarios.* Washington, DC: Island Press.

——. K. Chopra, R. Leemans, P. Kumar, and H. Simmons (eds.) 2005c. *Ecosystems and Human Well-Being, III: Policy Responses.* Washington, DC: Island Press.

——. D. Capistrano, C. Samper K., M.J. Lee, and C. Randsepp-Hearne (eds.). 2005d. *Ecosystems and Human Well-Being, IV: Multiscale Assessments.* Washington, DC: Island Press.

Micklethwait, J. and A. Wooldridge. 2000. *A Future Perfect: The Challenge and Hidden Promise of Globalization.* New York: Random House.

Miller, G. and K.S. Babiarz. 2016. "Family planning program effects: Evidence from microdata," *Population and Development Review* 42(1): 7–26.

Montgomery, M.R. and J.B. Casterline. 1998. "Social networks and the diffusion of fertility control," Policy Research Division Working Paper No. 119, Population Council, New York.

Moore, F.C. and D.B. Diaz. 2015. "Temperature impacts on economic growth warrant stringent mitigation policy," *Nature Climate Change* 5: 127–131.

National Research Council. 1986. *Population Growth and Economic Development: Policy Questions.* Washington, DC.

Newman, K., S. Fisher, S. Mayhew, and J. Stephenson. 2014. "Population, sexual and reproductive health, rights and sustainable development," *Reproductive Health Matters* 22(43): 53–64.

Norberg, J. 2016. *Progress: Ten Reasons to Look Forward to the Future.* London: One World.

O'Neill, B.C. et al. 2010. "Global demographic trends and future carbon emissions," *Proceedings of the National Academy of Sciences* 107(41): 17521–17526.

Pritchett, L.H. 1994. "Desired fertility and the impact of population policies," *Population and Development Review* 20(1): 1–55.

Rees, W.E. 2001. "Ecological footprint, concept of," in S.A. Levin (ed.), *Encyclopedia of Biodiversity, Vol. 2.* New York: Academic Press.

——. 2006. "Ecological footprints and biocapacity: Essential elements in sustainability assessment," in J. Dewulf and H.V. Langenhove (eds.), *Renewable-Based Technology: Sustainability Assessment.* Chichester, UK: John Wiley & Sons.

Rees, W.E. and M. Wackernagel. 1994. "Ecological footprints and appropriated carrying capacity: Measuring the natural capital requirements of the human economy," in A.M. Jansson et al. (eds.), *Investing in Natural Capital: The Ecological Economics Appropriate for Sustainability.* Washington, DC: Island Press.

Ridley, M. 2010. *The Rational Optimist: How Prosperity Evolves*. London: 4th Estate.

RSPB et al. 2013. *State of Nature 2013*. Report issued jointly by the Royal Society for the Protection of Birds and 19 other UK conservation and research associations. London: RSPB.

Sen, A. 1982. "Approaches to the choice of discount rates in social benefit-cost analysis," in R.C. Lind (ed.), *Discounting for Time and Risk in Energy Policy*. Baltimore, MD: The Johns Hopkins University Press.

Sonfield, A., K. Hasstedt, M.L. Kavanaugh, and R. Anderson. 2013. *The Social and Economic Benefits of Women's Ability to Determine Whether and When to Have Children*. New York: Guttmacher Institute.

Starbird, E., M. Norton, and R. Marcus. 2016. "Investing in family planning: Key to achieving the Sustainable Development Goals," *Global Health Science and Practice* 4(2): 191–210.

Temple, J. 1999. "The new growth evidence," *Journal of Economic Literature* 37(1): 112–156.

Thaler, R. and C. Sunstein. 2008. *Nudge*. New York: Penguin.

Tsui, A.O., R. McDonald-Mosley, and A.E. Burke. 2010. "Family planning and the burden of unintended pregnancies," *Epidemiological Reviews* 32(1): 152–174.

UNDP. 1990. *Human Development Report*. New York: United Nations Development Programme.

UNFPA. 1995. *Programme of Action of the International Conference on Population and Development*. New York: United Nations Population Fund.

UNPD. 2016. *Model Based Estimates and Projections of Family Planning Indicators*. New York: United Nations Population Division.

———. 2017. *World Population Prospects: The 2017 Revision*. New York: United Nations Population Division.

Veblen, T. 1899 [1925]. *The Theory of the Leisure Class: An Economic Study of Institutions*. Reprinted. London: George Allen & Unwin.

Vitousek, P.M., P.R. Ehrlich, A.H. Ehrlich, and P. Matson. 1986. "Human appropriation of the product of photosynthensis," *BioScience* 36: 368–373.

Vitousek, P.M., H.A. Mooney, J. Lubchenco, and J.M. Melillo. 1997. "Human domination of Earth's ecosystem," *Science* 277: 494–499.

Vosen, P. 2016. "Anthropocene pinned down to post war period," *Science* 353(6302): 852–853.

Waters, C.N. et al. 2016. "The Anthropocene is functionally and stratigraphically distinct from the Holocene," *Science* 351(6269): aad2622.

Watkins, S.C. 1990. "From local to national communities: The transformation of demographic regions in Western Europe 1870–1960," *Population and Development Review* 16(2): 241–272.

Wiggins, D. 1987. "Claims of needs," in *Needs, Values, Truth: Essays in the Philosophy of Value*. Oxford: Basil Blackwell.

Wilson, E.O. 2016. *Half-Earth: Our Planet's Fight for Life*. New York: Liveright.

World Bank. 2012. *World Development Indicators*. Washington, DC: World Bank.

——. 2016. *Development Goals in an Era of Demographic Change*. Washington, DC: World Bank.

WWF (World Wildlife Fund). 2008. *Living Planet Report 2008*. Gland: WWF International.

——. 2012. *Living Planet Report 2008*. Gland: WWF International).

Contributors

Scott Barrett is Vice Dean of the School of International and Public Affairs and the Lenfest-Earth Institute Professor of Natural Resource Economics at Columbia University. He is also a research fellow with the Beijer Institute (Stockholm), CESifo (Munich), and the Kiel Institute of World Economics.

Aisha Dasgupta specializes in demography and family planning, and since 2016 has worked at the United Nations Population Division. She earned her PhD in 2014 on contraceptive use in Malawi, from the London School of Hygiene and Tropical Medicine.

Eric Maskin is the Adams University Professor at Harvard University. He received the 2007 Nobel Memorial Prize in Economic Sciences (with L. Hurwicz and R. Myerson) for laying the foundations of mechanism design theory. He has also contributed to game theory, contract theory, social choice theory, political economy, and other areas of economics.

Joseph E. Stiglitz is University Professor at Columbia University and a recipient in 2001 of the Nobel Memorial Prize in Economic Sciences. He is also co-president of the Initiative for Policy Dialogue at Columbia University, chief economist of the Roosevelt Institute, and the cochair of the High-Level Expert Group on the Measurement of Economic Performance and Social Progress at the OECD.

Robert Solow is Emeritus Institute Professor at the Massachusetts Institute of Technology. He was awarded the Nobel Memorial Prize in Economic Sciences in 1987 and received the National Medal of Science in 1999 and the Presidential Medal of Freedom in 2014.

Author Index

Bourdieu, P., 55n50
Bradley, S. E. K., 246–247
Bradshaw, C. J. A., 98, 101
Brander, J. A., 5n5, 239n13
Brock, D., 235n7
Brock, W. A., 139, 170
Brook, B. W., 98, 101
Broome, John, xxxv, 28–29, 46n39, 53n48, 74, 77, 80
Bryant, L., 226n1
Burke, A. E., 236, 271
Butz, W. P., 236, 244n17
Butzer, K. W., 114
Bykvist, Krister, xxxvi, 7n9, 54n49, 68n67

Caldwell, 239
Caldwell, J. C., 4, 237, 238
Caldwell, P., 237, 266
Campbell, Timothy, xxxvi, 171
Canning, D., 236, 266
Cardinale, B. J., 30, 97n95
Carlson, E., 59n55
Casey, J., 62n58
Cassman, K. G., 103
Casterline, J. B., 5n5, 241n15, 245, 247n21, 266
Cavendish, W., 32
Ceballos, G., 101
Chichilnisky, G., 11
Christiaensen, L., 113
Cleland, John, xxxv, 225, 236, 241n15, 245
Clemens, M., 17
Cline, W. R., 80, 81n78
Cochrane, Susan, xxxv, 5n5, 241n15, 267
Cohen, G. A., 21n16
Cohen, J. E., 96n93
Cohen, Joshua, xxxv
Colbert, E., 102n98, 171
Cottingham, J., 234n6
Cowen, T., 46n39
Cowie, Christopher, xxxv, 110n106
Coyle, D., 161n5
Crist, E., 5n5
Crutzen, P. J., 102n98, 253n27

Daily, Gretchen, xxxv, 97n95, 219, 257, 257n31
Daly, H. E., 159, 171
Daly, M. C., 65n63
Dannenberg, A., 103n99, 211–212
Dasgupta, Aisha, xxv–xxvi, xxxi, xxxiii, xxxv–xxxvi, xxxviii–xxxix, 1n1, 6, 35n28, 57n53, 104n101, 109n105, 121, 123, 207, 212, 217n5, 225–272
Dasgupta, Amiya, xxxvi
Dasgupta, Carol, xxxv
Dasgupta, Shamik, xxxv–xxxvi, 76n75
Dasgupta-Clark, Zubeida, xxxv
d'Aspremont, C., 43n35
Deaton, A., 227
Debpuur, C., 236, 267
Debreu, Gerard, xi–xii
Dewey, John, xiin2
Diamond, Jared, 113–114, 114n109, 203
Diamond, P., 85n82
Diaz, D. B., 254n29, 270
Diener, E., 65n63
Dixit, A., 131n1
Donaldson, D., 43n35, 53, 53n48, 71n70
Douglas, Mary, xxxv, 55, 57, 121, 173
Downey, S., 114
Downing, J. A., 99n96
Duraiappah, Anantha, xxxv
Dworkin, R., 21n16
Dyer, Jake, xxxvi

Edgeworth, F. Y., 39n31, 204
Ehrlich, A. H., 99, 101–102, 170, 253, 257, 257n31
Ehrlich, Paul, xxxv, 5n5, 33–34, 99, 101–102, 226, 239n13, 253, 257, 257n31
Ekanem, I., 244n17
English, J., 132
Enke, S., 95
Eno Belinga, S. M., 240

Fabic, M. I., 238
Fagels, Robert, 62n58

Subject Index